CRITICAL PERSPECTIVES

The purpose of the works in this series is to provide the teacher and student with the most important critical and historic commentary on major authors, themes, and national literatures of the non-western world.

In a period when vast realignments of power and long overdue reassessments of the cultures of the third world are occurring, the documents and polemics reflecting and often speeding these changes should be readily available.

Senior Editors of the Series: D. Herdeck, George-town University, Washington, D.C., and B. Lindfors, University of Texas, Austin

Subjects of the first works in the Series:

1. Amos Tutuola
2. V. S. Naipaul
3. Nigerian Literatures
4. Cuba South—A Panoramic View of Caribbean Writing Havana to Cayenne

Future Volumes

Chinua Achebe
Wole Soyinka
Christopher Okigbo
Aimé Césaire
Léon Gontran Damas
Arabic Literatures 1930-1975
Contemporary Iranian Literature

CRITICAL PERSPECTIVES

ON **AMOS TUTUOLA**

Edited by

Bernth Lindfors

Three Continents Press: Washington, D.C.

FIRST EDITION

3&P

Copyright © 1975
Three Continents Press

Three Continents Press
4201 Cathedral Ave., N.W.
Washington, D.C. 20016

ISBN 0-914478-05-2 (Hardcover)
ISBN 0-914478-06-0 (Paper)

Library of Congress Catalog Number: 75-13706

Library of Congress Cataloging in Publication Data

Lindfors, Bernth (editor)
Critical Perspectives on Amos Tutuola

Front cover from collage
by Susan Trumpower

ACKNOWLEDGMENTS

Acknowledgments

I wish to thank the following individuals and publications for permission to reprint the essays and reviews which appear in this book. Every effort has been made to trace copyright holders, but in a few cases this has proved impossible. I would be interested to hear from any copyright holders not acknowledged here.

Faber and Faber (London) and Grove Press (New York) for permission to quote from Tutuola's works;

Black Orpheus, The Listener, The New Statesman, The New York Times Book Review, The New Yorker, Nigeria Magazine, The Observer, Présence Africaine, The Reporter, The Spectator, The Times Literary Supplement, and *West African Review* for the reviews of Tutuola's books;

West Africa for the review of *My Life in the Bush of Ghosts* and the controversy that followed it;

Arthur Calder-Marshall and Arnold Goldman for their reviews in *The Listener*;

Cyprian Ekwensi for his review in *West African Review*;

Ulli Beier for his review in *Black Orpheus*;

Gerald Moore and *Black Orpheus* for "Amos Tutuola: A Nigerian Visionary";

Harold R. Collins and *Critique* for "Founding a New National Literature: The Ghost Novels of Amos Tutuola";

Eldred Jones and the *Bulletin of the Association for African Literature in English* for "*The Palm-Wine Drinkard*: Fourteen Years On";

Taban lo Liyong for "Tutuola, Son of Zinjanthropus";

E. N. Obiechina and *Présence Africaine* for "Amos Tutuola and Oral Tradition";

Omalara Ogundipe-Leslie, *Présence Africaine* and *The Journal of Commonwealth Literature* for "*The Palm-Wine Drinkard*: A Reassessment of Amos Tutuola";

Harold R. Collins and Twayne Publishers for "Tutuola's Literary Powers";

Charles R. Larson and Indiana University Press for "Time, Space and Description: The Tutuolan World";

Paul Neumarkt, *American Imago* and Wayne State University Press for "Amos Tutuola: Emerging African Literature";

A. Afolayan, Heinemann Educational Books Ltd. and Africana Publishing Corp. (a Division of Holmes & Meier Publishers, Inc.) for "Language and Sources of Amos Tutuola";

Robert Plant Armstrong and *Research in African Literatures* for "The Narrative and Intensive Continuity: *The Palm-Wine Drinkard*";

Sunday O. Anozie, Judith H. McDowell and *Cahiers d'études africaines* for "Amos Tutuola: Literature and Folklore, or the Problem of Synthesis";

Paul Edwards, Oxford University Press and the *The Journal of Commonwealth Literature* for "The Farm and the Wilderness in Tutuola's *The Palm-Wine Drinkard*";

Richard Priebe for "Tutuola, the Riddler";

and *Cahiers d'études africaines* for "Amos Tutuola: Debts and Assets."

I also wish to thank the African and Afro-American Studies and Research Center and the University Research Institute of the University of Texas at Austin for assistance in typing portions of the manuscript; Donald E. Herdeck for expert editorial advice; and Amos Tutuola for telling such marvelous stories.

B.L.

CONTENTS

INTRODUCTION

Introduction

The purpose of this book is to trace fluctuations in the literary reputation of Amos Tutuola and to provide a variety of critical perspectives on his work. Tutuola is one of the most controversial of African authors, and his six books have drawn reactions ranging from delirious enthusiasm to amused indifference to undisguised contempt. He is the kind of writer who attracts ardent fans and equally ardent foes, but his writing does not seem to be much affected by what critics say about him. There is a lot more continuity and consistency in his work than there is in the commentary on it. Despite fame and misfortune, Tutuola has remained basically the same simple storyteller, even while opinions about his literary abilities have changed.

The history of Tutuola's critical reception may be divided into roughly three phases: (1) foreign enchantment and local embarrassment, (2) foreign disenchantment and local reappraisal, and (3) universal but qualified acceptance. The initial reaction to Tutuola's first two books, *The Palm-Wine Drinkard* (1952) and *My Life in the Bush of Ghosts* (1954), was extremely favorable abroad but decidedly unfavorable at home. Indeed, Nigerians disliked Tutuola for the same reasons that Europeans and Americans treasured him: his subject matter was exotic and his grammar atrocious. Educated Africans suspected that the bizarre narratives of this messenger-turned-author appealed to foreigners because they projected an image of Africa as uncouth, primitive and barbaric—an image which happened to coincide with foreign stereotypes of the "Dark Continent." As a consequence, many of Tutuola's countrymen were convinced he was only being patronized by condescending racists and was really unworthy of serious consideration as a creative writer.

By the time Tutuola's fourth and fifth books (*The Brave African Huntress*, 1958; *Feather Woman of the Jungle*, 1962) appeared, however, his European and American readers were tired of his fantasies and fractured English. They expressed impatience with his inability to develop new themes and techniques and deplored his crippling limitations as a writer. Africans, on the other hand, were just beginning to appreciate his mythical imagination and extravagant sense of humor. In the mid-sixties a number of African literary critics wrote reappraisals of his work, probing his special strengths and weaknesses as a creative artist. By this time most sub-Saharan states had achieved political independence so African intellectuals were less self-conscious about their image abroad. Tutuola's books could therefore be evaluated more objectively than before, and many Africans discovered they liked them despite their oddities and obvious flaws.

In the early nineteen-seventies Tutuola became the subject of several penetrating studies as critics in Africa and other parts of the world began to try out new critical approaches to his work. By now Tutuola was recognized as a significant albeit curious author who had earned a special niche in the history of African literature. He was a singular, solitary figure who had arrived from nowhere and stumbled into greatness by the sheer vigor of his imagination. His works might be crude and unkempt but they possessed an elemental vitality which the polished writings of more sophisticated authors too often lacked. Tutuola was the naive prodigy of African letters.

The reviews and essays reprinted here are grouped chronologically so the reader may more easily follow the progress of Tutuola's literary career. Like his heroes and heroines, Tutuola has had many harrowing and happy adventures on his journey to respectability. He has been ambushed, assaulted and eaten alive by some critics and lionized and eulogized by others. But he has always survived these ordeals and proceeded on his way with confidence, determination and wit. African literature has been enriched immeasurably by the imaginative expeditions of this plucky pioneer.

Austin, Texas
January 1975

EARLY REVIEWS

Early Reviews

The initial reaction to *The Palm-Wine Drinkard* in England and America was astonished delight. Except for an anonymous critic in the *Times Literary Supplement* who grumbled that the book was "no more than a mass of unassimilated material," the first reviewers greeted Tutuola's unusual tale with wide-eyed enthusiasm, hailing the author as a primitive genius endowed with amazing originality and charming naiveté. Dylan Thomas set the tone with a rave review in *The Observer*, and a number of American critics followed suit a year later when the book was published in the United States by Grove Press. Indeed, were it not for the fact that Thomas's review appeared on the dust jacket of the Grove edition, it would be remarkable how many American reviewers parroted his sentiments—and occasionally his very words. Tutuola may owe much of his early notoriety to the endorsement of this famous Welsh poet.

Tutuola's second book *My Life in the Bush of Ghosts* was welcomed with the same mixture of awe, laughter and bewilderment that had greeted his first. It was published with a foreword by Geoffrey Parrinder, then Professor of Comparative Religion at the University of Ibadan, whose informative remarks about the book and its author may have helped both gain acceptance as literary discoveries worthy of serious critical attention. The *New Statesman and Nation* assigned the book to a prominent critic, V. S. Pritchett, and novelist Kingsley Amis reviewed it for *The Spectator*. But in Nigeria Yorubas reacted very negatively to a favorable review by Eric Robinson in *West Africa*, a weekly news magazine published in London and distributed throughout Africa. The controversy began with a letter to the editor from Babasola Johnson, a Yoruba reader who was dissatisfied with Robinson's evaluation. Robinson replied to Johnson's letter the following week, and a fortnight later the editor of *West Africa* published a biographical "portrait" of Tutuola which sparked further debate on his abilities as a writer. The entire controversy is reprinted here beginning with Robinson's review and including the informative portrait which was based on an interview with Tutuola.

The Palm-Wine Drinkard

From *The Observer*, July 6, 1952

Blithe Spirits

This is the brief, thronged, grisly and bewitching story, or series
of stories, written in young English by a West African, about the
journey of an expert and devoted palm-wine drinkard through a nightmare of indescribable adventures, all simply and carefully described, in
the spirit-bristling bush. From the age of ten he drank 225 kegs a day,
and wished to do nothing else; he knew what was good for him, it was
just what the witch-doctor ordered. But when his tapster fell from a
tree and died, and as, naturally, he himself "did not satisfy with water
as with palm-wine," he set out to search for the tapster in Deads' Town.

This was the devil—or, rather, the many devils—of a way off, and
among those creatures, dubiously alive, whom he encountered, were an
image with two long breasts with deep eyes; a female cream image; a
quarter-of-a-mile-long total stranger with no head, feet or hands, but
one large eye on his topmost; an unsoothing something with flood-light
eyes, big as a hippopotamus but walking upright; animals cold as ice
and hairy as sandpaper, who breathed very hot steam and sounded like
church bells; and a "beautiful complete gentleman" who, as he went
through the forest, returned the hired parts of his body to their owners,
at the same time paying rentage, and soon became a full-bodied gentleman reduced to skull.

Luckily, the drinkard found a fine wife on his travels, and she
bore him a child from her thumb; but the child turned out to be
abnormal, a pyromaniac, a smasher to death of domestic animals, and a
bigger drinkard than its father, who was forced to burn it to ashes. And
out of the ashes appeared a half-bodied child, talking with a "lower
voice like a telephone." (There are many other convenient features of
modern civilised life that crop up in the black and ancient midst of
these fierce folk legends, including bombs and aeroplanes, high-heel
shoes, cameras, cigarettes, guns, broken bottles, policemen.) There is,
later, one harmonious interlude in the Faithful-Mother's house, or
magical, technicolour night-club, in a tree that takes photographs; and
one beautiful moment of rejoicing, when Drum, Song, and Dance, three

7

tree fellows, perform upon themselves, and the dead arise, and the animals, snakes, and spirits of the bush dance together. But mostly it's hard and haunted going until the drinkard and his wife reach Deads' Town, meet the tapster, and, clutching his gift of a miraculous, all-providing Egg, are hounded out of the town by dead babies. (Here the sinister chapter heading is: "None of The Deads Too Young to Assault."

The writing is nearly always terse and direct, strong, wry, flat and savoury; the big, and often comic, terrors are as near and under-standable as the numerous small details of price, size, and number; and nothing is too prodigious or too trivial to put down in this tall, devilish story.

Dylan Thomas

From *The Listener*, November 13, 1952

The Palm-Wine Drinkard and his Dead Palm-Wine Tapster in the Deads' Town is the work of a thirty-two-year-old West African born in Abeokuta and educated first at the Salvation Army school in that city, later in Lagos High School. He served with the West African Air Force as a coppersmith and he now holds a minor position in the Department of Labour in Lagos.

One Sunday morning he went to see a very old man on his father's farm. The old man roasted a big yam for him and then offered him palm-wine.

> He started to serve the wine with bamboo tumbler. This bamboo tumbler was as deep as a glass tumbler, but it could contain the palm wine which could reach half a bottle. Having taken about four, my body was not at rest at all, it was intoxicating me as if I was dreaming. But when he noticed how I was doing, he told me to let us go and sit down on the bank of a big river which is near the farm for fresh breeze which was blowing here and there with strong power. Immediately we reached there and sat under the shade of some palm trees which collected or spread as a tent I fall aslept. After an hour, he woke me up, and I came to normal condition at that time.
>
> When he believed that I could enjoy what he wanted to tell me, then he told me the story of the Palm-Wine Drinkard.

Writing roughly with lead pencil three hours each day for five days, Mr. Tutuola then produced the first work of literature to be written in English by a West African and published in London. It is a very curious work, with an auroral quality of half-light, this herald of the dawn of Nigerian literature. How much was due to the very old man, how much to the influence of palm-wine and how much to the poetic imagination of Amos Tutuola, it is impossible to say. Its origin is already as confused as the authorship of the book of Genesis and its moods are as varied. Some of it is conceived with the extravagant

9

exaggeration of Rabelais. In other passages, one is reminded of *Tyl Eulenspiegel*; elsewhere of the magic metamorphoses of Arabian folk-lore. But though there is much in common with other primitive literatures, *The Palm-Wine Drinkard* is distinctive both by reason of its Africanness and by the author's incorporating into myth the parapher-nalia of modern life, such as telephones, bombs, and railways.

The story of the Palm-Wine Drinkard is the search for a master palm-wine tapster who is dead. Whereas other peoples, inhabiting lands more domitable, place the abodes of the dead either below the earth or in the sky, the equatorial African can readily imagine the dead surviving deep within the jungle. This gives to the book its peculiar horror. A young girl, for example, observes in the market place "A Complete Gentleman", with whom she falls in love. As she follows him into the forest, Complete Gentleman turns and warns her to go back. And with good reason, for as some Complete European Gentlemen hire their fine clothes from Moss Bros., this Complete African Gentleman has hired his limbs, and by the time that he reaches the hole in the ground where he lives, he is merely a Skull with other Skulls playing in the back-yard. Yet, remarks the Palm-Wine Drinkard, when set to win the lady back . . .

> I could not blame the lady for following the Skull as a complete gentleman to his house at all. Because if I were a lady, no doubt I would follow him to wherever he would go, and still as I was a man I would jealous him more than that, because if this gentleman went to the battle field, surely, enemy would not kill him or capture him and if bombers saw him in a town which was to be bombed, they would not throw bombs on his presence, and if they did throw it, the bomb itself would not explode until this gentleman would leave that town, because of his beauty.

The publishers have done well to avoid annotating this book as if it were merely an important anthropological document. They have resisted the temptation of commissioning a surrealist artist to illustrate, for example, Wife and Husband in the Hungry Creature's Stomach or the flight of the Red-people from the Red-town in the form of two red trees, all their leaves singing as human beings. They have left this strange, poetic, nightmare volume to seek for itself the staunch admirers it cannot fail to attract.

Arthur Calder-Marshall

From *The Reporter*, May 12, 1953

Palm-Wine Drinkard
Searches for a Tapster

In West Africa there is only one African novelist, as far as I could discover on a recent trip there, who has begun to write of his own volition in a manner that might be called African. Politically and psychologically, Africans enjoy a larger degree of freedom in West Africa than elsewhere on the continent, but in the arts and letters their development is not without difficulties.

The British are, by and large, indifferent to the African culture except as a museum piece, and the French, while more sympathetic, alternate between encouraging Africans to write and paint and being discouraged by results that are insufficiently Gallic. The enterprising African is much more likely to go to work for the government, where he can put on glasses and necktie and safely harass the white man with the white man's own weapons of legalism, bombast, and chicane.

But in Nigeria there is at least one African who has by-passed this adolescent stage in the growth of Africa into modern society and gone on to something altogether different.

His name is Amos Tutuola. His first book, *The Palm-Wine Drinkard*, was published in England by Faber in May, 1952, and had already achieved a passable success in Africa by November. It will be published here by the Grove Press.

The Palm-Wine Drinkard was on sale in the largest department store in Lagos, and also at the British Council in Accra, Gold Coast, where the original drawing of the dust jacket had been framed and hung on the wall. At the University College of Nigeria at Ibadan, I encountered British intellectuals who thought little of the book, but they had at least felt compelled to read it. Perhaps they were a little put out at the fact that the college bookstore had received letters from the author urging them to keep it in stock.

The Palm-Wine Drinkard is a work of fantasy, written in English but not an English of this world. The style is unschooled but oddly expressive. (The publishers reproduce a page of the manuscript to show the minor nature of their editing.) The story elements are almost wholly African, and few European derivations are apparent—unless the author was exposed to *Pilgrim's Progress* in childhood and had since forgotten about it. Here is the opening paragraph:

"I was a palm-wine drinkard since I was a boy of ten years of age. I had no other work more than to drink palm-wine in my life. In those days we did not know other money, except COWRIES [seashells], so that everything was very cheap, and my father was the richest man in our town."

The palm-wine drinkard's father engages for him an expert tapster, a man to climb the palm trees and tap the wine, and gives him a tree farm nine miles square, with 560,000 palm trees. "So my friends were uncountable by that time and they were drinking palm-wine with me from morning till a late hour in the night."

One day the tapster, working at the top of one of the tallest trees, "fell down unexpectedly and died at the foot of the palm-tree as a result of injuries." The drinkard and his friends bury him there, but afterward "my friends did not come to my house again, they left me there alone . . ." Unable to find a tapster "who could tap the palm-wine to my requirement," the drinkard has to take to ordinary water—"which I was unable to taste before"—and his friends avoid him.

"When I saw that there was no palm-wine for me again, and nobody could tap it for me, then I thought within myself that old people were saying that the whole people who had died in this world, did not go to heaven directly, but they were living in one place somewhere in this world. So that I said that I would find out where my palm-wine tapster who had died was.

"One fine morning, I took all my native juju and my father's juju with me and I left my father's hometown to find out whereabouts was my tapster who had died."

The rest of the book tells of the drinkard's supernatural wanderings on the way to "Dead's Town" and back. It differs from traditional descents to the Underworld in that the hero acquires a wife and they continue as a couple. (He rescues her from a Skull, who each day rents the necessary parts of a body to make himself into a "complete gentleman" and returns them in the evening.) They suffer many ordeals, overcome them by prodigies of magic, and eventually find the tapster—only to discover that he cannot come away with them, since he had "spent two years in training" and "had qualified as a full dead man . . ."

The narrative is imaginatively rich, with imagery drawn from both African legend and modern realities (like sandpaper, telephone, and football fields), and it seems to treat the racial relationship between black and white chiefly by ignoring it—which is not a bad idea. *The*

Palm-Wine Drinkard may not be, indeed, a product of genius, but it is certainly that of an unusual talent, seeking to express itself in spite of unusual obstacles.

The fame of the book, curiously enough, has not yet achieved fame for its author. Amos Tutuola is a messenger boy in the government Labour Department in Lagos. "Most people," the American consul told me, "don't know who he is or where he is." He is thirty-three years old and unmarried, a farmer's son from a large town sixty-odd miles north of Lagos. He had six years of elementary education and further training as a blacksmith; during the war he was a metalworker for the R. A. F. His present salary is eighty-five pounds (about $240) a year, and in November he had not yet received royalties from the book.

I had asked to have an interview with the author at the U. S. consulate, which may have been a mistake, for he was painfully shy and probably suspicious of my motives. The conversation was uncomfortable and inconclusive for both of us. It only occurred to me later that he might never have been interviewed before, and I wonder what he made of it all.

As an exercise in imagination, try to conceive of an author who (1) probably has never met another author, (2) owns no books, (3) is not known to his daily acquaintances as an author, (4) has no personal contact with his publisher, (5) is not certain where his book is on sale, and (6) does not think of himself as an author.

To Mr. Tutuola stories are things that exist; he merely puts them down. He is aware that the ability to do so is not universal—"Many people in Lagos cannot write stories"—but the act of composition as such has no creative aura for him. *The Palm-Wine Drinkard* came about because he used to go out on Sundays to a palm plantation, where there was an old man who told stories; presumably many of them are in the book. Mr. Tutuola "composed" it in two days and wrote it in three months, "just playing with it," during 1950, for lack of anything better to do. "I cannot sit down doing nothing," he said. The sale of writing as a commodity he understands, and I suspect he made the natural connection between America and commercial opportunity, but he himself is only its agent. When I asked him what his future writing plans were, he said that possibly there were more stories down on the farm and that if I liked he might be able to get some. "Leave the matter for me."

Mr. Tutuola's second novel, *My Life in the Bush of Ghosts*, has been in the hands of his publishers for nearly a year. It seems to him perfectly natural that they should wait "until they have seen the reception of this one." Press clippings of *The Palm-Wine Drinkard*'s reviews in England have been sent to him, and he is conscious—perhaps too conscious—of minor flaws, of his own naivete, of being treated as a curiosity. "The grammar is not correct at all. I made many mistakes."

One wonders how a man like this can become important in Nigeria except by becoming pretentious. I went to the Labour Department later, to get him to sign my copy of his book, and found him sitting in a corner in his loose-fitting uniform, asleep. I had to get to him past row on row of bespectacled Nigerians, sitting at their desks in bureaucratic self-satisfaction and palpably annoyed at the breach of decorum in a white man's calling on a messenger. He asked me what I wanted him to write and then, after signing the inscription, he said: "I think, when you reach there, the U. S. A., you write a letter to me." I said I would, but why did he want me to?

"So I know you not forget me."

Eric Larrabee

From *The New York Times Book Review*, **September 20, 1953**

If you like Anna Livia Plurabelle, Alice in Wonderland and the poems of Dylan Thomas, the chances are you will like this novel, though probably not for reasons having anything to do with the author's intentions. For Amos Tutuola is not a revolutionist of the word, not a mathematician, not a surrealist. He is a true primitive. And the pleasure a sophisticated reader will derive from his un-willed style and trance-like narrative is akin to the pleasure generated by popular painters like Rousseau or Obin, whose surface subject-matter is our world of artillery pieces, Coca-Cola bottles and soccer, but whose innocence and quasi-academic technique remind us so movingly of the fabulous lost worlds of Sassetta and Pisanello, Carpaccio and Breughel.

However, Tutuola's world, having no connection at all with the European rational and Christian traditions, has qualities foreign to all these artists and writers. The narrator who calls himself "an expert palm-wine drinkard" lives on a farm containing 560,000 palm trees and employs a palm-wine tapster (is there even such a thing as palm-wine, one wonders—and one finds that there is) who taps 150 kegs of the stuff every morning, which our hero drinks "before 2 o'clock p.m." The tapster falls from a tree and is killed and the remainder of the book consists of the indescribable adventures of the narrator as he searches for his tapster in "Deads' Town" and lots of stranger places, finds him, is given a miracle-working Egg which feasts a houseful of guests, and then, when they've overstayed their welcome, flogs them to death—"especially old people and children and many of my friends."

Whether an ethnologist or a psychologist could "explain" any of this in terms that would relieve the perplexity of our literal minds, only a dullard who has buried his childhood under several mountains of best-selling prose could fail to respond to Tutuola's naive poetry. Such a one would be like the man described as "walking toward his back or backward." Whereas, the narrator, being one of those he calls "the alives" and traveling down "the really road," is never stopped from getting where he wants to go by time, space, or even death: "I myself had changed into a flat pebble and was throwing myself along the way to my home town." The author of this unique book is a West African, 33 years old. He had six years of elementary education, further training as a blacksmith and (during the war) as a metal-worker for the R.A.F. As Dylan Thomas says, he writes in "young English." Eric Larrabee, who interviewed him and described his book in *The Reporter*, observed that "it seems to treat the racial relationship between black and white chiefly by ignoring it—which is not a bad idea." But there is a sentence in the book which may belie this, though it purports to be no more than a description of "9 terrible creatures 3 feet high," encountered by the narrator, in a paper bag: "Their skin was as sharp as sandpaper, with small short horns on their palms, very hot steam was rushing out of their noses and mouths whenever breathing, their bodies were as cold as ice and we did not understand their language, because it was sounding as a church bell."

Selden Rodman

From the *New Yorker*, December 5, 1953

Amos Tutuola's *The Palm Wine Drinkard* is called on its jacket "a novel from Africa," and a distinguished critic has declared that it explores a path American writers might profitably follow. All this indicates that an enjoyable piece of effervescence is being taken a great deal too seriously. Mr. Tutuola, like Daisy Ashford, is a natural storyteller, and his principal strength is much the same—the lack of inhibition in an uncorrupted innocence. Sir James Barrie's young friend, in telling the story of Mr. Salteena, set down whatever came into her head in the order in which it came, because she thought that is how storybooks are produced. Mr. Tutuola, a literate English-speaking West African, has encountered the novel and its freedom of invention after being brought up on the folk story, which combines rigidity of form with freedom of embroidery. He has scrambled the two and let the results flow onto paper. They will seem startling and new only to those who were not lucky enough to be raised on the old-fashioned nursery literature of Grimm and Andrew Lang's Blue, Red, Orange, and Green books of fairy tales. Those who received this painless grounding in folklore will meet one familiar character after another in Mr. Tutuola's story, from the man who goes to the house of Death to fetch back a friend to the miracle child who is stronger than a hundred men. What gives the book its great charm is that its time-honored material is treated without any trace of antiquarianism or of the folklore collector's inevitable self-consciousness. Mr. Tutuola tells his story as if nothing like it had ever been written down before, and he gives his themes the pristine quality they must have had when they were the living substance of the cultures that produced them and before they were demoted to the nursery. One catches a glimpse of the very beginning of literature, that moment when writing at last seizes and pins down the myths and legends of an analphabetic culture.

You will remember when I mentioned the three fellows, namely:—"DRUM, SONG AND DANCE." So when this lady (Dance) saw that I helped them greatly, and they

were also in a comfortable place . . . she sent for the two
other fellows (Drum and Song) to come to their new town
for a special occasion. But how could we enjoy those three
fellows? Because nobody could beat drum as "Drum" could
beat himself, nobody could sing as "Song" could sing
himself, and nobody could dance as "Dance" could dance
herself in this world. Who would challenge them? Nobody
at all.

This sounds naive and barbaric, and it is. It is true that when the
Muses of our culture, part birds and part women, first frequented Horse
Fountain, before the Greek poets made them respectable and neat-
ankled young women, their apparently elegant names—Euterpe,
Calliope, Terpsichore, and so forth—meant things as simple as Drum,
Song and Dance, and that they were conceived in those terms. But it
was a fact only because the poets had not yet written their poems, and
it is not possible to recover that simplicity. It is only possible to envy
Mr. Tutuola his good luck in being a castaway on a little island in time
where he can be archaic without being anachronistic. His situation,
however, is unique, and it would be as fatal for a writer with a richer
literary inheritance to imitate him as it would be for a sculptor to adopt
the idioms of Benin or Mycenae. *The Palm Wine Drinkard* must be
valued for its own freakish sake, and as an unrepeatable happy hit.

Anthony West

My Life in the Bush of Ghosts

From *New Statesman and Nation*, March 6, 1954

In *The Palm Wine Drinkard*, published last year, a modern West African imagination was working with a lazy freedom in the English language. A soft, amazed voice led us easily out of real life into a fantasy life as barbarous, bloody and frightening as the masks of the tribal ceremonies. Now, in a second "novel" we can know more about this extraordinary writer. He is a Nigerian from Abeokuta, born in 1920 of Christian parents. He was educated by the Salvation Army and at high school, became a coppersmith and is now a civil servant in Lagos. The Rev. Geoffrey Parrinder, who writes a good introduction to the new book, points out one advantage which Tutuola has had from a brief education: he has not fallen into that stilted English which so many educated African writers use, but has worked out a loose, talking prose, close to "pidgin." (I have found only one piece of literary dead wood in the whole tale—"Without more ado I took to my heels"). Strange verbs like "transparented" are used; mission hall adjectives like "sceptical" for "pagan." One cannot tell whether works like Tutuola's are freaks that mark a linguistic crisis or rebirth in a culture, or whether they are the forerunners of a powerful outburst of oral literature. In many English-speaking countries where masses of unlettered people are now receiving education, it looks as though the exceptional imaginations will (from the examination point of view) be driven underground into "bad" English.

This new book is an Odyssey and though, after a few pages, it runs into nightmare, there is a true course and meaning to it. The last line is "This is what hatred did." The hatred began in the jealousies of the polygamous life: the narrator is, at first, a boy of seven, the son of his father's third wife. The other two wives have only daughters and, fearing that the boy will inherit, they try to poison him. Then a tribal war breaks out and they purposely leave him, hoping he will be killed. He runs off to the bush and there he is captured by ghosts. Millions of these "deads," often no more than fragments of bodies and generally repugnant, inhabit the bush and for 27 years he wanders among them—

tortured, punished and abused. All the time his main quest is for his home and his mother. At the end of the tale, he achieves his aim, partly by the aid of a television ghostess who shows him a picture of his home and family in the sores on the palm of her hand. (Tutuola has never seen television; odd that he has imagined the nasty, crumbling, decaying texture of the television pictures.) In a violent, bizarre but quite simple talking manner, Tutuola is describing universal experience in a way that will be deeply interesting to psycho-analysts and anthropologists, but he ought not to be read for scientific reasons: he has the immediate intuition of a creative artist working by spell and incantation.

The important thing in Tutuola is his power to set down the collusion of dream and person. The startled critic will find moments of *Alice in Wonderland*, Bunyan and the Bible, in the story-telling and a groping, Christian jubilation. His ghosts are apocalyptical yet local. He is carried off by a "smelling ghost" to be eaten alive by him. Obscene as a cess-pit, crawling with insects and snakes, smeared with urine and rank blood, this thing carries the child off and turns him into a horse. The story goes from one repulsive terror to another, from city after city of the dead, where river ghosts, insect ghosts, burglar ghosts, the ghosts of the Nameless town and the Hopeless town conspire to punish him or to eat him. In each episode the narrator is enslaved and beaten, in one buried alive, in another half roasted on a fire, in others crushed or bitten by snakes. There are one or two sardonic moments and there is a little happiness when he lives with the monstrous "flash-eyed mother", whose eyes light up town and jungle, or when he marries a ghost called the "super lady"; but in general the pilgrimage is emotional—through guilt, terror and despair. The mother figure is a monstrous imaginary idol. Her body occupies a whole town which is six miles round and is as "clean as a football field", and she is fed by the ghosts of babies. Millions of babies' heads with eyes like fireflies appear on her body and if the heads talk "their voices would be sounding as if somebody strikes an iron or the church bell ... if all of them are talking together at a time, it would be as a big market's noises, they were arguing, flogging and reporting themselves to their mother."

This would be intolerable because preposterous reading but for two things: the dramatic idea of compulsion in an animistic culture. The boy cannot move, for example, "because the bush wanted me to be in one place"; at another point he is betrayed in his flight by "the talking land", which speaks as he runs over it and so exposes him to his enemies. These inventions are poetic and alarming. The barbarous fantasy is not free, but is ruled by the dreadful conspiracy of primitive belief and sensibility. The other strength of the story is simply its seriousness. The marvellous is domesticated. The tale of the Spider's Web Bush, for example, describes how a ghost captures him and believes he is his dead father who has never had proper burial. He is bound in web and buried alive. But a grave-robber digs him up in order to eat the spiders which were hidden in the coffin to give the dead something to eat on the way to heaven. Other ghosts want to join the feast and to eat him as well. A fire is lit, but the web is wet and he does not burn. But soon, while the ghosts are quarrelling, he resourcefully lies on the red hot fire, gradually dries the web and so bursts it open and escapes. That night he finds a soft warm safe place—a house he thinks it is—and wakes up to find he is sleeping in the pouch of an animal.

Fear of the jungle, fear of the dead, fear of being eaten, despair in suffering and disgust, are the main emotions of the book, but occasionally there is a slightly comic note and a suggestion of symbolism or allegory. Hopeless-land seems to come from Bunyan. Here people do not talk; indeed it is a crime to do so, but simply communicate by shrugs of the shoulders. The narrator cries out "Oh!" when his foot is trodden on, and he is at once hauled up before the king:

> Then he was asking me these questions with a shrug of his shoulders, as follows—"Who are you?" But as I did not understand what he was asking me with the shrug of his shoulders, so to set myself free I began to reply as well with a shrug of my shoulders as he was doing, which means to him "You are a bastard king." And again, on the same spot that I stood before him I mistakenly raised up and down the lids of my eyes which means "You are a fool" and this is contrary to the law of the town.

And there is the Loss-or-Gain river crossing—so called because the traveller leaves his clothes on the bank and, swimming naked over, picks up the clothes left by travellers in the opposite direction. Here the narrator and his wife, the super-lady, lost, for they found only baby clothes waiting for them.

Tutuola's fancy is endless; yet it is controlled by the tribal folklore. It discernibly expresses the unconscious of a race and even moments of the nightmare element in our own unconscious. The slimy or electric movements of nightmare, its sickening logic, its hypnotising visual quality, its dreadful meaningfulness, are put down by an earnest and ingenious story-teller. One feels one has been taken back thousands of years to the first terrors of human nature. A book like this disposes at once of the illusions, so useful to settlers, that "the African is a child." Tutuola's voice is like the beginning of man on earth, man emerging, wounded and growing. He is not the specimen of the folklorist and anthropologist, but a man living out a recognisable human and moral ordeal.

V. S. Pritchett

From *The Spectator*, February 26, 1954

Like *The Palm-Wine Drinkard*, its predecessor, *My Life in the Bush of Ghosts* is a kind of writing difficult to define and even to describe. At the age of seven, its narrator wanders into a hole in a hill, under the impression "that it was an old man's house who was expelled from a town for an offence." This is soon disproved by the appearance of a golden-ghost, a silverish-ghost and a copperish-ghost; and the arrival of Smelling-ghost ("his nose and eyes were very hard to look at as they were very dirty and smelling") puts it beyond doubt that the scene is the mythical Bush of Ghosts. This is a self-consistent world complete with towns, currency, wars, husbandry, its own Directorate of Medical Services and a special branch of the Methodist Church. There are some ex-human ghosts, but most are non-human living creatures, not always immortal. In appearance they vary from near-human to such monstrosities as the flash-eyed mother: "Millions of heads which were just like a baby's head appeared on her body. . . . She had a large mouth which could swallow an elephant uncut." It is no surprise to learn that "90% of ghosts hate any of the earthly persons to enter this bush," and the narrator, as he wanders in and out of captivity and from one ghost-town to another, is starved, defiled, thrust into proximity with mosquitoes, snakes and spiders, confined for long periods to a tree-trunk, a food-bag, a pitcher and an animal's pouch, turned into a horse and a cow, and given a ghost's head in error ("this head was smelling badly") after being decapitated in battle. In the intervals, however, he is befriended to the extent of marrying twice and begetting a son by the Super-lady, and is almost reluctant to leave the Bush of Ghosts and return home after twenty-four years.

What sort of book is it, then? In the face of a tissue of un-fathomable African myth and fairy-story, written in a completely new English idiom, for, presumably, a native audience, a European reader will blench at this question, and only feel a fool if he mutters: "Nightmare . . . primitive unconscious . . . episodic allegory without a key reminiscent of Kafka . . . poetry . . ." Certain emotions can at any rate be identified: physical misery, horror, fear, despair and a unique grotesque humour that seems not to be felt by the author as humour in our sense at all, not as "relief" or as an indication that human ideas still prevail in his ghost-world, but as just another serious, fantastic and violent effect. Mr. Tutuola's book is a severe test of our originality as readers, of our ability to throw all our preferences and preconceptions out of the window when the need arises. It will probably only go to show that I can't do this if I say that my interest flags when I read something that so rarely evokes anything in life as I know it, and if I anticipate a possible objection by pleading that even misery, pain and the rest cannot be universal and become blurred in a strange context. But this book clearly needs repeated readings before its extraordinariness can be fully noted, let alone mastered, and there is no doubt of the size of Mr. Tutuola's talent, which makes the average "modern novel" look jejune and vapid. Try this bit.

> But as the bush which surrounded this pond was very quiet without any noise of a creature whatever it might be so I began to feel much cold without being cold, and when my heart was not at rest for the quietness of that place then I went to the place that I spread the skin in the sun and began to warm myself in this sun perhaps my body would be at rest, but when there was no change at all until the skin was dried then I took it and left that area as quickly as possible. So I wore it as a cloth, of course, it could only reach from my knees to the waist, so I was going on with it like that.

Kingsley Amis

The Controversy in *West Africa*

From *West Africa*, **February 27, 1954**

Amos Tutuola's first book, *The Palm-Wine Drinkard*, was enthusi-astically received by a number of English critics, including Dylan Thomas, V. S. Pritchett, and, in her latest book, Elspeth Huxley. *My Life in the Bush of Ghosts* (Faber, 12s. 6d.) is the same mixture of devilishness, grotesque adventure, and naive story-telling. The book is firmly rooted in West African folk-lore; a number of the stories can be identified in the recent Penguin edition of West African folk tales. As Dr. Parrinder tells us in his introduction, the stories are "genuine African myths, such as are told in countless villages round the fire or in the tropical moonlight." Mr. Tutuola's English is a very unreliable instrument but it has its gusto, and there can be no question that the stories come over with a greater pungency in his two books than if his English had been "correct" but lifeless. His images seem to come from direct observation:

"there I saw a very short ghost who was not more than three feet high but very corpulent as a pregnant woman who would deliver either to-day or to-morrow."

The same comparison occurs, however, several times and so becomes ironed out "as flat as a football field"—another phrase which is overworked. Nevertheless his work is scattered with striking phrases, though this book is not as powerfully written as *The Palm-Wine Drinkard*. I particularly remember from that book the story of the Skulls where Tutuola's narrative is unusually plain and perspicuous;

"But one day, the lady attempted to escape from the hole, and at the same time the Skull who was watching her whistled to the rest of the Skulls that were in the backyard, the whole of them rushed out to the place where the lady sat on the bull-frog, so they caught her, but as all of them were rushing out, they were rolling on the ground *as if a thousand petrol drums were pushing along a hard road.*

We may parallel the last few words with a sentence from *My Life in the Bush of Ghosts* which might have been written by Sean O'Casey;

29

> "If all the heads and herself were eating at the same
> time their mouths would be making noises as if one
> hundred winches are working together."

Mr. Tutuola has a great talent for using these phrases which bring
modern West Africa immediately before us.

Nevertheless one is forced to remember V. S. Pritchett's remark
that *The Palm-Wine Drinkard* was "a freak." Now the freak has been
repeated, and we are told that still other manuscripts exist, presumably
of a similar kind. Is there sufficient strength in Mr. Tutuola's work to
justify publication of further works; do they point the way for a true
Nigerian literature in English? There must be grave doubts whether
there is a strong possibility of development in or from the two books.
Dr. Parrinder's anecdote is in fact a very telling criticism because not
only the author but also the reader must re-live the experience of a true
work of literature: "I realised how deeply he lived in his own narrative
when I asked Tutuola the reason for the apparently haphazard order of
the towns of the ghosts. He replied, quite simply, 'That is the order in
which I came to them.' " Tutuola's words are in any case ambiguous.
Then there is no doubt that *My Life in the Bush of Ghosts* is still very
repetitious even after Dr. Parrinder's prunings. Finally this book is
much less sustained than *The Palm-Wine Drinkard*. The Methodist
Church in the Bush of Ghosts is as methodical as the Methodist Church
in the clear—but it is less inspired.

I do not wish to discourage anyone from reading these two
extraordinary books from which any imaginative reader will experience
a frightening, monstrous and vigorous world. Mr. Tutuola is undoubtedly hag-ridden. But I think that the way to West African
expression in English will have to be different from this. The neat and
careful nought out of ten school of West African English will come to
an end but it may be a preliminary to the full control of English. In the
meanwhile Mr. Tutuola, native of that most fascinating city, Abeokuta,
gives us the true macabre energy of Africa, and we are very much in his
debt.

Eric Robinson

From *West Africa*, April 10, 1954

Sir,

I do not know if Mr. Eric Johnson reviewed Mr. Tutuola's first book in your journal. I remember the reviewer paid such glowing tributes to this book that those of us who nursed a genuine desire for that type of book rushed to buy it. Alas, what did we find? A long tale written in a language we did not understand. I hold your reviewer and others of his ilk accountable for the impact of this second book on the reading public.

Now let us face facts. *Palm Wine Drinkard* should not have been published at all. The language in which it is written is foreign to West Africans and English people, or anybody for that matter. It is bad enough to attempt an African narrative in "good English", it is worse to attempt it in Mr. Tutuola's strange lingo (or, shall I say, the language of the "Deads"?). The language is not West African Patois as some think. Patois is more orderly and intelligible than the language of *The Palm Wine Drinkard*. Patois does not contain such words as "unreturnable", "weird" or such expressions as "the really road". To illustrate, you may compare the construction of the Kroo proverb—"When massa thief 'e take. When boy take 'e thief," with the construction of the simile "as flat as a football field".

Readers who have read *The Palm Wine Drinkard* will perhaps notice that Mr. Tutuola's attempt consists largely of translating Yoruba ideas into English in almost the same sequence as they occur to his mind. The example quoted by Mr. Robinson well illustrates this. The expression "to-day or to-morrow" is well-known in Yoruba. The book would have been more readable if Mr. Tutuola had stuck to this method of direct translation, but he mars it by occasional inclusion of words taken from the dictionary at random, by comparison with objects which are foreign to Yoruba speech, and by incorrect and too literal translations. How many English readers know that "Unreturnable Heaven's Land" is Mr. Tutuola's version of "The undiscovered country from whose bourne no traveller returns"?

31

The book ought to have been written in West African Patois proper, or in Yoruba, but then Mr. Tutuola's literary tactics would have been exposed. Besides the fact that his stories are well-known, and have been published in one form or another, most of his plots were borrowed from Fagunwa's *Ogboju Ode*. He even gave himself away when he referred to this book in one of his chapters as "The Brave Hunter in the Bush of the Ghosts".

Perhaps your reviewers will try to be more factual. The tributes they pay to Tutuola's books compared with the hard remarks about *The New West Africa* suggest that an obscure connection exists between the "brain" encouraging publication of the first types of book and the "brain" attempting to discourage the latter.

Babasola Johnson

Editor's note following Babasola Johnson's letter

Mr. Johnson is entitled to his opinion about the literary quality of Mr. Tutuola's books: but his remark that *Palm Wine Drinkard* should never have been published suggests that he thinks he is entitled to dictate to Mr. Tutuola how he should write and to the public what they should like or read. There is no connection of the kind suggested between the reviews in *West Africa* of Mr. Tutuola's books and others. Mr. Robinson is a former lecturer in English at University College, Ibadan, the reviewer of *The New West Africa* is an economist. That book was criticised on "factual" grounds and the reviewer did not discourage such books but welcomed its appearance: he regretted that it wasn't better. It is difficult to see how works of imagination, like Mr. Tutuola's, can be assessed "factually".

Editor

From *West Africa*, April 17, 1954

Sir,

I was most interested to hear Mr. Johnson's views of Amos Tutuola's novels (*West Africa*, April 10 issue). There are some matters, however, which he has confused. First, I was not, as you know, the reviewer of *The Palm Wine Drinkard*. Secondly, I do not know the reviewer of *The New West Africa*, and I regret to say that I have not read that book. This disposes, I think, of the suggestion that there is a scheme, in which I am involved, to encourage one kind of book and to discourage another. Thirdly, and this interests me most, Mr. Johnson does not seem to have read my review of *My Life in the Bush of Ghosts* very carefully. In it I made some very serious reservations to my recommendation of Tutuola's work;

> "There must be grave doubts whether there is a strong possibility of development in or from the two books"

and

> "I do not wish to discourage anyone from reading these two extraordinary books . . . But I think that the way to West African expression in English will have to be different from this."

I pointed out moreover that Tutuola's work is based on Yoruba folk tales.

Yet in fairness to Mr. Tutuola one cannot accept Mr. Johnson's standards of criticism. It is no detriment to Mr. Tutuola's work that he has woven well-known stories into his own version of a spiritual pilgrimage. Many of Chaucer's fabliaux were equally well known in his time. Nor is it the critic's function to dictate to the author what mode of language he shall employ. The basis of judgment is surely whether the language used is a sufficient instrument for the writer's purposes. Now Mr. Tutuola's language is often clumsy and often repetitive, but it is remarkably vigorous at its best. It makes no difference, to my mind, that much of that vigour is carried over direct from the Yoruba. In this case it is clear that much of the vigorous phraseology is Tutuola's own.

Yours sincerely,

University of Bristol   *Eric Robinson*

From *West Africa*, May 1, 1954

Portrait: A Life in the Bush of Ghosts

"To compose the thing is not hard for me. Even at work I compose, for I cannot be pleased to do nothing, and messenger does not always have work to do in the office." Those are the words of Amos Tutuola, whose first book, *The Palm-Wine Drinkard*, sent a mild cyclone of excitement through the surfeited minds of leading literary critics.

Who is this spinner of strange, compelling fantasy, to whom "composing the thing" is not difficult? Tutuola looks like a thousand other junior government clerks. He seems much younger than his thirty-four years. His speech is slow and diffident, and his manner shyly polite. Only when he narrates one of his own stories, such as *Dola With Her Kola-nut Tree*, does he reveal a little of himself. As his expressive hands gesture impatiently, miming the words he has such difficulty in articulating, you realise that the homely face and pleasant smile, the messenger's brown uniform, portray nothing of the real man at all. They are the dream; the tales seething in his mind are the reality.

Almost all children everywhere are told legends, and fairy tales with a moral, by their mothers. To Tutuola his mother and his aunt, with whom he lived in the township of Iporo-Ake, Abeokuta, related all the folk tales they had heard from their mother. In 1930, when he was ten, Amos became a pupil at the Salvation Army School, where he was by no means a distinguished "scholar". He always longed for the holidays, to escape to his father's farm where, when work and play were finished for the day, he and his young friend would sit in the darkness and tell one another stories; ghost stories, moral tales; any narrative that entertained.

His mother and aunt wanted Amos to continue his education but they could no longer afford to feed and clothe the growing boy and keep him at school, so they let him work as house-boy to a government clerk who promised to look after the child in return for domestic services. His new master enrolled him at the Central School, Ake, where he remained for three years. Later, when the clerk was transferred to

Lagos he took the boy with him and sent him to Lagos High School. After two years young Tutuola decided he should learn a trade, and chose that of blacksmith. With his training he got a job as a metal worker with the R.A.F. at Oshodi. He liked working with heavy substances. He enjoyed making metals bend under his skilled hands.

After the war there wasn't such a demand for people of his calling, so Amos was unemployed for a year, during which his father died. Then in 1948 he became a messenger with the Labour Department in Lagos. He was now for the first time conscious of the weight of hours. To free his mind from the boredom of clock-watching he reverted to an almost forgotten childhood habit of story-telling. But an office worker cannot very well tell stories through the spoken word, even with the indulgent employers Tutuola seems to have had, so he wrote them on scrap paper. Of his first written story, *The Wild Hunter in the Bush of Ghosts*, he says "in a day I cannot sit down doing nothing. I was just playing at it. My intention was not to send it to anywhere."

Tutuola might never have changed this intention had he not read an advertisement in a local paper, in which the advertisers had set forth a list of their latest publications. A few days before Amos had written *The Palm Wine Drinkard*. This extraordinary book was completed during forty-eight hours' febrile work. He spent the next three months enlarging on the original. When he felt satisfied that he had obeyed all the dictates of his imagination, he laid aside his pencil, wrote a final copy in ink, and trustingly sent it off to the organization whose advertisement he had safely kept (The United Society for Christian Literature). They can be considered the "finders" of an author who wrote as no one with whose works they were familiar had ever before written. They replied to Amos, pointing out that they were not publishers but book sellers. However, they kindly volunteered to help to find a publisher. Faber and Faber published *The Palm Wine Drinkard* in 1952. It was subsequently published in the U.S.A., and in a French edition.

Although his book met with instant success abroad, Tutuola had as yet no ambition to devote his life to writing. He still wanted to be a blacksmith. But that avenue remained obstinately closed to him, though he passed a trade test successfully. Perhaps to dull the edge of his frustration, or maybe because he married and needed a little more money to support his wife and mother, or more likely just because he had a compulsion to write, he started *My Life in the Bush of Ghosts*. After the now almost familiar two days spent on drafting the entire volume, and three months on revision, Tutuola sent his second book to his publisher. It appeared in print this year.

Since then this eager author has sent some short stories, based on folk-lore, to the B.B.C. Three have been broadcast: interesting when you remember that a convention has been established that script writing is quite a different art form from written matter meant to be read silently. Tutuola has succeeded in both fields, using precisely the same technique. His own spoken and written English are identical and he writes exactly what presents itself to his mind. His revision is not of the painstaking, scholarly kind, where the author suffers intensely over a thousand subtle details. While Amos is aware that the language he uses does not conform to standard Queen's English, he is helpless to do anything about it in his semi-literate state (he did not go to school until he was ten, and seven years spent at various schools did no more than teach him the elements of the three Rs). He can only re-write passages that fail to portray in word pictures the ghostly creatures of his imagining as vividly as he sees them.

Tutuola confesses that he more than half-believes the tales he writes and he can, without mental trauma, reconcile this quasi-belief with his strong Christian views. His belief seems to supply a clue to the compelling nature of his books. The reader, however sophisticated, enters into the illusion and fantasy and momentarily believes with him.

After much thought Amos has decided to attend evening classes to "improve" himself, so that he may develop into what he describes as "a real writer". "I am not telling the story as it is in my head all the time, but I cannot speak good English for them yet" is his moving self-condemnation. While an intensive course in English would naturally extend Tutuola's vocabulary, it is doubtful if it would also widen the range of his vision. If his books were couched in stilted, grammatically correct English, would they not lose their excitingly imaginative texture, and degenerate into just another collection of fables?

This author's written style is unique among present-day writers. It seems a valid vehicle for the expression of his particular obsession: ghosts, both quick and dead; for he merely translates in a literal fashion from the Yoruba in which all the old legends are still verbally told. If he does "improve" himself educationally, I hope Amos will not come forth too far from his dream world, peopled as it is by creatures an imaginative child might create. The essential difference between them is that the average child's creative powers are dulled by the impact of adultness: the vision is blurred, then lost for ever. Tutuola, by chance or genius, has preserved the vision. Even so, he feels "written out" and intends to return to Abeokuta for a short time to rest and draw fresh inspiration from listening to old people re-telling Yoruba legends. He will then decide whether to write another "ghost" book, or to try something different.

Very few Nigerians seem to have heard of Tutuola and fewer have read his books. He is gregarious and spends almost every evening with friends, mostly tailors, blacksmiths, carpenters, and other tradesmen. Many of them are illiterate, and have no idea that when Amos leaves them he goes home to read the newspapers and pictorial magazines and then settles down to write until midnight. Among those acquainted with his works young intellectuals predominate. Even they, for the most part, have not fully realised that although Tutuola's perceptiveness has not been overtaken by scholarship, or indeed, in his case, perhaps because of that, he has all the promise of a great imaginative writer if little of the conventional paraphernalia. It is, therefore, not unlikely that for some years to come he will have a wider reading public outside his own country than within Nigeria. Taken by and large, the reading public confines itself to improving works and text-books. In a country where people are poor and almost everyone is filled with a burning desire to become "somebody" there is little time and less money to spend on light literature. When the present trickle of courageous apostles of a national culture broadens into a lively stream, all literate Nigeria, and not just the appreciative few, may regard Amos Tutuola with pride as pioneer of a new literary form, based on an ancient verbal style.

from a Nigerian correspondent

From *West Africa*, June 5, 1954

Sir,

I have followed the points so far (*West Africa*, April 10 and 17 issues) on the books of Amos Tutuola. Having read *The Palm Wine Drinkard* and *My Life in the Bush of Ghosts* I must express my disagreement with Mr. Johnson's views and state how I came to regard Tutuola's books as works of literary merit.

Mr. Johnson was not pleased with the language and contended that the reviewer's tributes were misplaced. To me, the language employed in the two books does not (without being influenced by fondness of palm wine) read strangely. One has to look into a recently published book called *Folk Tales and Fables* to grasp fully the point I am making.

Mr. Tutuola writes on folk tales; to write these successfully demands real ability on the writer's part so that he can carry his readers with him. To do this his style must attune to the subject matter. Mr. Tutuola has, in my opinion, achieved this; the style is romantic.

Whilst agreeing with the views of his reviewers, I believe that Mr. Tutuola's style already sets a pattern for West African folk-tale writing.

Yours faithfully,
Ade Sodipo

From *West Africa*, June 5, 1954

Sir,

The "portrait" of Amos Tutuola in your May 1 issue has stirred my interest in the work of this "new author". Unfortunately (or perhaps fortunately) I have not read any of his two "extraordinary books", as Mr. Eric Robinson described them.

But the news that *A Life in the Bush of Ghosts* has been translated into French is really startling.

From the "portrait" it is clear that the author is not an academic man and therefore I submit that it is not a high literary standard that has attracted so many European and American readers. What then? The writer of the "portrait" suggests that it is mere love of light reading. But I think there is another reason.

Most Englishmen, and perhaps Frenchmen, are pleased to believe all sorts of fantastic tales about Africa, a continent of which they are profoundly ignorant. The "extraordinary books" of Mr. Tutuola (which must undoubtedly contain some of the unbelievable things in our folklores) will just suit the temper of his European readers as they seem to confirm their concepts of Africa. No wonder then that they are being read not only in English, but in French as well. And once this harm (I call it harm) is done, it can hardly be undone again. Mr. Tutuola will get his money and his world-wide fame all right, but the sufferers will be the unfortunate ones who have cause to come to England or Europe. I am not being unduly anxious.

Mr. Tutuola is perfectly free, as you suggested earlier, to write and publish anything he likes but I would suggest that undue prominence is being given to these two books which, as far as I can gather, are of no literary value in spite of the "author's written style" being "unique among present-day writers"; books which show no marks of possible future development and which at best are incapable of giving accurate information about Africa (or Nigeria for that matter).

Yours, etc.,

Durham   *I. Adeagbo Akinjogbin*

From *West Africa*, May 8, 1954

Sir,

I read with great interest and sympathy the letter from Mr. Babasola Johnson on the subject of the books of Amos Tutuola. There are a great many West Africans who agree with Mr. Johnson, and deplore the high praise that has been given to this writer's work.

For more than two generations Africans have found it necessary, to find a publisher, to express themselves in a foreign medium, English. This has naturally resulted in the loss of natural expression. The struggle to acquire the English idiom has often resulted in set phrases, long words and cliches which have killed the writing as literature even if not for the interest of its content. This temporary stultification applied also to other arts, and it was a shock, to some an unpleasant shock, when critics suddenly recognised the live beauty of African sculpture which has now, we hope, brought about a revival of the ancient art. Indigenous music suffered in the same way, but a revival of that too is now in force thanks to inspired drummers like Philip Gbeho of Achimota, and enthusiastic recordists like Hugh Tracey of the African Music Society.

Now, like a bombshell, into the literary world comes the extraordinary talent of Amos Tutuola. The translation of well known and rather horrific folk stories into ungrammatical and incomprehensible English is naturally shocking to an African (or a European) who has laboured with his grammar and got prizes for his essays at school, but the whole secret of this new writer's success is explained by Mr. Johnson himself. He says: "Mr. Tutuola's attempt consists largely of translating Yoruba ideas into English in almost the same sequence as they occur in his mind." This is surely the whole essence of art in any form, spontaneity, the art of pouring oneself out into whatever the medium without contrivance or artifice. The talented writer who has had his grammar instilled into him (which takes very many years in a foreign language) gets his writing grammatical without thinking about it, but a writer who has no grammar just does without; but the flow and the colour and the rhythm remain, even if some comprehension is lost.

It is perhaps already safe to say that Amos Tutuola's books can be regarded as another beacon to light the road to true West African nationalism. They have been genuinely hailed as literary gems by people who have surely no political axe to grind, the highbrow literary critics of Europe and America, and they are books that no one in the world but a West African could possibly have written. What is more, like the Ife Bronzes of Nigeria, and the xylophone music of the Wachopi of Portuguese East, they will raise the prestige of African peoples in the world of art, and kill for ever any idea that Africans are copyists of the cultures of other races.

Mercedes Mackay

EARLY CRITICISM

Early Criticism

The earliest articles one finds on Tutuola date from the mid-fifties, when he was known as the author of *The Palm-Wine Drinkard* and *My Life in the Bush of Ghosts*. The commentary tends to be descriptive rather than evaluative, as each writer attempts to explain Tutuola's significance or to account for extreme differences of opinion on his creative work. The emphasis in these articles is on informing the outside world of the existence of a sensational literary freak in Africa.

Serious literary criticism begins in 1957 with the publication of Gerald Moore's perceptive essay in the first issue of *Black Orpheus*. A few years later Harold Collins introduces Tutuola to American academia in *Critique*. Both critics try to come to terms with Tutuola's tenacious hold on the imagination through his unconscious exploitation of universal mythic patterns and motifs.

A NIGERIAN VISIONARY

BY GERALD MOORE

The young Yoruba writer Amos Tutuola has now published three books in England and has made a considerable reputation for himself throughout Europe and America. Enough material exists for some attempt at a careful and serious assessment of his work; even those who have always been inclined to dismiss him as a "freak" will at least admit that he is now too sizable a freak to be ignored.

The most remarkable feature uniting all three of Tutuola's books is his apparently intuitive grasp of basic literary forms. All his heroes or heroines follow out one variant or another of the cycle of the heroic monomyth, Departure — Initiation — Return *(1)*. In his first books the *Palm-Wine Drinkard*, the variant form is that of the deliberate, limited Quest. The whole book may best be seen as the story of the Drinkard's quest for his dead palm-wine tapster and the trials, labours and revelations he experiences in the course of it. It is thus of the utmost significance that the first of all the trials imposed upon him in his journey is the binding and bringing of Death. The naivety and directness with which this tale is told (Death, for example, is discovered digging in his yam-garden) should not obscure its importance. It stands as a clear enough indication that the Drinkard's adventure is not merely a journey into the eternal African bush, but equally a journey into the racial imagination, into the sub-conscious, into the Spirit World that everywhere co-exists and even overlaps with the world of waking "reality." Or, to express it mythically, he is descending, like Gilgamesh, Orpheus, Heracles or Aeneas before him, into the Underworld, there to confront death itself and attempt to carry off some trophy to the living as a symbol of his mastery over the two worlds.

Once the Drinkard is embarked on his adventure, the familiar figures of heroic myth make their appearance one by one. There are the task-masters who impose certain labours upon him as the price for giving information about

---

1. For a study of the monomyth see Joseph Campbell. *The Hero With A Thousand Faces*, Bolingen Series XVII, Pantheon Books (New York, 1949).

Reprinted from *Black Orpheus*, 1 (September 1957), 27-35. An expanded version of this essay was later published in Moore's *Seven African Writers* (London, 1962), 39-57.

the dead tapster's whereabouts; there is the ever-faithful and helpful female companion (Dante's Beatrice, Theseus' Ariadne, Jason's Medea) in the shape of the Drinkard's wife, whom he rescues from the terrible "complete gentleman" and marries as the reward of his exploit; there is the devouring monster (the Red Fish) who must be slain in order to lift the curse from a whole community and free them from the burden of annual human sacrifice. If the Drinkard encounters fewer magic helpers than his European counterpart would probably need, that is because his own "ju-ju" powers are constantly accumulating; for this book reflects the widespread African belief that whenever a magician is overthrown his powers are immediately transferred to the conqueror. Some of the most interesting episodes, from the point of view of comparative mythology, are the birth of the half-bodied baby from the swollen left thumb of the Drinkard's wife, the meeting with Faithful-Mother in the White Tree, and the Hungry Creature which swallows both the Drinkard and his wife during their homeward journey. The half-bodied baby is a very close parallel to the Tom Thumb of European folklore (the same figure is known in Yoruba as Mogbon juba or Child-Wiser-Than-His-Father). The idyllic stay with Faithful-Mother seems a clear enough example of what Campbell calls the "Meeting with the Mother Goddess" (1), while the White Tree may be identified as the usual tree symbol for the World Navel (Ygddrasil, the Bo Tree, the golden apple-tree in the Garden of the Hesperides, the Tree of Knowledge in the Garden of Eden). The sojourn in the belly of the Hungry Creature is certainly the familiar motif of the Whale's Belly from which the hero must emerge reborn, and the manner of the Drinkard's escape is also familiar; he first shoots the Creature dead from inside with a musket and then hacks his way out with a cutlass.

When at last the Drinkard reaches the Deads' Town — the lowest level of Hades — he does not, like Orpheus, enjoy even the chance of getting back to the waking world with his tapster. The tapster sadly explains to him that the dead cannot return with the living, neither can the living dwell with the dead; this is the Drinkard's real Initiation, for thereby he learns the true meaning of life and death. There is an interesting parallel in the ancient Japanese myth of Izanagi and Izanami, told in the "Records of Ancient Matters," though there the unreturning one pursues her would-be rescuer with destructive fury till he is safely back in the land of the living. Nevertheless, the Drinkard does not return empty-handed from his Quest. He wins a boon, though not the one he set out to get, for the tapster gives him a magic egg which will perform anything he asks of it (it may not be too fanciful to see in these magic eggs of folk-lore a regenerated version of the Cosmic Egg from which, according to many mythologies, the whole world was created). So the Drinkard, now a changed man whose past life is dead, for he has undergone his "rite of passage" or education of the soul, sets out on the direct path to his home town. Here Tutuola gives us one of his most appalling visions, for this direct path

---

1. op. cit., Chapter II, 2.

is filled by an unending stream of deads; but the characteristic twist he gives to this Dante-like prospect is that the most terrible of all the deads are the babies, who ferociously assault everyone in their path. As the Drinkard and his wife near their home they fall in with the Mountain Creatures, who become annoyed and pursue them. There follows a typical example of the Transformation Flight, in the course of which the Drinkard turns himself into a pebble and succeeds in hurling himself across the river which separates them from his town. This river is, of course, the Return Threshold, and in accordance with all the rules of mythology the hero's pursuers can never cross it. It is also in accordance with these rules that the boon-bearing hero shall find his community in a state of anarchy and distress, for otherwise his whole adventure might appear wasted. The Drinkard finds his town suffering from a terrible famine and for a while he is able to relieve it by the use of his egg. But soon human greed and folly defeat him and in a fit of anger he turns the power of his egg against the people. Meanwhile the real cause of the famine remains untouched, for Earth and Heaven, once fast friends, are quarrelling over the seniority, and Heaven is demonstrating his greater power by withholding all rain and dew from the Earth. The Drinkard advises that the famine can only be ended by sending a slave to Heaven with a present acknowledging his seniority. In other words, from henceforth the supreme deity will be the male Sky God and not the old female Earth Goddess, protectress of matriarchy. Thus the famine is ended. One of the most powerful moments in the book is the return of the ghost of the sacrificed slave:

> But when the slave carried the sacrifice to Heaven and gave it to Heaven he could not reach halfway back to the earth before a heavy rain came and when the slave was beaten by this heavy rain and when he reached the town, he wanted to escape from the rain, but nobody would allow him to enter his or her house at all. All the people were thinking that he would carry them also to Heaven as he had carried the sacrifice to Heaven, and were afraid.
>
> But when for three months the rain had been falling regularly, there was no famine again.

In this way the resolution of the Drinkard's individual development as hero is linked with the restoration of harmony between man and his gods, for it is the Drinkard's new understanding, won by the hard way of adventure, which enables him to settle the cosmic quarrel through which man is suffering.

Tutuola has managed to impose an extra-ordinary unity upon his apparently random collection of traditional material. The unity is that of intense vision, for Tutuola is a visionary writer and must be seen as such if he is to be understood or effectively judged. A good deal of the criticism of his books has apparently taken it for granted that they are novels, which argues an astounding lack of literary education in the critics concerned. Tutuola's affinities are with Bunyan, Dante and Blake rather than with the Western novel, for the novel as we know it deals with man in society, while Tutuola is concerned with man alone, suffering and growing amid the images thrown forth by his own mind and by the imagination of his race. He is something much rarer and more interesting than another novelist.

There is an interesting confirmation of the visionary character of his work in Dr. Parrinder's Foreword to *My Life in the Bush of Ghosts*. Dr. Parrinder recounts how he once asked Tutuola why he had described the various towns in the Bush of Ghosts in that particular order. Tutuola simply replied, "Because that is the order in which I came to them." He has *lived* through his material before ever he sets it down; the many fragments of folk-lore, ritual and belief embedded in it are not just things remembered (whether from individual or racial knowledge), but things already experienced; they have all passed through the transmuting fire of an individual imagination and been shaped for its ends.

The comparison with Bunyan is a fruitful one, for both writers are men of little formal education who seize upon the images of the popular imagination.

Take this passage from the "Pilgrim's Progress":

"hidious to behold, he was clothed with scales like a Fish (and they are his pride), he had Wings like a Dragon, and out of his belly came Fire and Smoke, and his mouth was as the mouth of a Lion ......

This rises into literature from the same great sources as Tutuola's Red Fish in the *Palm-Wine Drinkard*, whose :

head was like a tortoise's head, but it was as big as an elephant's head and it had over 30 horns and large eyes which surrounded the head. All these horns were spread out as an umbrella. It could not walk but was only gliding on the ground like a snake and its body was just like a bat's body and covered with long red hair like strings...... All the eyes which surrounded its head were closing and opening at the same time as if a man was pressing a switch on and off.

This description of the eyes is a brilliant instance of Tutuola's easy use of the paraphenalia of modern life to give sharpness and immediacy to his imagery. The comparisons with the branching stems of an umbrella frame and with hanging pieces of string are equally effective, if less striking than the switch or perhaps the finest example of all is the Drinkard's description of the "complete gentleman," whose beauty was such that even bombers would respect it :

I could not blame the lady for following the Skull as a complete gentleman to his house at all. Because if I were a lady, no doubt I would follow him to wherever he would go, and still as I was a man I would jealous him more than that, because if this gentleman went to the battlefield, surely, enemy would not kill him or capture him and if bombers saw him in a town which was to be bombed, they would not throw bombs on his presence, and if they did throw it, the bomb itself would not explode until this gentleman would leave that town, because of his beauty. At the same time that I saw this gentleman in the market on that day what I was doing was only to follow him about in the market. After I looked at him for so many hours, then I ran to a corner of the market and I cried for a few minutes because I thought within myself why was I not created with beauty as this gentleman, but when I remembered that he was only a Skull, then I thanked God that he had created me without beauty ......

If we examine the formal structure of Tutuola's second book, *My Life in the Bush of Ghosts*, we shall find that here there is no deliberate quest or definite objective. The Initiation is not sought but is imposed upon the boy-hero as the process of his development into manhood. The whole book may thus be seen as a kind of extended Initiation or "rite of passage". At the beginning of the story the narrator is a boy of eight and is in a state of innocence. He is just starting to know the meaning of "bad", for he is the victim of the jealousies among his father's wives, but he does not yet know the meaning of "good". Fleeing from his deserted town before a slave-raiding army, he becomes separated from his brother and accidentally rushes into the terrible Bush of Ghosts, which he enters through a hole in a large mound, in a manner somewhat reminiscent of Alice falling into Wonderland. Like Alice again, he immediately undergoes a series of transformations, though his are certainly the more radical; at various times he becomes a cow, a ju-ju stuck in the neck of an immense pot, a horse and a monkey. As he travels or is carried from town to town, deep in the Bush of Ghosts, the boy suffers a breathless variety of experiences, mostly horrible or fearful in character. His status is usually that of a slave or, at best, a resented intruder, though he has rare intervals of peace and gradually becomes more and more contented with his extra-ordinary life. At one time he is even happily married to a ghostess for a few months and later he lives for four years with a beautiful Super Lady, who bears him a son half-ghost, half-mortal, over whose upbringing they finally quarrel.

To the uninitiated European reader the word "ghost" is likely to be rather misleading, for the ghosts of this book are not the individual spirits of those who once lived on earth; they are the permanent inhabitants of the Other World, who have never lived as mortals, but who have intimate knowledge of that life and are in constant intercourse with it. At the same time, it appears that earthly witches and wizards hold their meetings among these ghosts and that it is from there that "spirit-children" are sent to dwell among men and act as agents for the ghost world. None of this is worked out with theological exactitude, for Tutuola assumes this kind of knowledge, but so much at least is clear.

After twenty-five years in the Bush of Ghosts the hero has become so accustomed to life there that he no longer has any wish to escape, but when at last the chance is presented to him by the Television-Handed Ghostess he decides to take it. After still further misfortunes at the hands of his long-lost, unrecognised brother, he returns to normal life with his family. Like Adam, he has lost his innocence and has fallen into a full knowledge of good and evil: he is ready to begin adult life. The closing words of the book, "This is what hatred did", pick up again the hints of the opening pages and confirm its nature as an extended division of Initiation or Purgatory—though we must understand that this is a purgatory undergone by the living and not by the dead; a preparation for life and not a payment for its past mistakes.

Tutuola's last book, *Simbi and the Satyr of the Dark Jungle*, was published in 1955. Here the heroic figure is that of a young girl, born with conspicuous advantages of every kind, who comes to feel that these must ultimately be paid for in comparable abasement and suffering. This is a theme as universal in literature and myth as that of the deliberate quest, to whose grand object such abasement and suffering may appear as incidental and subordinate; but in reality they are two different ways of expressing the same life-renewing, regenerating experience. The belief that expense must somehow be balanced by equivalent earning or sacrifice, by a "storing-up", is perhaps the mythic version of the Law of the Conservation of Energy, intuitively apprehended. But in myth it is seen that *man himself*, by heroic action or sacrifice, must renew the energy of his world and keep it in equipoise. This, the theme of *Simbi*, is seen particularly clearly in the great English medieval poems "Sir Gawayne and the Grene Knight" and "Wynnere and Wascoure." For an individualist society it has lost its meaning.

Simbi, we are told, was the only daughter of the wealthiest woman in her village:

> She was not working at all, except to eat and after that to bathe and then to wear several kinds of the costliest garments.- Although she was a wonderful singer whose beautiful voice could wake deads and she was only the most beautiful girl in the village.

One day her two friends Rali and Sala are kidnapped and soon after this Simbi begins to yearn to experience the "Poverty" and the "Punishment" because she had known "neither the poverty nor the difficulties of the punishment since she was born." Ignoring the warnings of her mother and others, she consults the Ifa priest (the professional diviner of Yoruba society) and he advises her to make a certain sacrifice at that familiar starting point of mythical adventure, "the place where three paths meet". While she is sacrificing, the terrible Dogo comes from behind her and carries her away on the Path of Death. Then she begins to experience the poverty and the punishment with a vengeance, and immediately regrets her obscure impulse, but once embarked on the adventure she must suffer it to the finish. Dogo sells her as a slave in a far town and there she meets again with Rali and Sala and several other girls of her village, 'nameless refugees', who have been kidnapped before her. But Simbi is the only one who has voluntarily brought her sufferings on herself, and the others make her feel it. The little group wanders on from place to place and is several times threatened with human sacrifice and other dangers, but each time they are saved at the last moment by the heroic efforts of Simbi. Sometimes with her companions, more often alone, Simbi struggles on through her self-imposed agonies. When at last she wins home to her village again, only Rali is left alive to accompany her.

The central experience of the adventure is Simbi's sojourn in the Dark Jungle, the empire of the Satyr. Here ends the Path of Death, and the only way of escape from the Jungle is to return by it. Simbi wanders here for a long time and has many bruising encounters with her terrible enemy the Satyr before she finally conquers and kills him by flying up his nostril in the form of a water-fly (Iromi) and biting him to death. The Satyr of the Dark Jungle is Tutuola's greatest creation, at once comic and terrible. Here he is talking to himself after his first humiliating brush with the resourceful Simbi:

> "I believe, the two ladies shall come back to this jungle and I shall kill both of them at all costs at any day I meet them. It is certain, they are my meat!....By the way, what is the meaning of 'Iro....'? of course, I know the meaning of 'Iromi' that is an insect of water, but what of 'Iro...' into which that lady (Simbi) said she could change? Anyhow, we shall meet again and then continue our fight."

The use of the word "lady" in such a context heightens the comedy of the scene. Gentility is a disease in modern Nigeria; no-one is ever described as a "woman", even by a Satyr.

The Satyr's greatest stratagem is when, knowing Simbi's love of singing, he creates a vast hall in the Jungle made entirely of singing birds, so that it is literally built of pure music. Yet even this delightful trap, though Simbi falls into it all right and it rather endears the Satyr to the reader, fails to give him control of her for long. The Satyr carries her to a high rock and, after embedding her in it by turning her partially into stone, proceeds to beat her. But Simbi escapes by the aid of a magic helper and turns herself into a water-fly. Unrecognised by the Satyr, who knows that she can become "Iro...", but not "Iromi", she flies up his nose and kills him in the manner already described.

In *Simbi*, Tutuola has tightened his grasp of narrative, heightened his dramatic sense, and displayed a new speed in the handling of the big scenes. There is far more dialogue than in the earlier books, and the frequent adverbial "stage directions" add greatly to the dramatic interest and humour of the conversation:

> "Of course, my wish before I left our village was to seek for the "Poverty" and the "Punishment" but I have regretted it since when Dogo kidnapped me and sold me," Simbi explained coldly. "But before you will regret your wish will be when you return to our village," Bako replied and then she asked sharply from the rest "or is it not so?" "Yes, it is so!" the rest confirmed loudly.

The occasional *longueurs* of Tutuola's earlier books arose from the wholesale application of an oral narrative technique to written narrative. Writing of the *Palm-Wine Drinkard*, Mr. V. S. Pritchett said, "Mr. Tutuola's first paragraph knocks one flat." This is how Tutuola opened his first story:

> I was a palm-wine drinkard since I was a boy of ten years of age. I had no other work more than to drink palm-wine in my life. In those days we did not know other money, except cowries, so that everything was very cheap, and my father was the richest man in our town.

The impact of this is that of a warm African voice beginning a tale. Tutuola wrote exactly as if he were entertaining a group of friends with his fantasies on a moonlit night. This purely oral narrative method has many advantages but some pitfalls too. The "live" narrator who has his audience actually round him can afford (if he is a good story-teller) any amount of long-winded digression and embellishment—indeed, that is part of his art. The writer who bases his work on the same method must be much more ruthless with himself, and there were places in Tutuola's first two books where even the appreciative reader might begin to nod a little. It is all very well to knock the reader flat with one's first paragraph, but it is important that none of the later ones should render him comatose. Tutuola has now shown in *Simbi* that he can prune his exuberance fairly drastically without sacrificing any of the warmth and rich-ness of his speaking human voice. When the *Drinkard* first appeared many were inclined to salute it as a once-for-all miracle and to raise a doubt whether even Tutuola could do it again. But in *Simbi* he has not only done it again; he has gone on to show that he can sharpen and refine the expression of his unique prolific genius.

There remains the important question of Tutuola's reputation in Africa itself. No amount of international acclaim, gratifying though it be, can count for as much in the development of such a writer as the enthusiasm and support of his own people. The progress of his reputation in Africa has been gravely hampered by the manner in which his books have appeared. The imprint of a leading English publisher, though an assistance in the London market, may even be a hindrance in the local one. His books are expensive by Nigerian standards; 10/6 or 12/6 are prices that young Nigerians may be accustomed to pay for a text-book that will help them directly in examinations but not for "a mere story-book." Moreover, his publishers are a firm generally associated with the "high-brow" in literature and the dust-jackets of these books, excellent in themselves, reflect this. For these reasons the number of Nigerians who have discovered Tutuola from the bookshelves unaided must be fairly small. Last year I had the experience of lecturing to a large audience of adult students and finding that few of them had even heard Tutuola's name and not one had read any of his books. On the other hand, these same students reacted with delighted wonder and amusement to the reading of extracts from the *Drinkard* and at the end of the lecture were clamouring for copies to buy. Many educated Nigerians, however, are embarrassed by the "mistakes" they find in Tutuola's English, which some of them seem to regard as an undeserved reflection on the African race in general. Their ears, being less sensitive than those of an English-man to all that has become jaded and feeble in our language, are likewise less able to recognise the vigour and freshness that Tutuola brings to it by his urgency of expression and refusal to be merely correct. A similar stage to this had been gone through even by the American reading public, though to them English was their native language, and the racy American vernacular, as opposed to "polite" English, did not become respectable till the enormous popularity of Mark Twain had made it so. In view of all these factors, a great service would be done by any publisher imaginative enough to produce cheap paper-backed editions of Tutuola's books and distribute these widely to the little bookshops in West Africa.

Tutuola's value to the rising generation of young African writers is probably that of an example rather than of a model. There are not likely to be two Tutuolas in Africa today, and to write in his manner without comparable visionary power and imaginative intensity would not only be foolish but, for a more fully educated writer, affected as well. The most valuable part of Tutuola's example is his confidence. This confidence transforms even his apparent disadvantages into special virtues, for his fragmentary education is seen to have left him in tune with the great imaginative life of his race, whilst his command of West African idiom enables him to create a style at once easy and energetic, naive and daring. By going into himself Tutuola has rediscovered the great common soil of literature, which mere imitation of its currently branching peculiarities and variations in England or America could never have shown him. Imitativeness is the besetting temptation of Nigerian writers at present; but Tutuola has set all chance models aside and, refreshed like Antaeus by contact with his abiding Mother Earth, has forged matter, form and style again for himself.

Founding A New National Literature:
The Ghost Novels of Amos Tutuola

HAROLD R. COLLINS

I should like to give my impression of the "ghost" novels or mythical romances of the Nigerian writer Amos Tutuola and defend these remarkable works from the disparagement of his own educated countrymen, offering by the way some brash speculations on how Nigeria, or any other Commonwealth nation similarly situ- ated, can get itself a new national literature. Although I am aware of the contributions of the writers Aboderin, Ekwensi, Gbemi and Achebe toward founding a Nigerian literature in English, I should like to turn my attention exclusively—in this first year of Nigeria's independence—to the very special and exciting contribution of the shy, polite young Yoruba (with some six years of formal schooling) who has been honored by the enthusiastic reviews of Dylan Thomas, V. S. Pritchett, and Selden Rodman; French, Italian, German, and Yugoslav translations, and such impressive, though momentary, world acclaim as to rate mention in the magazine *Vogue*.[1]

A prophet can be without honor, even in dynamic, increasingly literate Southern Nigeria. John V. Murra, in his sympathetic review of Tutuola's *The Palm Wine Drinkard* and *My Life in the Bush of Ghosts,* conveniently summarizes the West African intel- lectuals' complaints against the work of Tutuola. They deplore his "crudities," his lack of inhibitions, and the folk-tale basis of his stories. They accuse him of plagiarizing from the traditional Yoruba folk tales, of encouraging a useless, impractical mythical way of thinking, of leading West African literature up a blind alley, and of providing the supercilious westerner with an excuse for continuing to patronize the allegedly superstitious Nigerian.[2]

The indictment is pertinent and thorough-going, and even if it does not turn out to be a true bill, it will serve nicely as a formula for our examination of the four "ghost" novels of Tutuola—*The*

Reprinted from *Critique*, 4, 1 (1961), 17-28. For a fuller elaboration of this argument, see Collins's *Amos Tutuola* (New York, 1969).

Palm Wine Drinkard (1952), My Life in the Bush of Ghosts (1954), Simbi and the Satyr of the Dark Jungle (1955), and The Brave African Huntress (1958).

It is not hard to understand what the educated West Africans mean by Tutuola's "crudities." His language, for instance, whatever its power and grace may be, is not the Queen's English. Paul Bohannan, writing in the Listener of May 13, 1954, has called it a combination of schoolboy English, officialese, and West African pidgin.² The officialese element, however, is not very conspicuous, and the vocabulary would be too extensive for any but Macaulay's schoolboy. And Tutuola's English, though furiously non-standard, is distinctly English; a true pidgin is an entirely new language, with its own peculiar grammar. Geoffrey Parrinder, lecturer at University College, Ibadan, Nigeria, simply calls it, "English as it is spoken in West Africa."⁴ A Nigerian exchange teacher of the writer's acquaintance, possibly not wishing to offend by too severe a judgment, mildly observed that Tutuola's language was such as might be expected of an intelligent African who had not attended secondary school.

The unconventional features of Tutuola's grammar and vocabulary are plain for all to see: composition teachers will shudder for his neologisms, his unidiomatic verbs and pronouns, his syncopations in syntax, his fragments (the bad kind), his typographical oddities. The student of literature will also deplore his mispunctuation of indirect quotation, his lack of analysis or commentary and of developed scenes, his wooden conversational exchanges, his very loose episodic structures, his anticlimaxes. In a series of very lively coffee-break arguments with Mr. S. Akanji Dawodu, another Nigerian exchange teacher, entertaining the views on Tutuola summarized in the Murra review, this writer felt obliged to confess that the crudities of Tutuola's books were quite undeniable, that in an ideal world, founders of national literatures would have more than six years of education, that more education might have made Tutuola a better writer (if it didn't spoil him altogether). On the other hand, Mr. Dawodu went so far as to confess that he had probably been blind to some of Tutuola's positive merits.

But now that we have pleaded guilty to the charge of crudity, a few rejoinders are in order. For all the crudity of language, we are as much struck by the clarity, directness, vigor, and felicity of this Anglo-Nigerian language of Tutuola's as we are by its unconventionality. Murra characterizes Tutuola's language as a "terse, graphic, and personal" kind of "young English." This is an understatement. Tutuola's English is a perpetual delight. Here's a taste of it:

> I did not satisfy with it . . . . she looked thereabouts perhaps somebody might be near . . . . beat him greedily . . . . she never acrossed such a wonderful orchestra . . . . the rest warned her whisperly . . . . I was shaking together with my voice . . . . I did not leak out the secret . . . . I fed up to be alive any more . . . . no shoes could size his feet in this world.

Unfortunately, it is just this stylistic vitality, this *con brio* exuberance, that Mr. Dawodu could not appreciate. Perhaps he was too upset by the "crudities" and the misconceptions they would give rise to, to observe the vitality. Or perhaps one needs to be native to the English language to understand the vigor of this non-standard dialect.

Another rejoinder: for all the ineptness of method and construction, Tutuola's major characters are credible and substantial. In *The Palm Wine Drinkard,* in spite of the first person point of view and the very awkward conversation, Drinkard is clearly established as a shrewd, witty, easy-going Yoruba. The wanderer in the bush of ghosts, very like Drinkard though explicitly distinguished from him, is even slightly more credible in that he usually exercises his wit and pluck without the almost inexhaustible store of ju-ju that Drinkard has at his command. Simbi, the girl satyr-killer, is more substantial and credible than Drinkard's wife or the wanderer's two wives, probably by virtue of the author-omniscent point of view, the better developed scenes, the more plausible torments she suffers, and her companionship with her all-too-human "refugee" friends. But surely Adebesi, the Brave African Huntress, is the most successful and engaging of all of Tutuola's characters. Perhaps she is so partly because she is sparing of the ju-ju, partly because she has human, though not cordial, relations with the pigmies, the bachelors of the woman-less town, the old man, and his persecutor Ajantala. In these two female characters Tutuola has brought into world literature the spunky, practical, comradely Nigerian woman of strong initiative and impressive militancy, like the Nigerian trading woman, or lady warrior in the Women's Wars against harassed colonial officials.

And we might remind ourselves that the methods of character-ization in romances must be different from those in realistic novels. Northrop Frye has observed that "subtlety and complexity are not much favored" in romances, because the "general dialectic struc-ture" of quest and conflict polarize the characters into those who are *for* the quest—these are "idealized as gallant and pure"—and those who are against the quest—these are "caricatured as simply villainous and cowardly.'" This analysis describes the basic strategy of characterization in Tutuola's works, though there are some wonderful individualizing touches and *un*-ideal traits in his characters.

One more rejoinder: Tutuola's episodic structures are pretty much determined by the tradition he is working in; they accurately reflect the structure of the folk tales that have inspired him. Furthermore they fit very ancient folklore patterns. Drinkard's search for his dead tapster friend in Dead's Town is the folklore Quest to the Underworld; the quest involves Drinkard and his wife in "uncountable" ordeals and adventures—mostly preternat-ural—with monstrous marvels and marvelous monsters, all of which constitute the traditional folklore test of their courage and resourcefulness. *My Life in the Bush of Ghosts* describes the hero-narrator's twenty-four years of wandering on his way home through the frightful jungle of odd and malevolent ghosts and is thus a kind of quest in reverse, or West African Odyssey. *Simbi and the Satyr of the Dark Jungle* describes a quest, Simbi's search for the "poverties and punishments of life." (Incidentally, she is enslaved, beaten by other slaves, assaulted by a crazed companion, almost "sacrificed to the head" of a king, nailed in a coffin and dumped in a river, trapped in a hollow tree, and almost swallowed by a boa constrictor.) *The Brave African Huntress* relates a sort of one-woman siege of a jungle Troy. Adebesi, daughter of a great hunter and, contrary to custom, the inheritor of his traditional occupation, starts out to find her four hunter brothers who have been killed or "detained" by the hostile pigmies in the Jungle of the Pigmies; she means to "kill or drive the whole pigmies away from that jungle" and to kill all the dangerous wild animals. And she does just that, for she is a doughty little huntress, female wrestler, and female boxer.

Most of the West Africans' objections to Tutuola's work have to do with its basis in traditional Yoruba folklore. West Africans have complained of the "commonplace" character of his tales; they have heard such stories from their grandmothers, they say. Some have gone so far as to suggest plagiarism from a printed collection of folk tales. Such objections are understandable, as we shall see, but they are misguided. Aren't these critics, though entirely correct about the mythical, folklore content of his tales and about his adapting folk tales they have heard from their grandmothers (Tutuola has admitted all this, it is obvious) nevertheless completely mistaken when they complain of "commonplaceness" or plagiarism? Their complaints are founded on an erroneous but widespread misconception of literary originality that equates it with novelty of theme, action, setting, and so on. The brilliant Yoruba folktales are a common possession of the Yoruba people, and since they *are* folk property and not copyrighted private property, it would seem that a gifted individual artist like Tutuola has every right to adapt them, sophisticate them, make of them what he can. The Yoruba folk tales, no matter how familiar they were, could never be "commonplace" to anyone with literary taste and without special bias, any more than the Oedipus tale or the Prometheus tale could be. And as for plagiarism, we might simply say that Tutuola came by his folklore in just the same way the editors of the collections did.

An examination of such collections of West African folk tales as Phebean Itayemi and P. Gurrey's *Folk Tales and Fables* (Penguin, 1593) and Elphinstone Dayrell's *Yoruba Legends* (Sheldon, n.d.) will turn up a score or more of parallels and "sources" for incidents in Tutuola's novels, including some of the most striking.

If we examine such collections of West African folk tales we readily learn what the real relation is between Tutuola's work and the folk tales. First, we are surprised to find how often there are parallels for wildly imaginative incidents that we might have been tempted to suppose were pure inventions of Tutuola's. But, more important, we are impressed with Tutuola's rare gift for capturing the spirit and manner of the traditional tales, including the word-play, which does not come through very well in the collected tales. His last novel, we might add, even includes a song, as did many of the traditional tales in their original form.

Anyone at all familiar with the Yoruba folk tales will attest to their high value, their wonderful unrestrained humor and high

63

spirits, their quite sensible celebration of such precious human virtues as shrewdness, good management, common sense, good-natured kindness, steady loyalty and courage. Would not such brilliant oral literature make a good foundation for a national literature? As we shall see, the adapting, modifying, sophisticating, deepening, humanizing that Tutuola works upon these tales, together with what we shall call his syncretism, suggest that he knows exactly what he is doing.

In the terms of Northrop Frye's brilliant and useful theory of fictions, Tutuola is writing naïve quest-romances, in which the hero "moves in a world in which the ordinary laws of nature are slightly suspended: prodigies of courage and endurance, unnatural to us, are natural to him, and enchanted weapons, talking animals, and talismans of miraculous power violate no rule of probabilities, once the postulates of romance are established." Since Drinkard calls himself a god and all of Tutuola's heroes and heroines are very potent and his monsters very malevolent, we might say that Tutuola's romances verge on another, an even more primitive mode of fiction—the myth. Frye has neatly anticipated just such a possi-bility: "The nearer the romance is to myth, the more attributes of divinity will cling to the hero and the more the enemy will take on demonic mythical qualities." Since, as Frye has reminded us, there is a significant analogy between naïve romances and dreams of wish fulfilment or nightmares and since, in spite of the humor, Tutuola's romances are distinctly nightmarish, we might call the "ghost" novels naïve mythical romances with nightmarish inci-dents.[6] But such a rather technical designation would rather sim-plify matters: there are in these romances certain modernizations and sophistications, scarcely to be anticipated in even the most brilliant theory, and these will be described later in some detail.

However, even if the educated West Africans were persuaded of the originality of Tutuola's work, they would, we may presume, still object strenuously to his "immersion in the mythical past with its gods, ghosts, wars, sacrifices, and submerged terrors"; they feel that such a preoccupation "delays progress." We might admit the truth of this charge and then say that the extenuating circumstances are more important than the charge itself. It is true that one of the most conspicuous qualities of Tutuola's ghost novels is the pristine, pagan, old African atmosphere of them. None of the four novels has a white character or explicitly mentions a white person. The last two novels seem to make no mention of any Western institution, unless "touting man" in *Simbi* would qualify, or the "custody" and "pesters" in *The Brave African Huntress,* which do strongly suggest the Nazi concentration camps and the cruel Nazi guards. The Africa of all four novels is basically the old-time Africa of communal working in the king's fields, cowrie shell money, interminable law suits, polygamy, slavery, uninhibited palm-wine drinking, and dancing to drum music, "general wars, tribal wars, burglary wars, and the slave wars," and frequent human sacrifice.

But for all of this pagan African background, white man's customs, techniques and artifacts infiltrate into the novels in a most interesting way. In *The Palm Wine Drinkard,* for instance, guns and bottles are mentioned and Faithful Mother in the White Tree looks like a strangely indulgent missionary and her establishment like an oddly undisciplined missionary hospital: she serves liquor and offers her guests cigarettes. *My Life in the Bush of Ghosts* has the most of this—pardon the expression—anachronistic syncretism of the old and the new. A Rev. Devil is pastor to a kind of "anti-church" of evil doers and baptizes converts with "fire and hot water." Super Lady, the narrator's second wife, lives in an elegant European-style house complete with bathroom, kitchen, parlor and dressing room with full length mirror; she gives her husband, besides a full wardrobe of European clothes, a costly wristwatch. The hero's dead cousin, a self-appointed bishop, rules over a thousand churches (with their parochial schools) and a diocese served by teachers, headmasters, education officers, nurses, and medical officers; and boasting such features of civilization as police stations, courts and prisons. Among the Western-style activities mentioned in the novel are an exhibition (of smells!), a conference (of ghosts), and a professional meeting (of witches and wizards). With the last two novels there are fewer of white man's ways and gear. *Simbi and the Satyr of the Dark Jungle* mentions only guns and a "weighing scale"; if the gnome, the satyr, the myrmidon, and the phoenix are cultural imports they are Western only in name. The Satyr, for instance, is a sort of African Hairless Joe, and the gnome acts very much like a Yoruba animal hero. The Western imports in *The Brave African Huntress* are few and rather incongruous, among them a "shakabulla" gun (named from the sound of the discharge), "special concerts," chocolates and ice cream.

In the first two novels Tutuola has curiously de-emphasized the white man's ways and works by making them elements in figures of speech to describe his mythical marvels, almost as though he were leading his partially Westernized compatriots out of the modern world back into the old mythical world of heart's desire and heart's terror. The hideous Red Fish opens and closes its multiple eyes "as if a man was pressing a switch off and on." "Mouths would be making noises as if one hundred winches were at work." The device has considerable graphic vigor, and we may wonder why Tutuola abandoned it in the last two novels.[7]

We should also note that Tutuola's monsters, his bogeymen, who (or which) are even more flamboyant than those in the folk tales, are often *technicalized, mechanized,* made into "techno-bogeys," as it were. Silverish Ghost can, with his silver light, "transparent" a person, presumably like a fluoroscope. A snake "vomits" colored lights. Flash-eyed Mother, an immense hydra-headed female who "fill[s] the town as a vast round hill" and "does not move to anywhere at all," executes those who displease her by flashing fire out of her "two fearful large eyes" in her principal head, reminding us of flame throwers. The Television-handed Ghostess, as her name indicates, has a TV screen in her hand.

Tutuola's ghost novels are indeed "immersed in the mythical past." But are the educated West Africans wise to expect their new literature to turn so completely and abruptly from the old culture, even if it were barbaric and primitive? The role of folk-lore, or mythology as we call it, in Greek literature is a common-place: the Greeks were too self-assured to be ashamed of their remote ancestors' legendary atrocities, bacchanalian orgies, and human sacrifices, their fanciful titans, minotaurs, sphinxes, harpies, gorgons, furies, and other bogeys. (Eric Larrabee has reported, in the *Chicago Review* of Spring, 1956, that Tutuola was interested in reading Edith Hamilton's work on mythology, and we are tempted to suspect some echoes of Western mythology in his work.)[8] Any English graduate student could tell the West Africans how much our English literature owes to mythology, brandishing proof out of the careful studies of Douglas Bush.

What does it matter that Tutuola's ghost novels are not realistic? After all, the realistic tradition of the English novel may have been determined by the social and intellectual conditions of the eighteenth and nineteenth centuries, and the realistic novel may be an exotic in Nigeria. Perhaps the Nigerian novel may turn out to be different, more poetic, more fantastical. Perhaps the Nigerians will develop a more sophisticated kind of romance than Tutuola's, with "African-gothic" marvels and terrors and a manner Poesque, Hoffmanesque. And the educated West Africans' insistence upon realism is probably one more instance of that prejudice in favor of mimetic literary art that has long plagued the criticism of fiction.

And does it really matter that the ghost novels do not suggest ways to educate, hospitalize, and industrialize Nigerians? Surely Tutuola's novels do something just as important: they show the spirit in which these high-priority works should be achieved.

Nigerians will of course read great quantities of technical or "useful" books (apparently Tutuola does himself),[9] and there will probably be many realistic social-problem and "culture-contact" novels like Chinua Achebe's *Things Fall Apart* (Heinemann, 1958), hailed by a reviewer in *West Africa* magazine as Nigeria's first "straight" novel. Incidentally, Achebe's novel, like Elspeth Huxley's *Red Strangers* (1939) a study of the breaking of the tribe with the advent of the whites, is nostalgic about the old order, for all of its terrors and cruelties, rather caricatures the whites, is certainly not properly hopeful about technological progress, as Tutuola's novels are, in their strange way. Cyprian Ekwensi's *People of the City* (Dakers, 1954) incidates another possible avenue of exploration for Nigerian fiction. *People of the City* is a light-hearted urban-picaresque novel dealing with the straits and scrapes with the girls and the anxious apartment-hunting of a young man about Lagos town, together with some rather incongruous reflections of that young blade on national pride and social solidarity. But after we have read Achebe's and Ekwensi's rather more conventional novels, Tutuola's strange tales still linger bright and splendid in the memory.

Possibly the Nigerians will have to build their literature on their own story-telling traditions, eschewing Western models, lest they perpetrate such literary curiosities as the Burmese version of *Count of Monte Cristo*. Possibly they will adapt the various English novel forms to their own needs. At any rate, they must not be ashamed of their old way of life, if they are to produce a literature worthy of their own aspirations. (Europeans are not ashamed of *their* barbaric past!)

It might be plausibly argued that Tutuola is writing in the wrong language. Perhaps it is not certain that English, the second language of educated Nigerians, will be the language of Nigeria's literature. Hausa, a *lingua franca* with nine million speakers in Northern Nigeria and neighboring areas, and Tutuola's Yoruba, with five million speakers,* might be serious contenders.

The West Africans have deplored Tutuola's "lack of inhibitions"; probably they refer to his very frequent graphic descriptions of cruel beatings, torturings, and mutilations, and to his images of nastiness, figures of filth, excrement and disease. A few specimens of Tutuola's nastiness will show the extent of his offenses against good form: the "unknown creatures" "started to spit, make urine, and pass urine on their heads"; the Television-handed Ghostess, a bald lady "almost covered with sores" in which "uncountable maggots" are "dashing here and there," will show the wanderer in the bush of ghosts the way home, if he will lick her sores daily for ten years; Simbi's arch-enemy the Satyr is "gobbling the spit of his mouth as if he had already started to eat them." The five-foot-long navel of the "huge stern pigmy" is "sounding heavily as when water was shaking in a large tube."

It would seem that objections against atrocities and nastiness in literary art involve two critical fallacies: the confusion of the moral standards by which we judge the actions of persons in real life and the artistic standards by which we should judge a work of art, and the notion that the ugly and painful should be excluded from fiction. Surely conduct which in real life ought to be condemned as morally offensive may be represented in fiction if it serves a literary purpose there; only very naïve readers—and persons who have a psychic need to censor other persons' reading— project the hypothetical morality of novels out into the real world. And perhaps we should not admit that *any* human concern, no matter how taboo-ridden in our culture, should be excluded from literature, unless for very good literary reasons. If the unpleasant and the ugly are systematically excluded from literary works the result is likely to be a sort of pollyanna sentimentality, a prettification. Besides, the fastidious readers are not making the proper reading adjustments for romance: as Northrop Frye points out, romance "turns fear at a distance, or terror, into the adventurous; fear at contact, or horror, into the marvelous. . . ."[10]

We may suspect that the educated West Africans are suffering from a kind of colonial pecksniffery, that they are hungering and thirsting after a respectability that will impress Europeans. Perhaps they are disturbed by the fear that white men—even white nonentities—may think them uncultivated, barbarous, backward, childish, inferior. The notion that foreigners should like Tutuola's ghost novels only because these novels confirm them in their stereotyped views of Africans as barbarians, is something of a giveaway on this state of mind. The growing political and industrial power of the African peoples will probably cure this pecksniffery—and properly impress even white nonentities.

We can certainly sympathize with the educated West Africans' fears about the effects of Tutuola's work. In the current cliché, West Africans want to produce in world opinion an image of themselves as modern, civilized, enlightened persons with progressive and sensible views. No doubt about it, the ordinary heedless reader would be badly misled about Nigeria and Nigerians by Tutuola's works. But this is a social, a political, a public relations consideration—Mr. Dawodu, with some urging, admitted as much to the writer—and such a consideration does not touch on the literary merits of Tutuola's romances.

If West African critics cannot understand why foreigners have made so much of Tutuola's work, the foreigners might well retort that they cannot understand how West Africans can fail to be captivated by Tutuola's graces and powers. His uninhibited humor should be able to do the job by itself. Though explaining humor is not a very promising business, humor is one of his most engaging qualities, and we must try to illustrate the quality before we rest our case. Drinkard earns badly needed funds by changing himself into a canoe and ferrying passengers across a river. A "debiter" who has "never paid any of his debts since he was born" meets a bill collector who "has never failed to collect debts since he has begun the work"; the two fight and kill each other; a curious bystander commits suicide so he can go to heaven and see how the affair turns out. When the wanderer in the bush of ghosts screams during his baptism by fire and water, the ghosts coolly remark, "You may die if you like, nobody knows you here." In Hopeless Town the wanderer does poorly trying to communicate by the shoulder-shrugging language that is locally current; he shrugs to the monarch of the place the rather unfortunate confused message: "You are a bastard king."

Who of us would dare to say that we are positively sure just how a national literature should be founded in a so-called backward country with a rich oral tradition? Surely we must not be dogmatic. But for all the crudity, the mythological benightedness, the "lack of inhibitions" in Tutuola's work, one lover of literature with a fairly catholic taste is convinced that, for the verve, the assurance, the creativity in matter and technique, the human values sustained, and the gay humor of the work, Amos Tutuola of Abeokuta deserves to be called the founder of Nigerian Literature.

KENT STATE UNIVERSITY

NOTES

1. Eric Larrabee, "Amos Tutuola: A Problem in Translation," *Chicago Review*, X (Spring, 1956), 40. The Nigerian writers mentioned are all represented in Peggy Rutherfoord's African anthology *Darkness and Light* (London, 1958).

2. "The Unconscious of a Race," *Nation*, CLXXIX (September 25, 1954), 261-62.

3. "Translation: a Problem in Anthropology," *The Listener*, LI (May 13, 1954), 815-16.

4. Foreword, *My Life in the Bush of Ghosts* (London, 1954), p. x.

5. *Anatomy of Criticism* (Princeton, 1957), p. 195.

6. *Ibid.*, pp. 33, 187, 107.

7. It might occur to the reader, as it did to this writer, that the Tutuola novels would make an effective Disney fantasia. In a letter of May 7, 1958, a representative of Disney Productions reported that the studio had in fact considered making a movie of Tutuola's books.

8. Larrabee, p. 41. It is easy to be wrong in such source hunting. The episode concerning the Ibembe king's horns in *The Brave African Huntress* is very similar to Ovid's Midas story, retold in Chaucer's Wife of Bath's Tale (III; 951 ff). When the writer wrote to ask Tutuola if he knew of these supposed sources, he answered quite simply, "The king who has horns is in the traditional story of my town." (Letter of May 11, 1958)

9. Besides the evidence in the ghost novels, in his letter mentioned in the note above, Tutuola asked to have these books sent to him: J. R. Eaton's *Beginning Electricity* and Alfred Morgan's *The Boy's First Book of Radio and Electronics*.

10. Frye, p. 37.

LATER REVIEWS

Later Reviews

Reviews of Tutuola's later books reveal that his reputation as a writer suffered a sharp decline in the late fifties and early sixties but rose again in the middle and late sixties. Readers had tolerated his third book *Simbi and the Satyr of the Dark Jungle* (1955), but they began to react negatively when *The Brave African Huntress* (1958) appeared, and they were quite openly hostile to *Feather Woman of the Jungle* (1962), which was published in the same year as the first paperback edition of *The Palm-Wine Drinkard*. Reviews of *Feather Woman of the Jungle* were frequently retrospective, recalling the magic of Tutuola's first books and comparing their authentic bright glow with the dull artificiality of what Tutuola was producing now.

At the same time that European and American readers were getting tired of him, Africans were beginning to rediscover Tutuola. A Yoruba ballad opera version of *The Palm-Wine Drinkard* was so enthusiastically received in Nigeria in 1963 that it went on tour in Ghana and parts of Europe and was later revived for performance at the First Pan-African Cultural Festival in Algiers in 1969. A number of African critics wrote reappraisals of Tutuola's work in the mid-sixties, recognizing him as an odd but important literary figure. By the time *Ajaiyi and His Inherited Poverty* (1967) was published, Tutuola's reputation was fairly secure both in Africa and abroad. Foreign critics began to salute him as an eccentric old friend, and Nigerian reviewers hoped that his fantastic stories would someday be available in Yoruba. Fifteen years after the publication of *The Palm-Wine Drinkard*, Tutuola had finally gained universal acceptance as a significant African writer.

Simbi and the Satyr of the Dark Jungle

From *The Times Literary Supplement*, **October 21, 1955**

Mr. Amos Tutuola is not merely an original writer, but also an original: a wayward, fanciful, erratic creative artist from West Africa, whose fertile imagination works gaily just within (and occasionally outside) the confines of English grammar and language. In *Simbi and the Satyr of the Dark Jungle* he tells, with a simplicity so artless that at times it appears calculated, a fairy tale about a young girl who, against the advice of her mother, sets out to discover "the Poverty and the Punishment," and experiences them in various, painful forms. At times Mr. Tutuola's voice might almost be that of Damon Runyon. Simbi, after her capture and ill-treatment by Dogo, "an expert kidnapper of children," tells him:

> I had wanted to know the "Poverty" and the "Punishment" and to experience also their difficulties. But I have now declined from my wish in respect of the severe punishment which you are giving me continuously since when you have caught me about one hour ago.

The fact is, not that Mr. Tutuola writes like Runyon, but that Runyon's mock-innocence echoes something of the West African writer's genuine primitive simplicity. Simbi's adventures will have particular interest for the psychoanalyst—in, for instance, the tale of Bako, a girl who steals goats, rams and cocks, and when questioned says that they have been stolen by her Siamese twin sister at home. Bako's punishment is to be turned into a cock, with a huge comb and beak and "shoulders and arms full of strong wings." One likes also the Satyr himself, who greets Simbi and her friend Rali with the words: "Come along, my meat, I am ready to eat both of you now!"

From *West African Review*, **January, 1956**

Frankly I do not know what to make of this latest offering by Amos Tutuola. To review a book is—as far as I know—to give your audience your own honest estimation of the work: an estimation based upon (to say the least) vague standards. The fact that these standards are identifiable when positively present accounts for the surprising unanimity with which critics acclaim a work as good or bad.

When, however, there are no standards by which to judge an offering, a critic has two choices. "Chuck it out, it's no good." (An attitude unfortunately adopted by most Nigerians towards Tutuola.) Or, out comes the trumpet; and hiding behind this horn the critic blows his loudest, aiming by his own noise to drown and deafen his ignorance of the facts. After all, who *knows* Tutuola's world of "deads" and "satyrs"?

I stand in between. Tutuola has imagination. If you heard "The Human Age," by Wyndham Lewis on the B.B.C.'s Third Programme or "Johnson Over Jordan," by J. B. Priestley on the B.B.C.'s Home Service, you would automatically rank Tutuola with the most imaginative writers at work today. He may not possess their subtlety, but he can hold his own for sheer invention. He has now reduced his work to a formula: something happens to disturb the normal life cycle. (In this case the girl Simbi is dissatisfied with a life of wealth and comfort.) Follows a search, usually in the land Tutuola knows best. The result of this is that Tutuola's writing is identifiable and distinct in itself. It is not surprising that translators clamour for his work. The "ungrammatical" style is excellent French, German or Italian!

Simbi's encounter with the Satyr—a fearful creature on the path of death, ten feet tall, king of the dark jungle "wanting to kill them for his food" is horrifying.

Another African fairy tale for adults who excuse themselves for their indulgence in the macabre by all kinds of attitudes including Third Programme snobbery.

C. O. D. Ekwensi

The Brave African Huntress

THE BRAVE AFRICAN HUNTRESS Illustrated by Ben Enwonwu.
BY AMOS TUTUOLA Faber and Faber, 1958.

When Tutuola's first book, "The Palm Wine Drinkard", appeared in 1952 an eminent British critic wrote: "The first paragraph knocks one flat". And what a magnificent opening it was indeed:

> I was a palm-wine drinkard since I was a boy of ten years of age. I had no other work more than to drink palm-wine in my life. In those days we did not know other money except COWRIES, so that everything was very cheap, and my father was the richest man in our town.

Who could fail to be intrigued by this opening paragraph, who could resist the slow rhythm of these sentences? And the book amply fulfilled the promise of this opening. The language of the "Palm Wine Drinkard" is quaint, but it is rhythmical and poetic, and the tale is a strange mixture of vision, humour and myth. How disappointing, in comparison, is this last book of Tutuola, "The Brave African Huntress". Just compare the opening paragraphs:

> I, Adebisi, the African huntress, will first relate the adventure of my late father, one of the ancient brave hunters, in brief:
> My father was a brave hunter in his town. He had hunted in several dangerous jungles which the rest hunters had rejected to enter or even approach because of fear of being killed by the wild animals and harmful creatures of the jungle.

The rhythm and the magic are gone. The sentences do not flow. As prosaic as this opening paragraph is the whole book. In vain one searches here for the poetry and vision of Tutuola's earlier books. Adebisi, the brave huntress goes to the bush of the pygmies and overcomes there a series of horrible giants. But none of the creatures she meets are as memorable as "the complete gentleman", or the "red fish", "the four hundred dead babies", "the flash eyed mother" or the "satyr" of his earlier books. It is as if his vision had failed him. Compare the description of this monster from "The Brave African Huntress" with the "red fish" from the "Palm Wine Drinkard":

> It was as big as an elephant. I had never seen the kind of this animal before. Because he had a very big head. Several horns were on his forehead. Each of the horns was as long and thick and sharp as cow's horns. Very long black and brown hairs were full this head and they were fallen downward, they were also very dirty. All the horns were stood upright on his forehead, as if a person carried a bunch of sticks vertically. His beard was so plenty and long that it covered his chest and belly as well.

Tutuola goes on to describe this animal for half a page, but in the end we fail to "see" it, and therefore we are not horrified. How much more visionary is this description in the "Drinkard":

Reprinted from *Black Orpheus*, 4 (October 1958), 51-53. Akanji was a pseudonym for Ulli Beier.

His head was like tortoises head, but it was as big as an elephant's head and it had over 30 horns and large eyes which surrounded the head. All the horns were spread out as an umbrella. It could not walk, but was only gliding on the ground like a snake and its body was just like a bat's body and covered with long red hair like strings......
All the eyes which surrounded its head were closing and opening at the same time as if a man was pressing a switch on and off......

This failure of vision is noticeable not only in the descriptions and the imagery but also in the tale itself. "The Palm Wine Drinkard" is full of symbolism. (For an analysis of this I must refer the reader to Gerald Moore's article in "Black Orpheus" No. 1). The closing chapter describing the conflict between heaven and earth rises to the level of a great universal myth. The whole book, in fact, has a kind of cosmic setting, and Gerald Moore did not exaggerate when he classified the "Drinkard" as a variant of the great heroic monomyth. "The Brave African Huntress" has lost all mythological significance. There is no symbolism, it is a mere adventure story, or rather a string of adventure stories, very loosely knit together. Surprisingly ,there is even very little humour in the book. nothing to compare with the conversations between Simbi and the Satyr in Tutuola's preceding book. The lack of inspiration which is so noticeable may be due to the fact that Tutuola has derived nothing from Yoruba folklore in this book. (The story of the king of Ibembe town being the only exception.) He apparently tries to make up for this by quoting many Yoruba proverbs, and attempting to coin some new ones as well. This is quite a charming innovation. Unfortunately the proverbs are not always very meaningful to non-Yorubas in Tutuola's translation. For example:

The thief who steals bugle. Where is he going to blow it?
In this world of the white men or in heaven?

The joke is rather lost on anybody who does not know that "bugle" is Tutuola's translation for "kakaki trumpet", an instrument that can be played only for the king.

Finally a word about the editing. We appreciate the fact that the publishers do not wish to tamper with Tutuola's style. To translate "The Palm Wine Drinkard" into "correct" English would mean to destroy the rhythm of it. One of the great excitements of reading Tutuola is in fact his fresh West African idiom, the colour and imagination of his language. But it is rather unfair on the part of the publishers to leave even spelling mistakes uncorrected. Tutuola's language will lose none of its poetry, his style will not lose character if he is told that "gourd" is not spelled "guord". It is mere sensationalism on the part of the publishers not to correct a mistake like the following: "I thank you all for the worm affection you have on me." The publishers are in this case no longer interested to preserve Tutuola's originality, they are inviting the readers to have a good laugh at his expense. I wonder whether the publishers realise how much harm they do to Tutuola's reputation in West Africa through this kind of thing? There has been a great deal of opposition to Tutuola on the part of young West Africans. They suspect that his success in Europe is not based on literary merits but on his curiosity value. They feel that Europeans merely laugh at the "funny" language and the "semi-literate" style of Tutuola. The publishers attitude confirms these suspicions in the eyes of the younger generation and helps to blind them to Tutuola's genuine literary merits.

One also fears that this new book will confirm Tutuola's critics in their view that his books are mere hackneyed story telling. But those who say "Let us have books about real people at last from West African authors" I advise to go back and read Tutuola's first three books again after reading "The Brave African Huntress". Nothing could be more "real" than Tutuola's great creations of the imagination. "Death" digging up the yam garden, "earth" sending a sacrifice to heaven, "Child-Wiser-than-his-father", "the beautiful superlady", "the skull", "the silvery-ghost" and the "flash-eyed mother" have rather more life than the "real" people in the "real" town of Lagos in "People of the City". Tutuola at his best is not a mere story teller but a creative poet whose creatures of imagination are unforgetable.

AKANJI.

From *New Statesman*, April, 1958

Tutuola's English is that of the West African schoolboy, an imperfectly acquired second language. In what other age could bad grammar have been a literary asset? And how has it preserved its wonderful badness? These queries are unavoidable when one reads *The Brave African Huntress*. It is Tutuola's fourth, the most straightforward and the thinnest. Adebisi, the daughter of a great hunter, goes to the Jungle of Pigmies to kill the pigmies and rescue her four brothers. Her adventures are no more fantastic than those we know in legends from other countries, though they lack the consistency that makes it easier to suspend disbelief. These is none of the primeval nightmare fascination of the earlier books, little to attract the psychoanalyst and the anthropologist. Were it not for the difficult language, the book could be given to children.

V. S. Naipaul

Feather Woman of the Jungle

THE MIXTURE AS BEFORE

AMOS TUTUOLA: *Feather Woman of the Jungle.* 132pp. Faber and Faber. 15s.

Mr. Amos Tutuola's first two books, *The Palm-Wine Drinkard* and *My Life in the Bush of Ghosts,* caused quite a literary sensation when they appeared some years ago. There had been nothing quite · like them before, and the strangeness of the African subject matter, the primary colours, the mixture of sophistication, superstition, and primitivism, and above all the incantatory juggling with the English language combined to dazzle and intoxicate. Novelty-seekers, propagandists for the coloured races, professional rooters for the avant-garde—any avant-garde, anywhere, and at any time—were alike delighted, and none more vociferously than the thinning ranks of the Apocalypse. ‹ "This tall, devilish story ", Dylan Thomas wrote of *The Palm-Wine Drinkard,* but while in one sense this was merited and suggestive praise, in another it carries for the cognoscenti the clearest of clear warnings. And these, as clearly, *Feather Woman of the Jungle* will reinforce. The more critical 1960s require something sharper to the taste than just the mixture as before.

For this very much is the mixture as before. It consists of ten African Nights' Entertainments, ten adventures related by a chief-to-be to the assembled villagers. Main ingredients are the Jungle Witch herself with her birds and whips, Hairy Giants, the Savage Men, the Goddess of Diamonds, mad people, " dump " people—a kind of zombie—and other people who are turned into images. The nights are full of ghouls, the " town of wealths " is far away, babies born to the dump are killed at birth, and Death, accompanied by his wife whose breasts reach the ground, wanders around twelve feet high on the look-out for victims.

He talks like this:

" Who are you ? Who are you eating my mangoes ? Stop in one place and let your death meets you there or be running away and let your death chase you ! Please, choose neither of the two ! Because I am the death who is coming to kill you all now ! Willing or not all of you will go in my soup pot tonight ! "

As for the style more generally, and for the atmosphere, here is a typical sample:

Hardly in the following morning, when the Jungle Witch rode her usual ostrich to the hut. When she came down from it, she put one bunch of whips down before us (images). After her birds were perched on our heads and shoulders, she walked into the hut and met Ashabi in the corner as she was weeping bitterly. Then without mercy, she asked from her: " Where are your two brothers ? " . . . But Ashabi, with tears rolling down her cheeks, pointed finger to us and said: " Look, old mother, my two brothers had changed into the images last night ! " Then the Jungle Witch turned her fearful eyes to us and hastily

Reprinted from *The Times Literary Supplement*, May 25, 1962.

interrupted without mercy: " Oh, very good! I am very lucky indeed that my images are increased by two! Very good! " . . . She dragged the bunch of the whips nearer.

Now how one responds to this is up to the individual. It is pointless, certainly, to look for any exact symbolism, though occasionally one glimpses something meaningful in much the same way as one follows the coils of the snake in the darkness of the tree in Douanier Rousseau. But increasingly one's reaction is irritation, a desire to say " So what ? " in quite the rudest way, and to protest against what is dangerously near a cult of the *faux-naïf*. And why just ten African Nights' Entertainments ? Why not one thousand and one ?

TWO VIEWS OF AFRICA

Feather Woman of the Jungle, by Amos Tutuola (Faber, 15s).

TUTUOLA is the most controversial novelist to come out of Africa, in the post-war period anyway. His style is the bane of English Language teachers in Nigeria since the very features of his style which have so endeared him to the critics, are those considered to be faults in the student of English grammar.

For all the controversy Tutuola is a delight to read. His story is that of a seventy-six-year-old chief who entertains the people of his village for ten nights with the saga of his adventures as a young man and how, through them, he became rich. These adventures are thrilling and mysterious, full of the frightening night creatures of the forest and Tutuola's imagination. One after the other the figures of myth and traditional tales appear to the brave young man as he journeys in search of wealth; the Jungle Witch and her birds and images, the dump lady, the bush of quietness, the goddess of diamonds on the mountain and the wife he won and who was taken from him, the hairy giant and giantess and a host of others.

The tales have Tutuola's childlike innocence of the earlier books that make him unique. One can scarcely doubt that this is a contrived quality for certainly the author is conscious of the real meaning of his tales and their symbolism. Like Chinua Achebe, he is mature enough to see that the literature of Nigeria should concern itself with life and problems among Nigerians rather than excessive preoccupation with the "man of two worlds" theme which, as an article in a recent issue of this magazine pointed out, has been an obsession of Nigerian writers for the past few years. It is this combination of maturity and innocence which make Tutuola's writing so interesting. However, one hopes he is not stranded in this vein of myth and fairy-tale and that in his next book he will show us his unconventional talents in a novel cast in the conventional mould.

S.D.D

Reprinted from *West African Review*, August, 1962.

Ajaiyi and His Inherited Poverty

From *New Statesman*, **December, 1967**

Amos Tutuola's strange sagas have engendered a select but unexclusive cult. When Palm Wine Drinkards accidentally meet and disclose themselves to each other, they are only too eager to pass on the gnosis to a bystander. There is something about the prelogical plausibility of the adventures that can charm and beguile people who couldn't tell a Yoruba carving from an Ife bronze. I get an impression from Africans that they prefer a more modern image for their various countries and I can see their point. But I continue to hope vainly for a tolerant coexistence between fearful monsters and oil refineries. Despite the somewhat forthright revivalism of Mrs. Alice Lenshina and others, the Goblin world is shrinking and soon there won't even be a plaster cast of an indigenous ghoul in an African folk museum.

In order to leave the road thoroughly clear for uninhibited goblins, Ajaiyi, the tragic hero of Tutuola's latest book, describes a previous birth, two hundred years ago, when his parents die, leaving him a bequest of poverty. The rest of the odyssey describes his lengthy quest for various gods and cacodaemons to have his inheritance annulled. He escapes from the idol worshipper, only to run foul of the Fire Spirit, and escapes from Firetown with the help of the more benevolent River Nymph. Both these entities exist, I suspect, in the Ethnological section of the British Museum where they may be recognised by innocent eyes devoid of pedantry. On his way to petition the Creator he is hi-jacked by one-legged demons, but spurred by the proverb "when the head is cut away from the neck the body is entirely useless," he cuts his way free, only to find that the Creator doesn't deal in fiscal matters and refers him to the Devil. Disappointments abound after terrifying encounters, until he robs a witch doctor's clerical benefice, pays his debts and craftily builds churches to square himself with God Almighty. Tutuola's atavistic Yorubaland would have been familiar to our own ancestors, who cheated the hag Ceridwen in the Mabinogion and cheered Cuchulain in bed and battle in the Irish Tain

BoCuailnge. Such writing makes more sense and gives more pleasure if taken almost literally, and this applies to Tutuola.

Desmond MacNamara

From *The Listener*, December, 1967

Amos Tutuola is being like these French songstresses who sing in this land for decades of years but whose English speaking is still being broken as much after all the time passing as when coming off the boat at first. He is writing the inspired Higher School Certificate paper for the satisfying of English Masters, which is to me the better when staying in the culture and not in the spirits, gods etc for too long exclusively. Naturally the spirits, gods etc are talking like the people, that is the joking part, but dear me sometimes they are sounding not like the energies of the myth of them which filters through the speaking English but sounding like the building up of them by schoolchild to a pretend of myth. Spirit of Fire cries: "What? You have no right at all to ask such a nasty question from me! You hopeless Queen of the River! Go out from my town now otherwise I shall burn you and your followers into ashes now!" But this is being more of this writer's joking, whether he is a myth story or is Yoruba Daisy Ashford.

Ajaiyi and his "junior sister" Aina watch their impoverished parents die and set out from their village to seek freedom from their "inherited poverty." It is a reverse *Rasselas*, an unroyal pair leaving an Unhappy Valley. The typical episode puts Ajaiyi in possession of a fortune only to have him lose it through a likeable gullibility. Poverty, though he does not see it, is the mother of all things good, and his short-term wealth only attracts misery in the form of witch-doctors, cruel kings, jealous friends. That Ajaiyi gets free of his poverty by a last-minute conversion and the largesse of parishioners is disappointing, but is accomplished in a sufficiently slapdash manner to seem a kind of parody of the native writer belatedly reminding himself to please the missionaries. I hope it's parody.

Arnold Goldman

AJAIYI AND HIS INHERITED POVERTY by Amos TUTUOLA (Faber & Faber).

Amos Tutuola was once described by a critic as « a wayward, fanciful, erratic, creative artist ». His fifth novel, **Ajaiyi and His Inherited Poverty,** is further proof of Mr. Tutuola's skill as a novelist. It is the story of the adventures that befall a youth and his younger sister after the death of their parents. They are first kidnapped by a man who sells them to an idol-worshipper but they manage to escape into the forest just before they are due to be sacrificed. There, they fall foul of an evil being, the Spirit of Fire, but they finally escape from his clutches. After some more adventures, they return to their village where Aina gets married. Ajaiyi sets off once more in search of fortune and, having teamed up with two other poverty-stricken youths, he travels to the land of the Supreme Being. There they learn that wordly riches can only be obtained from the Devil, and they decide to turn to him for help. However, Ajaiyi has the wisdom to refuse to sell his soul to the Devil in exchange for money. He finally returns home, marries and obtains wealth through piety and unselfishness.

Ajaiyi and His Inherited Poverty is an outstanding novel in many ways. Its most striking characteristic is perhaps the way in which Mr. Tutuola deliberately turns his back on everyday logic. For instance, the first words we read are : « I, as Ajaiyi by name, was fifteen years of age, my junior sister, Aina by name, was twelve. Both of us were born by the same father and mother, in a very small village... This story happened about two hundred years ago when I first came to this world through another father and mother. By that time I was a boy and not a girl, by that time I was the poorest farmer and not a story-teller... » Right from the start, the reader is drawn into a magical world in which events occur exactly as the subconscious mind would represent them in a dream. The best example of the surrealistic nature of Mr. Tutuola's novel is certainly the following description of the Spirit of Fire : « ... his head was three times bigger than his body and it was about six feet long and tapered towards the end. The whole head was curved towards his back, and it was so both edges of it had long and wide feathers which were also curved together with the head. His nose was thicker than a round pillar of about three feet diameter and it was so much curved like a sickle that it was touching his chest. Each of his ears was as big as a hat. Both his eyes were at the point where his curved head started... »

Ajaiyi lives in a world where real and imaginary meet on equal terms. In his many wanderings, he meets with a number of strange beings, ranging from ghosts to witches and evil spirits. There is, for instance, the « human dead-body eater », who is described as an ape that has two long sharp horns on its head, or the unicorn that takes Ajaiyi and his companions to the Devil's abode. What is most captivating about Mr. Tutuola's novel, however, is its moral aspect. Ajaiyi's

Reprinted from *Présence Africaine*, 65 (1968), 180-81.

adventures are a long, lonely search for truth and inner purity. He progressively learns a great deal about life, for instance that « money is the father of all evils and the creator of all insincerities of the world », or that « the rope of the truth is thin but there is nobody who can cut it ; the rope of lie is thick as a large pillar but it can easily be cut into a thousand pieces », or even that « no one claims relationship with a poor man ; but when he is rich, everyone becomes his relative ».

Many passages of this novel remind one of Dante's **Divine Comedy.** Mr. Tutuola's vision of Hell is very striking indeed : « ... I began to distinguish a number of the people who had died in my village long ago... All were burning repeatedly and thousands of the thunderbolts were dashing on each of them at a time. Some of the people that I knew before they died in my village, and who were in this big flame, were judges who were not honest in judging cases, except when bribery was offered. The murderers, liars, thieves, deceivers, etc. etc., and many politicians who had embezzled the State's money, lands, etc... »

One cannot perhaps help feeling that having to write in English somehow impoverishes the author's style and that he would probably have expressed himself far better in Yoruba, his native tongue, but **Ajaiyi and His Inherited Poverty** is undoubtedly a highly imaginative novel that is well worth reading.

Ola BALOGUN.

From *Nigeria Magazine*, March/May, 1968

This novel makes very light and easy reading and would be more interesting to those who know Yoruba mythology and understand Yoruba idioms, philosophy of life, life after death, the spirit world and the different types of gods and their media.

Briefly, the story tells of how the hero of the novel and his loyal junior sister set out on the death of their parents to find deliverance and what they suffered in the hands of those who cheated and deceived them. However, Ajaiyi, with the help of his wife who outwitted their antagonists, succeeded in freeing them from bondage.

Of course, I would strongly recommend *Ajaiyi and His Inherited Poverty* to be read by those who really understand the English language. To those who do not this novel will confuse them owing to the author's peculiar use of words some of which do not exist in the English language, and his direct translation from Yoruba to English as shown in this . . . "A hunch does not hinder the progress of the person who has it on his back," as well as unnecessary embellishment like . . . "Of course when Aina said that she was hungry for food, we discontinued the arguments AT THE SAME TIME . . . ."

I wish it could be translated into Yoruba for it will certainly make an enjoyable reading for Yoruba readers.

Gladys Agbebiyi

REAPPRAISALS

Reappraisals

In the middle and late sixties there were at least four attempts by African critics to reassess the value of Tutuola's work. All agreed he was a compelling storyteller much misunderstood and underappreciated by African readers who were put off by his bad grammar and utilization of traditional oral narratives. Each then sought to define the nature of his idiosyncratic strengths and weaknesses and to explain his significance as a writer. Meanwhile, across the Atlantic, an American critic was completing the first full-length study of Tutuola's writings and coming to similar conclusions on his own. These reappraisals are included here in the order of their publication.

The Palm Wine Drinkard: Fourteen Years On

Eldred Jones

Tutuola's *Palm Wine Drinkard* was published by Faber in 1952 and would probably have passed largely unnoticed but for a rave review by Dylan Thomas in *The Observer*. The exoticism and utter fantasy, the almost cavalier disregard for English as she is spoke, appealed to the imagination of Dylan Thomas. He praised this as a "brief, thronged, grisly and bewitching story . . . . Nothing is too prodigious or too trivial to put down in this tall, devilish story". This, remember, was before even Ekwensi's *People of the City* had been published. Many West Africans could not share the general enthusiasm because they feared that Tutuola's language would be taken as being representative of West African English, and also because recognizing, as they no doubt did, the folk stories which Tutuola so grotesquely embroidered, they gave his imagination less credit than would someone who came fresh to these fantastic adventures. And so it appeared that once again East and West had demonstrated that "Ne'er the twain shall meet".

I think now, over a dozen years later and so many African novels later, we can take a second look at Tutuola's achievement.

First there is no doubt that both in his material and in his structure Tutuola is indebted to African folk-lore. (But remember, we can make similar statements with regard to Shakespeare and English folk-lore—Shakespeare and Greene, Shakespeare and Holinshed, Shakespeare and Sir Thomas North without seriously undermining Shakespeare's reputation as a creative artist.)

Tutuola makes use for example of the story of the girl who refused all suitors and then enthusiastically marries a complete stranger only to find him a devil. This is what he embellishes into the story of the "curious creature who turned into a skull". In the Krio version of the story told in Sierra Leone, the unknown man turns out to be a "devil". As he and his bride journeyed towards his home, he started shedding his clothes one by one. As each item dropped off and the bride pointed to it, he would reply: "Lef am de, na de ya mit am".

Reprinted from *The Bulletin of the Association for African Literature in English*, 4 (1966), 24-30.

(Leave it there; you found it there.) Finally when he had shed all his borrowed clothes he stood revealed as a devil. The girl was ultimately rescued by her despised younger brother who had followed his sister against her wishes. The traditional moral ending is: "This is why girls should marry the men chosen by their parents and not marry strangers, however handsome."

The changes Tutuola makes to this story are indicative of his method. He amplifies and exaggerates details. The man in the traditional story was always dressed to kill, and in European clothes—top hat and morning dress in the Krio version. Tutuola's "curious creature" is similarly dressed:

> He was a beautiful "complete" gentleman, he dressed with the finest and most costly clothes, all parts of his body were completed. . . . As this gentleman came to the market that day, if he had been an article or animal for sale, he would be sold at least for £2,000 (two thousand pounds). (p. 18)

But Tutuola's mind goes deeper than clothes. His "complete gentleman" sheds part of his body. Tutuola itemizes the grisly disintegration of the "complete gentleman" down to his returning of "the skin which covered his head ... now the complete gentleman in the market reduced to a 'SKULL'." Of course at this point as at a similar point in the traditional version, the lady repents her decision. But now we are well and truly in Tutuola's world. Apart from the attributes of this particular skull—"he could jump a mile to the second before coming down"—Tutuola soon devises a whole race of skulls. Like his gods and ghosts these skulls live in families apparently marrying and being given in marriage. The details of the lady's captivity are also the products of Tutuola's imagination: "At the same time that they entered the hole, he tied a single Cowrie on the neck of this lady with a kind of rope, after that, he gave her a large frog on which she sat as a stool, then he gave a whistle to a skull of his kind to keep watch on this lady whenever she wanted to run away." (p. 22) The cowrie had a function too: "but the lady could not talk at all, because as the cowrie had been tied on her neck, she became dumb at the same moment." The cowrie also was an alarm. (p. 23)

Tutuola also brings his imagination to work on the method and process of rescue by our hero, the Drinkard, and here we are even deeper in the realms of fantasy. The Drinkard, by means of his "juju" was able to turn himself into a lizard and trail the "curious creature" (p. 26), turn back into a man (p. 27), then into air (p. 27), again into a man (p. 27), and finally when the unearthly chase was at its height with the chasing skulls "rolling on the ground like large stones and also humming with terrible noise, ... then I changed the lady to a kitten and put her inside my pocket and changed myself to a very small bird which I could describe as a 'sparrow' in English language."

Tutuola thus transforms the simple tale into a horror comic by a technique of exaggeration and transformation. Tutuola employs several tales and motifs from folk-lore in a similar way, exaggerating details and inventing even more grisly ones of his won. He preserves the structure of the folk-tale with its moral interjections and moral ending. Halfway through the story of the curious creature, and in capital letters, this warning occurs:

DO NOT FOLLOW UNKNOWN MAN'S BEAUTY.

When at the end of the episode he marries the girl he has rescued we have a familiar summary remark: "This is how I got a wife" (p. 31).

Tutuola's stories touch folk-lore in many details, but depart from folk-lore as often. There is a transforming as well as a creative imagination at work which makes use of traditional ideas as well as details from the new and changing urbanized African world. His use of money is interesting. The curious creature had inventoried £2,000 in the market place. In the manner of an official receipt, Tutuola writes the sum out in words as well as in figures. This interplay of the world of hard commerce with the world of fantasy combine to give Tutuola his bizarre dream effect. On one occasion when he was penniless, the Drinkard turned himself into a canoe which his wife then employed as a ferry-boat "to carry passengers across the river, the fare for adults was 3d (three-pence) and half fare for children. In the evening time, then I changed to a man as before and when we checked the money that my wife had collected for that day, it was £7. 5s. 3d." (p. 39). His final total at the end of the month was £56. 11s. 9d.

In another bizarre transaction, "we ... sold our death ... for the sum of £70. 18s. 6d. and lent our fear ... on interest of £3. 10s. 0d. per month" (p. 67). He is similarly concerned with dimensions and weights. The extraordinary tree which houses the "faithful mother" was "about one thousand and fifty feet in length and about two hundred feet in diameter" (p. 65). The miraculous baby weighed "at least 28 lbs." (p. 37), and one of the fantastic creatures he encountered had "over 30 and large eyes" (p. 79). Tutuola gives times of day—5 o'clock, 7 o'clock (p. 78)—and numerous other details from urban life. He has a fondness for statistics no doubt born of his work in a government office. This sort of detail makes up the warp and weft of Tutuola's embroidery.

Sometimes Tutuola's source is not a complete narrative; it is a unit of popular belief or custom. The Drinkard's experiences in "The Wraith-Island" exemplify this. The whole episode seems based on two commonplaces of life in agricultural Africa. The first, that animals attack crops at harvest time, and the second that it is customary for first fruits of the harvest to be offered to the local deity. Out of these commonplaces Tutuola makes a fantastic creation. By means of exaggeration the marauding animal becomes a nightmare figure:

> . . . he was as big as an elephant. His fingernails were long to about two feet, his head was bigger than his body ten times. He had a large mouth which was full of long teeth, those teeth were about one foot long and as thick as a cow's horns, his body was almost covered with black long hair like a horse's tail hair. He was very dirty. There were five horns on his head and curved and levelled to the head, his four feet were as big as a log of wood. (p. 48)

It turns out that this was the "owner" of the land. All he required was a token sacrifice. As soon as he got this, the animal became quite benevolent. He carried the Drinkard on his back and gave him some wonder seeds which produced fruit in ten minutes (p. 48).

It is in ways like this that Tutuola's imagination is fired by his traditional background. Tutuola's world is complex. It contains elements of traditional folk-lore and belief, of Christian belief (there is an implicit faith in the Christian God in phrases like "God was so good," etc.), elements of an urbanized money civilization, western judicial practice, and indeed anything that comes his way. He binds all this into a unified world different from each of its constituent parts.

The structure of the book is simple. It is a series of adventures in quest of the Drinkard's deceased tapper. In his quest he encounters tremendous obstacles which he overcomes with the combined help of juju, benevolent spirits and native cunning. The end of the story is interesting for it underlines a moral which had been made earlier. At the start of the story, because he can offer them unlimited palm wine, the drinkard is very popular. When his tapper dies and he can no longer offer this lavish hospitality, the friends pointedly disappear (pp. 8-9). The moral is obvious—friends are fickle. This point is made again at the end of the story. The Drinkard returns after his quest, without the tapper who is irrevocably dead, but with a magic egg (another borrowing from folk-lore) which produces unlimited food on demand. With the help of the egg he relieves a famine and earns the gratitude of people for miles around. When the egg fails, however, they abuse and desert him. He manages to restore the egg, but this time it can only produce whips. Using the new power he punishes the people for their ingratitude, and the egg disappears. The Drinkard is left without resources, and the land with the famine which had been caused by a quarrel between Land and Heaven (another folk tale idea). A sacrifice borne to heaven by the best of the King's slaves placates heaven and the famine ends. This end seems to have very little structural connection with what has gone before. It is true an earlier moral "not too small to be chosen" is repeated but this does not affect the essential irrelevance of the end.

This is indeed a feature of Tutuola's writing. All the energy is spent on the individual episodes which are loosely strung together. There is no attempt at any meaningful inter-connection or over-all point of view. The Drinkard seems no different for his adventures. Life continues as before. For all the incidental morality (often a mere repetition of the moral formulas attached to the tales he uses) Tutuola seems to have no conscious moral position. There is no new vision for all the suffering. In a similar way Simbi in *Simbi and the Satyr of the Dark Jungle* returns from her all-conquering mission carried out in defiance of all the traditions of the village, only to say at the end: "Hah, my mother, I shall not disobey you again!" Tutuola thus disappoints all feminists looking for the emancipation of village womanhood, as he disappoints anyone who looks for a message in *The Palm Wine Drinkard.*

Reading Tutuola must be a very different experience for an African who knows the stories and motifs he exploits, and a non-African to whom these ideas come fresh and strange. For the African there is a large element of recognition. The language is likely to be as puzzling to him as to a European, for Tutuola's merit is *not* essentially linguistic, though few can fail to thrill at some of Tutuola's more fortunate coinages—"drinkard" and "gravitiness" being two of my favorites. For the non-African there is the sustained element of surprise and of strangeness. The fantasy is undiluted by the little subtraction sums that are clicking in the African's head.

113

TABAN LO LIYONG

Tutuola, son of Zinjanthropus[1]

Teachers of English language and educated Africans who pride themselves
n their mastery of English will be surprised to learn that in creative writing
rammar does not count very much. In art, too, perspective, proportion,
ymmetry, have very little importance to great artists. And, in modern electronic
nusic, the innovations are such that Ludwig van Beethoven would have raged
ɔ madness were he to come to life today. Perhaps the arts are undergoing a
reater revolution than they went through in the romantic period. Now, some
f these modern artists who are transforming our sensibilities, burdening
ınguage with a tug and a twist, mangling limbs, experimenting with colour,
nd time, and tone, and surface, and space—some of these people are ordinary
ıortals like you and me; they steal away to their artistic world and then come
ack to us. But some of them live in one world only—their artistic world, full
f Alices, Guernicas, Joseph K's, Finnegan's Wakes, and Complete Gentlemen.
`heir world is not balanced, not as orderly as we would have designed it.

Now, in all that he has done, Amos Tutuola is not *sui generis*. Is he ungram-
ıatical? Yes. But James Joyce is more ungrammatical than Tutuola. Ezekiel
Aphahlele has often said and written that African writers are doing violence
ɔ English. Violence? Has Joyce not done more violence to the English language?
Mark Twain's *Huckleberry Finn* is written in seven dialects, he tells us. It is
cknowledged a classic. We accept it, forget that it has no "grammar", and
o ahead to learn his "grammar" and what he has to tell us. Let Tutuola write

---

This article is written in order to stimulate a fresh look into the writings of Amos Tutuola.
Very litle of Tutuola's work is mentioned directly. Instead, points of view are provided
hrough which Tutuola's true greatness may be appraised.

Reprinted from *Busara*, 1, 1 (1968), 308. A revised version of the same essay
ıter appeared in Liyong's *The Last Word: Cultural Synthesis* (Nairobi, 1969),
'p. 157-70.

"no grammar" and the hyenas and jackals whine and growl. Let Gabriel Okara write a "no grammar" *Okolo*. They are mum. Why?

Education drives out of the mind superstition, daydreaming, building of castles in the air, cultivation of yarns, and replaces them with a rational practical mind, almost devoid of imagination. Some of these minds, having failed to write imaginative stories, turn to that aristocratic type of criticism which magnifies trivialities beyond their real size. They fail to touch other virtues in a work because they do not have the imagination to perceive these mysteries.

Art is arbitrary. Anybody can begin his own style. Having begun it arbitrarily, if he persists to produce in that particular mode, he can enlarge and elevate it to something permanent, to something other artists will come to learn and copy, to something the critics will catch up with and appreciate.

In 1952, then, we see our young David, clad only in a loin-cloth, and armed only with a sling, step into the arena to do battle with the philistine, the Giant, slayer of the Sons of Fame. I was young then—only another boy in Standard 7— otherwise I might have gone to drag David out of so unbalanced a match. As it was, my heart missed one beat—a beat I have never recovered. But, confidently, he swung his sling and lodged the stone in the Cyclop's eye. The great beast fell. I thought he was dead, but no, Cyclops had nine lives. May this missile, computer-directed, seventeen years afterwards knock him down once and for all!

Wale Olumide, a Nigerian who throws big names about without establishing a connection, accuses Tutuola of stealing his plots from Jung. This is an ironic flattery. But it must not stick, because: (a) I don't think Tutuola knows Jung, or knows him that much; in any case (b) Tutuola has no use for Jung, for his materials and tools are home-grown—the very ones that grow around the African shrine or fire-place; and (c) it is from native story tellers like Tutuola that Jung got the evidence for his conclusions.

Chief D. O. Fagunwa, a fellow Yoruba, preceded Tutuola in writing and publishing stories. The chief had the misfortune of being old-fashioned and writing in Yoruba. Now, he is suffering in the hands of inept translators. Undoubtedly there are very many African oral story tellers. Undoubtedly they could tell the stories better than Tutuola, just as other Greeks could have written (might have actually written, but their efforts got lost) better *Odysseys* than Homer. But we have no time for all these "could have", "might have" hypotheses. We demand immediate evidence, right now, into our own hands, so that even the Thomases among us can touch the scars.

If Tutuola trades in African myths and folk-lore, can we credit him with originality and imagination? Yea. For the artist's material is the very earth you tread on, the very traffic accident you see, the very mourning your unlucky neighbour is going through, the very turbulation that agonises lovers, the very fear of darkness and noise you had as a child. The artist appropriates all this common stuff, and in the depth of his imaginative funnel, transmits it, distils it, so that the finished material which emerges at the end of the conveyor belt is a gem whose lustre shines at the appropriate spots. There is nothing new under the sun, says Ecclesiastes the Preacher.

Hesiod did not plot the *Theogony*, although he put a Hesiodic outlook into it. Virgil's *Aeneid* is as Roman as Homer's *Odyssey* is Greek, though both told the same story. Had Ovid not been a rake, his *Metamorphoses* might have had less sensuality or passion and sex in them. Bertholdt Brecht's plays are transformations of other people's works. And the Great Shakespeare, how many plots did he steal?

When Ariosto presented his patron, the Duke of Ferrara, with his epic *Orlando Furioso*, the duke's only recorded compliment is the question: Where did you gather all these fantastic stories from? Maybe, the duke did not know. Amos Tutuola knows the exact order in which he *arrived* at the various towns in his novels.

Adolf Hitler did Tutuola the favour of starting World War Two. He went and worked as a blacksmith in the airforce division. Now, an aeroplane is noisy—and readers have to take their ears with them into Tutuola's jungles; there the very skulls make hideous alarms, audible from miles away. One of his heroes is so beautiful a work of art that the very Gods and Goddesses of Beauty bewitch guns so that they won't fire to kill him, however hard the triggers are pulled. If Burns borrowed Milton's *Paradise Lost* in order to study the character Satan, Tutuola borrows books on electricity in order to—to what?

Fagunwa's hero Olowo-aiye is the "Rich Man of the World", who periodically goes adventure-hunting in order to acquire more wealth. His motto is: Aim for the Best, the Most. Tutuola's hero wants to discover all the secrets of the Gods, aiming eventually at becoming wiser than the Gods. And he actually beats the Gods in their own game. Now, tell me, reader, which Greek God would have tolerated such human arrogance? Zeus of the Aegis? With his Thunderbolts he would have made a mince-meat of such a mortal as a lesson to other mortals, and to surfeit his thirst for blood. And Jehovah the Revenger would not only have smitten such a man, he would have punished the man's descendants to the *nth* generation.

Philosophies vary in their attitudes to abundance and scarcity. Where things—foods mostly—are hard to come by, austerity measures are adopted and stronger penalties imposed on malefactors—all in the name of Zeus or Jehovah. In the lush tropics, where fruits feed the hungry, one is assured of abundance, or near-abundance, and one can afford to defy society and the gods—one knows famine can't last for long, and, therefore, nature is playing a wasted game. Yoruba gods were weak because the Yoruba were stronger men. In their mythologies, man triumphs over the gods. Perhaps they defy the gods because they know the gods are fictions.

In our disdain—mistakenly all the same—of Amos Tutuola, we run the danger of disdaining the very material he worked with, to wit, African mythology. If we do that, we shall have cut our very umbilical cord, and disowned our mother. The social world as we know it originated in myths. Myths are the means of apprehending the world, comprehending it.

We went near and far in order to find parts with which to fit up Tutuola. We realise he has been seen "incomplete". And if we can now assemble the various limbs, fingers, eyes, ears, etc., together and assemble our hero, how does the Complete Tutuola look? Not as distorted as Moore thinks! What we behold is a modern ancient, the optimistic, daring, and defiant African of yesterday who could have walked with Beethoven to write this piece of impudence:

> Kings and princes can turn out as many professors and privy councillors as they please, grant titles and ribbons, but they cannot produce great men, minds that rise above the human herd and whose task it is to make themselves, for which they must be regarded with respect. When two men like Goethe and myself walk together, these great lords must be shown what we hold to be great. Yesterday, as we were walking back, we met all the Imperial family, we saw them coming from afar, and Goethe let go my arm to get out of their way onto the side of the road. No good arguing with him, it was impossible to make him take another step ahead. For myself, I pulled my hat down over my eyes and bore down on to the very centre of the company, hands crossed behind my back! Princes and courtiers parted and stood aside, the Archduke Rudolph took off his hat to me, the Empress was first to salute me; their lordships *know* me.

Lewis Nkosi, note this: Tutuola has the right to miss an appointment with you, or me. He is a genius and the Father of Modern African literature. West Africans woke up to write nervously because he was already in the field, and he is still ahead, far, far ahead. East Africans have lately entered the field. South African writing never shook Africa to its foundation the way Tutuola's has done. One day, and I wish it comes sooner, the Swedish Academy might begin to think seriously about awarding the Nobel Prize for literature to first-rate writers, and not to second-rate Peace fighters as they have done frequently. When that day comes, they should seriously consider Tutuola for the Nobel Prize for Literature. He merits it more than half-a-dozen winners I know.

Why should we continue to honour Homer dead and deny the laurel to a Homer alive?

A word to our writers.

Writers are supposed to be the most sensitive (with heightened awareness) part of the community; where was the sensitivity of (for example) Nigerians when their country was heading for the maelstrom? Writers are supposed to be the seers; where was their prophetic eye when danger was all around? As prophets who can see the present more clearly, they should have interpreted the signs, signs big enough for the blind to see, before the blows fell. As prophets who can see the most distant event, couldn't they have seen beyond *A Man of the People?*

The arts branched out of the esoteric mysteries of the kingly-aristocratic-priestly class in the beginning of society. When the artist served the noblemen, he had to use the language understood by them, he had to use words and expressions which did not offend them, he had to have an aristocratic theme, so he wrote on chivalry, and wrote epics. For a change, he wrote pastorals to acquaint the nobleman with the lives of his shepherds. Everything that could be done to satisfy "Our Most Gracious and Mighty Princes and Lords" was done.

Then, romanticism bursts upon the scene, democracy comes along, and what do we hear? William Wordsworth says the most revolutionary thing there is in the arts: the poet is "to choose incidents and situations from common life, and to relate or describe them, throughout, as far as... possible in a selection of language really used by men, and, at the same time, to throw over them a certain colouring of imagination, whereby ordinary things should be presented to the mind in an unusual aspect." —The encounter of kings in the Crusades is out, courtly love is out; the life of the beggar is in, polite language is out; the labourer's ungrammatical English is in, the Professor's English is out; Pidgin English is in, exact reporting is out; distorted imagination is in, classical poses are out; cubism is in, religious veracity is out; tall, grisly, thronged stories are in.

And yet Wordsworth did not really know the language spoken by men, nor did he know the lives of the common man of England. It is through Emile Zola in France that we view the lives of the new creatures spawned by the industrial age. It is Zola we must take with us as a guide around Kisenyi and the slums of Nairobi and Dar es Salaam. If we want to know the common American's speech, it is Twain's Jim, Huckleberry Finn, Tom Sawyer to whom we must listen.

Yet these were educated writers who left our educated world to record the secret lives of the poor across the street. Although they exhibited vulgar forms of life, communications in vulgar tongues, we realise our writers were putting on a show—for our benefit. We know they can speak "grammar" as well as we do, we know they know many things besides; we are comfortable in the knowledge that they are of our own class—writers who have struggled hard to master the language, master the art of writing, as well as master *their language of art, the language of the lower-classes.* Their art did not come to them by chance, it was acquired through the various hard stages we ourselves have gone through. So we respect them and we reward them.

To our surprise, one day, into the hall of fame walks a primary school boy, a naughty boy, a boy who knows no grammar, almost a total villager, and he claims a seat among the immortals. What? we shout. Who are you? When were you in Achimota? Perhaps you were at Ibadan with me? Are you a *been-to*? In a land where school knowledge is extremely important, our drop-out is meticulously analysed, weighed, and found insolvent. Our analysts pull their *agbada* up and set to *jollof*-rice and *gari* and chicken legs in their university halls and blame the whole thing on Dylan Thomas, Gerald Moore, and the whole White world. "If this fellow they mumble, (not even mentioning that name, to them accursed), had been to Oxford, and had then decided to use his mother-tongue's syntax, like Okara, perhaps we could believe him. But . . . ".

Unfortunately for them, art is a very strange beast, stranger than some of Amos Tutuola's. Art is no respector of education. Alexander Pope was already mumbling in numbers when he was a tot; Mozart played the piano when he could barely reach the keys; Walt Whitman—that expansive American visionary —who was he, wasn't he just another bum, but a bum who bumped on a face reader and was told that from the look of his facial features great things could be expected of him?

Art also changes its shape more than Proteus. With the classicists art was more exact than a photograph, her secrets were not for us to divine. Michelangelo Bournaroti and his predecessors glorified the perfect man in the name of a perfect, powerful God. But that cosmology has been shattered, the mirror of life has been broken. The world is in bits and pieces; the reflections from the broken mirror have so multiplied things that we are dazed. In the arts, we have seen (among others) Emily Brontë, Vincent van Gogh, Miro, Nietzsche, Chagal, Pound, Ionesco, Antonioni, Barth, Marshall McLuhan, L.S.D., and *bhang.* Not even Freud himself can assemble the various pieces on his magic couch.

To expect classical conformity is not the thing; to expect classical clarity is not the thing. You can't even expect to find order in language itself. What you can do is to stare at a glass at a time, catch a glimpse of the moving leg, another time stare at the heavens (if not yet clouded by smog), pass from one electrical terminus to the next, and, if you are strong enough, shut yourself in your desert mind and meditate awhile. Leave the search for order and meaning to the fools.

Today when the machine is taking up more and more of man's former dominion, isn't it refreshing to find a man who is man enough to stand up against the machines ? For what is language but a machine ? and learning grammar makes us more and more slavish to it. As Lewis Carroll's character asked, Who is to be the master ? Let men say their says. If there are things of importance in them, we the vegetables will be forced to learn their languages in order to get at their meanings. Each writer has his own language. Just as abnormal psychology has taught us more about life than normal psychology, so a complete system of abnormal language can shed more light onto some obscure parts of life.

Everything that goes on in the world has an effect on us, on how we see the world. We Africans have changed in many ways since the great encounter with the European pioneers. We have felt the impact of Europe, America, Asia. Asia, America, and Europe have not felt the impact of Africa very much. But they are beginning to feel it. I am not talking about politics. I am talking about ways of life and objects of common usage. Now, African fashions are copied by French designers. African languages are being taught abroad. African English, and, yes—even Tutuola's—is being taught in England. And those who learn these increase their stock of knowledge.

Unfortunately, Africans (of the Negritude breed) have always thought they are a different variety of mankind—they were the ones to produce perfection, and any African who did not answer to it had to be disowned. There are, we should remind our fellow brothers, virtuous Africans, vicious Africans, perverted Africans, meticulous Africans, lazy Africans, uneducated African geniuses like Amos Tutuola and Field Marshal Okello, the Father of Modern Zanzibar.

But when has a prophet met with honour in his country ? (Runners are a breed apart, since Kipchoge gets his dues.) Kinsmen stop aspiring prophets from yielding the palm to an especially dangerous competitor. What these foxes do is to clip our eagle's wings so that he may fly a middle course.

Writing about Robert Burns, another uneducated genius, Thomas Carlyle said:

> It is difficult for men to believe that the man, the mere man whom they see— nay, perhaps painfully feel—toiling at their side through the poor jostlings of existence, can be made of finer clay than themselves.

And didn't Ben Jonson (another university wit) make it a special point of telling us that Shakespeare "hadst small *Latine,* and lesse *Greeke*"—in the tradition of intellectuals (?) eclipsed by natural geniuses ?

Rare pearls have been thrown among us and we have trampled upon them.

Christina Aidoo, after blasting this spoiler of West African reputation in

121

English, this confuser of school pupils with his bad grammar, at least admits, grudgingly, that he possesses an abundance of imagination. But, it is IMAGI-NATION we seek in an artist.

E.N. Obiechina

Amos Tutuola and the Oral Tradition

A fairly detailed discussion of the distinction between folk-tales, legends and myths is necessary for a proper appraisal of Tutuola's works. Many of his critics have taken it for granted that he is a purveyor of myths (1). This opinion could not possibly be correct. Myths, as mentioned in a previous article, are a collective possession of the people and no single individual can lay claim to inventing them. If the West African reader of Tutuola rejects his claim to originality on the mistaken assumption that he has merely rehashed existing mythology, then Tutuola has the ignorance of his admirers to thank for it. His stories fall within the category of folk-tales. Myths are to a great extent sacred tales ; Tutuola's writing belongs to profane story-telling. As a result of their pseudo-religious significance, myths are rigid in form and content and so do not yield to individual creativity whereas legends are only slightly less rigid since the need to stick to the facts embodied within them has a limiting effect on the creative freedom of the narrator. Individual artistic creativity finds the greatest outlet in folk-tales because they have neither a ritual significance like myths nor a factual necessity like legends (2). As a result, folk-tales not only form the largest group of traditional narratives but they also have the greatest popular appeal.

Within the scope of the folk-tale, there is plenty of room for the exercise of individual imagination and originality. Within its tradition, only the outline of a story needs to be known. The narrator takes this outline and is completely free to embellish it with as much invention as he can muster and, in fact, much

---

(1) See Gerald Moore's *Seven African Writers* ; K.E. Sesanu in *The Commonwealth Pen*, edited by Mcleod ; Dr. Parrinder's Foreward to the Faber and Faber edition of *My Life in the Bush of Ghosts* ; Janheinz Jahn's *Muntu*.

(2) This distinction was pointed out to Herskovits by a Dahomean narrator (see *Dahomean Narratives : A Cross-cultural Analysis*, p. 16).

Reprinted from *Présence Africaine*, 65 (1968), 85-106.

value is attached to his resourcefulness in improvising new and interesting variations. His mode of delivery, dramatic gestures and verbal dexterity are the essential qualities that mark him out as a good story-teller. In view of this, it is difficult to see why anyone should refuse to acknowledge Tutuola's rights to originality and inventiveness. The conventional procedure at story-telling gatherings is something like this (and every West African who has lived in a village will agree) : the person whose turn it is to tell *his* story announces to the audience that he has a story to tell. The audience tells him to tell it. He then proceeds to tell *his* story. The important thing to note here is that the text of any story is public property until an individual whose turn it is to tell a story picks it up. Then it becomes *his* story. It would be suspected that the reverse process probably applied in balladry and epic narrative. These, requiring a more rigid formalistic structure than the folk-tale, probably depended on an original transmuting genius who, even though drawing heavily upon the cultural repertoire of the community, had to give formalistic shape to the material before it was ready for absorption into folk-literature. An epic narrative must therefore be the product of an original bard and a ballad that of an original ballad-maker (3). The folk-tale, on the other hand, belongs in its bare outline to the community until the individual picks it up and, during his process of narration, makes it his own. There is therefore no single authentic text. The skeletal text which embodies the well-known motif is there and, sometimes, the underlying exemplum. The individual narrator using the former builds it up by the use of his own methods. There could therefore be as many texts fo one story as there are narrators, some of them very good, some indifferent and others downright poor, depending on the competence or otherwise of the individual.

In written tradition with its fixed texts, it is possible to determine the indebtedness of one text to another. It is, for instance, easy to see how much La Fontaine's Fables incorporate details from Aesop's Fables by comparing the two. In the oral tradition, within which the quality of a story depends not only on verbal manipulation but also on dramatic devices such as gestures, facial expressions and voice modulation, textual comparison is not only unprofitable but impossible. Each text can be regarded as original because it bears a distinctive stylistic stamp. What Tutuola has done in his writing is to refurbish old tales by employing well-known motifs and narrative techniques. He is doing in writing what is perfectly justified in oral tradition — embellishing texts from his replete imagination which have become his own even though he has had to

---

(3) For a discussion of the problem of epic-making, the so-called « Homeric Problem », see Albert B. Lord : *The Singer of Tales*, p. 124.

write them down. If one has to look around for parallels, one may liken the situation to the problem of adaptation and borrowing in Elizabethan literature. Some of the best work produced at this period was by those who « borrowed » their themes from well-known classical and folk texts, or even from works of living authors, and imaginatively transformed them. Shakespeare made use of existing texts and in spite of Robert Greene's catty denunciation of « the upstart crow » who decked himself in others' feathers, the world is certainly much the richer for having Shakespeare.

To illustrate how much Tutuola's writing owes to oral tradition, it will suffice to examine *The Palm-Wine Drinkard* and *Simbi and the Satyr of the Dark Jungle* which most people regard as his best books. For the purpose of brevity, the titles are abridged to *The Drinkard* and *Simbi*.

⁎⁎

The Drinkard deals with the search by the hero for his dead palm-wine tapster. After a series of harrowing adventures, he succeeds in tracing him to Deads Town. He does not bring him back, however, but instead receives a gift of a magic egg with which he is enabled to produce anything he wants by merely requesting it from the egg. After further adventures, the Drinkard returns home and settles a dispute between the Sky God and the Earth Goddess, thereby putting an end to the drought which the Sky God caused to spite the earth. *Simbi* is the story of a pretty peasant girl and the daughter of a well-to-do mother who becomes dissatisfied with a life of slothful ease and decides, contrary to her mother's advice, to explore the real meaning of poverty and punishment. After stormy adventures, during which she experiences a great deal of both poverty and punishment, especially at the hands of the noxious Satyr of the Dark Jungle, she returns home a sadder and wiser woman.

The world of these stories is the undifferentiated universe of the traditional folk-tale within which intercourse between the living and the dead is possible. Within this universe, all nature is humanised. Tutuola recaptures the atmosphere of the immense intimacy between the different elements in nature in his description of the great carnival celebrating the resettling of the Red-people in a new town :

« ... when the day that they appointed for this special occasion was reached, these fellows (Drum, Song and Dance) came and when 'Drum' started to beat himself, all the people who had been dead for hundreds of years rose up and came to witness 'Drum' beating ; and when 'Song' began to sing, all domestic animals of that new town, bush animals with snakes, etc. came out to see 'Song' personally, but when 'Dance' started to dance, the whole bush creatures, spirits, mountain creatures and also all the river creatures, came to the town to see who was dancing. When these three fellows started at the same time, the whole people of the new town, the whole people that rose up from the grave, snakes, spirits and other nameless creatures, were dancing together with these three fellows... »

Such outbursts of vitality recur through Tutuola's stories. Man has to struggle hard to ensure a place in the universe. He must compete with the rest of animated nature. He is no absolute monarch exerting untrammelled authority over the rest of the universe. Fortunately, he is able to reinforce his vital force with magical power. He is able, by magic, to change himself into something else when hard pressed by his adversaries. Metamorphosis offers him both a means of protection and a facility to display his magical power. Tutuola employs the technique of metamorphosis extensively in both *The Drinkard* and *Simbi*.

As a result of this, some enthusiastic critics have referred to his writing as Kafkaesque. Kafka also uses the technique of metamorphosis in some of his short stories. The comparison between Tutuola and Kafka, even in respect of their use of metamorphosis, appears tenuous if not altogether misleading. In Kafka's stories, metamorphosis is a process of de-energization, a process demonstrating the deflated state of Man when confronted with inexplicable and portentous forces. Tutuola's tales reveal man as possessing the power and the ability to face up to or circumvent the menaces of those inimical forces. Man is not just a helpless and self-pitying cockroach, utterly isolated and rendered *incommunicado* with his kind ; he is not a wretched lamb-cat who is « left in the lurch », or the lost soul hovering perpetually and hopelessly between heaven and earth. In Tutuola, man becomes the consummate strategist who can turn himself into a bird, a lizard or a self-propelled pebble with the purpose of getting the better of his adversaries. In Kafka, man is the impotent victim of inexorable Fate ; in Tutuola, he is the proud possessor of great magical powers with which he defies even Fate itself. Kafka's metamorphosed men foreshadow the millions of helpless people in Europe who were to be trodden under the hooves of the most ruthless dictatorships. Tutuola's metamorphosed heroes and heroines show man struggling against the fearful and formidable forces of wild nature and the supernatural, but who, though often wounded and bruised in the struggle, nevertheless emerges victorious. Whereas metamorphosis in Tutuola emphasizes the dignity and vital energy of the human kind, in Kafka it stresses human futility and despair. Finally, Kafka uses metamorphosis parabolically for the purpose of giving a peculiar insight into the predicament of doomed man ; Tutuola uses it literally to demonstrate man's hope for survival even in the teeth of the hostile forces that surround him.

An important aspect of the world of Tutuola's books is the complete blending of fantasy with conventional realism, a quality which is also very characteristic of the traditional folk-tale. This aspect is clearly brought out in situations within which the principles of economic rationalisation are seen to operate within magical contexts. For instance, when pressed for hard cash, the Drinkard uses his inherited magical powers to turn himself into a canoe which his wife uses to ferry people across a stream at the rate of 3d. per adult and 1½ d. per child. Making an average daily turn-over of £7. 5s. 3d, the Drinkard and his wife are able to amass a handsome sum of £56. 11s. 9d at the end of one month. Again, just before the Drinkard and his wife enter the home of the Faithful-Mother in the White Tree, they carry out a brisk business transaction with « somebody at the door » selling their death to him for £70.18s.6d and lending him their fear on the interest of £3.10s.0d. When they finally leave the White Tree, they collect their capital (fear) and interest from the said « somebody at the door ». They, having sold their death, cannot from now onward be afraid of dying though they still possess the quality of fear, not having sold their fear at the time they sold their death. Within the arcadian Wraith-Island, and again in the new town of the Red-people, the Drinkard becomes an agricultural landlord making use of the mysterious little creature, the Invisible Pawn, to cultivate his extensive farm. Death is shown in *The Dinkard* as leading a sedentary and retired life in his farm and when the Drinkard visits him, he is busy tending his yam crops. Being Death, of course, he is living alone and is both his own master and labourer. In *Simbi*, the heroine pawns her services to the decrepit iconophile in return for shelter, food and clothing at a time when she is almost completely indigent in the Dark Jungle. She has to work very hard and devotedly to satisfy even her most elementary needs.

This essential economic rationalisation, which operates on the formula that material needs must be paid for either in cash or in kind, exists side by side with magical determinism which appears entirely antithetical to it. By the possession of the appropriate magical object (such as the egg which the Tapster gives to the Drinkard) and application of the proper spells, a man is able to procure his needs without physical labour or money payment. Very often, however, it turns out that fantasy merely subserves the interest of realism, and magical determinism in economic affairs only goes to strengthen the realistic principles of the *homo economicus*. To take the example of the magical egg again, after the parasitic neighbours of the Drinkard have been fed for sometime through the agency of the magic egg, an accident occurs and the egg breaks. The Drinkard patches it up but when it is commanded to produce food and drink, it produces whips which beat the idle parasites back to their homes. In the final analysis, this episode seems to suggest that there is really nothing like honest labour for honest returns. The predominance of economic rationalisation, whether by way of employment of labour, money-lending or commercialism, over magical determinism in economic matters is an essential aspect of the blending of fantasy and realism within the folk-tale tradition.

Another aspect of this blending is shown by the fact that, within the seemingly amorphous structure of Tutuola's universe, there are clearly defined boundaries as fully demarcated as modern national boundaries and a good deal more rigid since the folk-tale world, having no provision for the visaed traveller, has no means of admitting him from the outside except on terms of hostility. Within the Tutuolan jungle, therefore, the inhabitants, whether they are human trees or human animals or even spirit beings, know the extent of their own territory and do not violate the territorial integrity of their neighbours. Both the Drinkard and Simbi owe much of their suffering to the fact that they do not respect these « national » boundaries. But it is also an essential attribute of the protagonist that he cannot respect these boundaries because, if he does, the scope of his section could be unnecessarily narrowed. In fact, the action cannot even be expected to begin at all because the protagonist cannot leave his own territory if he is afraid to violate the integrity of other people's territory. The effect of a great immensity and variety of colour, character and idiosyncracy which one gets of Tutuola's world derives essentially from this geographical differentiation. Even though the unaccustomed eye of the hero cannot immediately recognize them within the dream-like half-light of the Tutuolan jungle, the inhabitants are acutely aware of them. Thus, the Faithful Mother stops short of the stream which separates her domain from the next territory when·she sees off the Drinkard and his wife. When the Drinkard and his wife are attacked by the army of horrible children along Deads' Road, they escape into the forest which turns out to be the territory of the wicked giant who catches them in his net and makes them his slaves. Again, when the Drinkard and his wife change into a pebble and propel themselves across the stream, they automatically put themselves beyond the reach of the angry mountain creatures hotly in their pursuit because, by conventional usage, the latter cannot cross the stream which forms the boundary between their territory and another territory.

There are distinctive physical and idiosyncratic differences between the inhabitants of the different parts of this world, and Tutuola gives the reader a quick insight into these differences by the use of remarkably cryptic descriptive terms such as the Sinners' Town, the Path of Death, the Town of the Multi-Coloured people, the Town Where Nobody Sings, the Satyr of the Dark Jungle, the Red-People of the Red-Town, Dead's Town, and so on. Differences in behaviour exist between different groups as shown in the absurd ways of the people of the Un-returnable Heavens' Town who would climb the ladder first before leaning it against the tree. Differential behaviour also exists between the living and the dead, as the Drinkard learns to his cost in Deads' Town. Differences in physical appearance sometimes form the basis of discrimination against the foreigner as shown by the racialist king of the Multi-Coloured People telling Simbi and her fellow refugees « We don't hate yourselves but your mono-colour ». The Tutuolan world is there-fore an undifferentiated universe only in the sense that within it all nature is humanised. In other respects, it shows clearly defined geographical and national boundaries and racial differen-ces. It is a part of the hero's prerogative that his activities carry him across these various barriers. His cosmopolitanism and absolute freedom from physical constraint enable him to move freely through the rigidly partitioned world of traditional folk-tale.

But it must also be stated that the hero is no brazen anar-chistic revolutionary, contemptuous of customary usages and impatient of established procedures. He violates the territorial rights of others because he is impelled by the circumstances of his single-minded pursuit to do so. He recognizes himself as an outsider in the new communities where his adventures take him. He is suspected and feared because, as a stranger, he is reputed to have a malignant and potentially dangerous influence over the well-being of the indigenous community. Not being a revolutionary, the hero does not set out to subvert the new community but the hostility of the natives puts him on the defensive and, in his effort to defend himself, he soon brings calamity upon them. The community is never quite the same again after the hero has made his way into it. The fate of the Red-People seems to justify the apprehension with which foreigners are regarded for the Drinkard turns out to be the instrument of their destruction after he has settled in their midst in the new town and Simbi's arrival in the Dark Jungle robs it of its colourful proprietor, the Satyr.

Hostility to the stranger is not just a case of morbid irra-tional xenophobia. The stranger is supposed to possess the evil eye which makes him a source of great danger to the community and the earliest opportunity is taken to get rid of him either by expulsion or by some more wicked means. Here, as in most other cases, cruelty stems from fear and apprehension. In a significant way, however, attitude to strangers in folk-tales differs from attitude to strangers in traditional society. Whereas in the former the stranger is an outsider and remains an outsider even after he has settled down, in the latter he could be, and often is, ritually incorporated into the community and ceases to be regarded as an outsider much in the same way as an alien who has been granted a country's citizenship ceases to be regarded as such. By the rites of incorporation, the erstwhile outsider now shares the common mystical bonds that bind the community. In folk-tales, he remains outside these mystic bonds and therefore has a destiny which is different from, and often in conflict with, the destiny of the community. This lack of a common destiny is the root cause of the inevitable disaster which the folk-tale hero brings to the community in which he finds himself.

.*.

This distinction between attitude to strangers in folk-tales and in traditional African societies is of some importance in view of the opinion sometimes expressed, especially by Western observers, that the tribe in traditional Africa is a closed association which recognises only itself and its interests and maintains purely negative and hostile relations with outside associations and persons. The concept of « them » and « us » is certainly strong in these societies (as in all others because it is by having identified common interests of its own that a society regards itself as a entity in contra-distinction with others of the same kind), and communities are aware of themselves by means of the common bonds of custom, beliefs, political identity and ritual obligations which unite their people in the same way that the possession of a national flag and anthem, common allegiance to a political authority and, to some extent, the existence of a national ethos, marks out and defines the existence of a modern Nation-State. But a traditional society is not quite as closed as it is made out to be, neither is it necessarily in a perpetual state of hostility with outsiders. Apart from the possibility of ritual incorporation of strangers, a traditional community has economic and sometimes ritual ties with neighbouring communities and this makes it imperative that friendly relations exist between collaborating groups. The practice of exogamy further increases the need for peaceful and friendly relationships and leads to the lessening of conflicts between different communities and peoples. In this connection, it ought also to be noted that the foreign wife motif in folk-tales hardly applies in traditional society. According to this, the foreign wife is marked out for discriminatory treatment and her children are victims of the injustice to which those of indigenous mothers are not subjected. In Simbi, for instance, we are told that the heroine has to leave her wood-cutter husband because the townspeople have sacrificed her two sons to their gods because she is not « a native ». Such wicked injustice is hardly possible in a traditional society and least of all in the Yoruba society to which Tutuola belongs. The Yoruba have a patrilineal system and marriage among them is patrilocal. The children of a marriage belong to the father's lineage group and there is no question whatever of their being regarded as strangers within their father's community.

The folk-tale world is therefore not a verisimilitude of the actual traditional world in every detail. What happens is that the potential tensions and stresses in traditional society which are taken care of by cleverly patterned social behaviour, are sometimes played up in folk-tales with the purpose of heightening the emotional effect of the narrative. From this point of view, exaggeration and sensationalism are the keynotes. Petty jealousies between siblings, co-wives and parents and children are constructed into elaborate machinations often ending in murder and fear, and suspicion of strangers leads inevitably to a monstrous sadism such as Simbi experiences as the wood-cutter's wife. This sensationalism elicits a feeling of horror, wonderment and fascination from the audience and Tutuola's genius as a story-teller manifests itself in his easy grasp of this aspect.

His stories recapture the essential humanism of the world of the folk-tale. Within it, all nature is not only imbued with vital force and is humanized, but *homo sapiens* is the pivot around which the drama revolves. He, in all his moods and fancies, in all his joys and tribulations, in all his goodness and nastiness, is the real centre of the Tutuolan world. Even where an animal is the hero of a story, it is invested with human qualities. As Léopold Senghor writes : « In the fable, the animal in seldom a totem ; it is this or that one whom everyone in the village knows well : the stupid or the tyrannical or wise and good chief, the young man who makes reparation for injustice... » (4). In Tutuola, we see man at grips with hostile elements, the jungle, vicious monsters and supernatural beings, struggling often by the skin of his teeth to save himself from the evils which surround him. Unlike the ballad whose preoccupation is with the thing done or the event that happened, Tutuola's story is only important in reference to the personality of the protagonist.

This aspect of the Tutuolan world view is worth emphasizing because the popular image of the traditional African as the helpless victim of his hostile environment is contrary to that held by the African of himself as reflected in traditional folk-

---

(4) Quoted by Jahn in *Muntu*, p. 221.

tales. The African is aware of the problems, physical and otherwise, which surround him and threaten his survival but he is immensely confident in his ability to face up to these problems by his courage and mental resourcefulness. This basic confidence is dramatised in many folk-tales where the triumph of the hero over hostile forces represents the triumph of mankind. The triumphant hero sees himself as a member of a community whose well-being and survival are also his own. Even though he recognises himself as an individual with an individual destiny, he is also aware that he cannot work out that destiny outside the framework of his community. The concern of the community becomes his concern and his egocentricity is strongly tempered with altruism. The traditional African draws strength from his group and then helps to sustain the group by his individual contribution. Both Simbi and the Drinkard are essentially individualists working out their personal salvation with courage and resourcefulness but they also realize that personal achievements, to be worth while, must be linked to the over-all well-being of the community. Both therefore clinch their adventures by performing some service of immense advantage : Simbi, by saving her town from the ravages of Dogo, the notorious slave-raider, and the Drinkard by settling the quarrel between the Sky God and the Earth Goddess and thereby putting an end to the famine which torments his town.

Judging from the folk-tale world, the individual's awareness of his membership of, and responsibility to, his society does not automatically make him a slave to its institutions. One may question the validity of what Durkheim calls the mechanical solidarity of tribal societies in the face of the many examples of freedom of action and free expression of individuality reflected in folk-tales. The individual is not a mere pawn within a rigid and ruthlessly authoritarian society — a blind unquestioning slave to his tribal institutions with neither individual will nor freedom of action and personal responsibility. Obviously, traditional society provides ethical and social guidance to its members through its mores, prohibitions and sanctions, but the individual has freedom of action and does exercise full responsibility for this. Both Simbi and the Drinkard's wife follow their own paths in spite of parental advice and they fully shoulder their responsibility. Of necessity, the hold which the community has over the individual cannot be so constrictive that the expression of his individuality is completely frustrated ; the individual cannot be so individualistic in his outlook that he regards his interests as entirely independent of those of the community within which he lives. Either case would have inevitably led to the complete impoverishment of both. In traditional society, a happy mean exists which imparts strength and unity. Its essential humanism, as exemplified in folk-tale narratives, arises from the awareness of an individual destiny within a larger, more inclusive communal destiny. The exploits of the folk-tale hero are expected to inspire the audience with courage, daring and mental alertness — qualities which are possible only within the context of a society which recognizes the existence of an individual will and freedom of action. Without this important element, traditional societies would have perished from a lack of stimulus and inspiration to overcome the hostile forces that surround them.

⁂

Tutuola makes use of the stereotyped character-types found in the folk-tale. Both Simbi and the Drinkard are quest protagonist and the quest-type character is one of the best known in West Africa. The pattern is very clear : first, there is the hero, then the well-defined objective of the quest and, finally, the taskmasters who are consciously or unconsciously operating to hinder the hero from attaining his objective. Among the most striking episodes of the two books are the rescue of the old man's daughter from the home of the skulls by the Drinkard, the trapping of Death, the birth of the Terrible Infant from the left thumb of the Drinkard's wife, the meeting with the Faithful Mother in the White Tree (all in *The Drinkard*) and Simbi's protracted and epic battle with the Satyr of the Dark Jungle (*Simbi*). The essence of the quest-tale is that everything is built on a heroic scale. The tasks imposed on the hero are formidable and dangerous and he succeeds in performing them by a characteristic combination of personal power (physical and magical), intelligence and bluff. In his mission to capture Death (a task imposed on the Drinkard by an old man in return for having shown him the way to his dead Tapster), the Drinkard displays these qualities. On his way to Death's house, he reaches a cross-roads. To find out which cow to follow, he lies down in the middle of the road with his head, legs and hands pointing in different directions. When, soon afterwards, some market-women arrive, their comments (as one may expect) solve the hero's dilemma.

« Who was the mother of this fine boy, he slept on the roads and put his head towards Death's road », they shouted. That is all the hero wants to know — his head is pointing « towards Death's road ». In Death's house, his struggle with Death is not only a matter of displaying physical or magical power, it is also a battle of wits and the Drinkard triumphs because he proves to be more nimble-witted and resourceful. In her struggle with the formidable Satyr of the Dark Jungle, Simbi displays great agility and astuteness. For instance, she confuses the Satyr by saying she would metamorphose into Iro... instead of Iromi.

The Satyr knows that Iromi means a waterfly but he has never heard of Iro (which at all events does not exist). When Simbi changes into a waterfly the Satyr is at his wit's end.

In this display of intellectual dexterity, the quest-hero shows an aspect of another kind of folk-tale hero — the trickster (or Picaro). The essential difference between the two is that the latter is something of a rogue, the former is not. Both move from one adventure to another (hence the term « picaresque » to denote the exploits of a travelling rogue-hero) but whereas the trickster's adventures are directed towards the aggrandizement of deep-seated perversities, the quest-hero is single-mindedly bent towards achieving a worthy objective. He is courageous, bold, resourceful, intelligent and pleasant whereas the trickster is clever, sly, intemperate and given to phallic obsession.

Tutuola's *Simbi* and *The Drinkard* have a picaresque quality without the rogue element. This is the sense in which the term was applied in the 18th century, especially to the prose epics of Fielding. Evidence of the picaresque nature of Tutuola's plot is that while structurally having a beginning, a middle and an end, it does not conform to the Aristotelian criterion of the well-constructed plot — that is, it does not represent a unity so closely-knit that the transposal or withdrawal of any of the incidents will disjoin or dislocate the whole. It derives its unity essentially from the protagonist whose participation in the incidents holds the plot loosely together. In this respect, the quest-tale plot is more structurally akin to the Spanish picaresque than to the 18th century English imitations with their more co-ordinated plots. In *Tom Jones*, for instance, the characters converge in London by a series of coincidences leading to the *dénouement*. Transposition of incidents (especially the middle ones) in Tutuola would not be of great structural consequence.

Tutuola makes use of the quest-type folk-tale because subsisting as it does on the marvellous and the sensational, and having a great deal of room for episodic development, it is the kind which allows his creative imagination the fullest play. One of the ways he exploits its possibilites is to build not only his protagonists but also his antagonists on a gigantic scale and imbue them with immense supernatural power (much in the same way that Milton builds up his Satan in *Paradise Lost*) to give a heroic quality to the ensuing struggle. Here, for example, is the description of the totemic Red Fish to whom the Drinkard is about to be sacrificed and whom he ultimately kills :

> « ... *its head was just like a tortoise's head, but it was as big as an elephant's head and it had over thirty horns and large eyes which surrounded the head. All these horns were spread out as an umbrella. It could not walk but*

*was only gliding on the ground like a snake and its body
was just like a bat's body and covered with long red hair
like strings. It could only fly to a short distance, and if
it shouted, a person who was four miles away would
hear. All the eyes which surrounded its head were closing
and opening at the same time as if a man was pressing a
switch on and off ».*

We see the hero faced with a being both physically gigantic
and appalling, endowed with an immense undefined power. Its
grotesque shape coupled with its gliding-flying propensity, its
electric-torch eyes and its loud voice reinforce the atmosphere
of terror. This use of the grotesque and larger-than-life aspect
is a universal characteristic of the epic narrative. The Red Fish
reminds one of Bunyan's Appolyion, the hideous giant with
scales like a fish, wings like a dragon and a mouth like a lion
out of which he belched fire and smoke. The loudness of its
voice can be likened to that of Stentor which, as Homer says,
could drown the waves.

The heroic stature of Tutuola's protagonists and, to some
extent, the advantures in which they are involved, has sometimes led to his being compared to Dante and Bunyan. One can,
in fact, see some resemblances to these authors though one has
to keep the comparison within reasonable limits without attempting to make normative judgments and realise that his writing
belongs to a different tradition. His heroes and the heroes of the
representative works of Dante and Bunyan are involved in some
kind of peregrination : the Drinkard goes from the world of the
living to Deads' Town in search of his dead Tapster ; Christian
goes to the Celestial City in search of salvation ; Dante makes
an imaginary journey that takes him to Hell, Purgatory and
Heaven in search of spiritual experience. These journeys span
the natural and the supernatural. Dante's poem and Bunyan's
prose fiction derive their motifs and inspiration from a Christian world-view and are clearly eschatological whereas Tutuola's
writing derives them from the traditional African *weltanschau-
ung*. The Christian works are allegorical whereas Tutuola's is immersed in the cultural consciousness of traditional Africa as
embodied in cosmology, moral values and attitudes. Finally, all
three writers, withing their different cultural milieux, have
successfully applied their creative imagination to producing
works of outstanding vigour, vividness and beauty.

∗∗

Apart from stock characters, Tutuola also uses well-known
motifs and themes which are derived from traditional values,
ideas of morality and norms of personal relationship. The motifs

include that of *L'Enfant Terrible*, derived from a belief that the abnormal child has a peculiar relationship with some supernatural agencies as a result of the circumstances surrounding his birth. *L'Enfant Terrible* is often a source of affliction to his parents in particular and the community in general. Within this category are twins, *revenants* and abnormally-born children : the Drinkard's son, born from his wife's left thumb, and Bako (the Siamese twin in *Simbi*) belong here. The first is as much a source of torment and affliction to his parents as is Bako to Simbi and the other « refugees ». Tutuola also makes use of the « popular godmother ». This motif deals with the character of those benign old people who help the young and needy with material sustenance. In folk-tales, they are often kindly, elderly women who emerge as if from nowhere to render succour to the hard-pressed hero. In *The Drinkard* the hero and his wife are much relieved by the Faithful Mother in the White Tree and Simbi is saved from starving to death by the decrepit iconophile.

He ingeniously employs the quarrel between the Sky God and the Earth Goddess in tying up the plot of *The Drinkard*. The myth of the Sky God, the *Deus otiosus*, is widely held in West Africa (5). He is supposed to be the Creator of the Universe but he has detached himself from this universe because man has polluted it with his sins. As a result of his distance from the world, he does not permeate the people's religious consciousness to the same degree as the ancestral spirits and minor gods. As a result, the Sky God has no shrines, no priests and hardly features at all in religious worship. People appeal to him only as a last resort when human justice has been denied to them and the other gods have turned their backs on them. The invocation of the Sky God is, in reality, a final gesture of despair and disillusionment. The explanation is that, by banishing himself to the sky, the Sky God puts himself beyond the immediate sphere of activities in purely agricultural communities where the Earth Goddess and the gods that control rain, fertility, diseases etc. are of more immediate significance. Christian missionaries, such as the Rev. John Taylor who guardedly admires the « this-worldliness » of traditional African religion (6), are intrigued by its materialistic orientation, essentially because the Sky God, who is held to be at the head of the Pantheon, is hardly made much of while the inferior gods and the ancestral spirits are much revered because they are directly involved in the people's struggles for material well-being.

Tutuola employs this belief to resolve the plot of his book. The Earth Goddess and the Sky God, once friends, are now

(5) See Ref. Fr James O' Connell's article « The Withdrawal of the High God in West African Religion : An Essay in Interpretation » in *Man*, May, 1962, pp. 67-69.
(6) Rev. John Taylor : *The Primal Vision*, p. 90.

involved in a quarrel over primacy and the latter has with-
drawn rain from the earth to demonstrate his superior power
(7). As a result, the earth is afflicted with drought and there is
a famine. The Drinkard returns from his quest to find his
country in a hopeless and piteous condition ; full of self-con-
fidence built up during his quest, he arbitrates the quarrel by
sending a tribute from earth to the sky, thereby establishing
the primacy of the sky over the earth and ending the famine.
It is typical of Tutuola's close adherence to traditional belief
that the carrying of the mediation sacrifice to the Sky God is
assigned to a slave because direct confrontation with the divine
is held to be highly dangerous. Everyone refuses to carry the
sacrifice except the slave who has no free choice. The accomplishment of the mission excludes him from communion with
other people : he has dealt directly with the divine and his
person has as a result become sacred and dangerous to the
security of ordinary folk. This view applies to the Osu, a slave
caste in Iboland which, in the remote past, formed a high priest-
hood that performed mediational rites to the gods. As a result,
their persons were regarded as sacred so that it was forbidden
to shed their blood, shave their heads or have any sort of
physical or social contact with them. The sacred nature of their
functions, which transferred to their bodies, had made them
social outcasts. Up to quite recently, the predicament of their
descendants was one of the most painful sociological problems
facing the Eastern Nigerian Government and legislation had to
be passed forbidding discrimination against them.

In both *Simbi* and *The Drinkard* we are made aware of a
society in which sacrifice is an important aspect of religion,
not just as a means of currying favour with the gods but as an
essential part of the pattern of life. Divination plays an active
part in the unravelling of the unknown. The Drinkard's wife,
who fulfils the dual function of philosophical companion and
prophet, expresses herself in gnomic pronouncements typical of
professional diviners. Simbi consults a diviner to know what
the future has in store for her. Kings have an important social
rôle as the benign protectors and counsellors of their people :
they are not blood-thirsty, arbitrary tyrants and when they have
to offer human sacrifice, they have often opted for foreigners
who do not partake of the mystic bond that unites the indigenous people. Human relations count for a great deal in traditional African societies and folk-tales emphasize their importance in sharply-pointed morals. Ingratitude, regarded by Dante
as one of the most reprehensible human sins, is severely pun-

---

(7) It is interesting to observe that in the Philippines, India and the
Malay Peninsula, the quarrel is not between the Sky and the Earth but
between the Sun and the Moon (*Folklore Studies*, 12-14, 1953-55).

ished. The whole population of Red Town in *The Drinkard*, and the ungrateful hunter in *Simbi*, pay for this sin with their lives while the ungrateful parasites of the Drinkard's town undergo severe flagellation. Obedience to parents and elders by children is a cardinal virtue ; disobedience is often visited by punishment and remorse. The whole story of *Simbi* is an extended moral treatise on the theme of parental obedience. The woman, who later becomes the Drinkard's wife, has to go through the horror of marrying a mere skull posing as a complete man after borrowing human parts from several clients. This combination of didacticism and entertainment satisfies one of the canons of neo-classical criticism : namely, that good literature should instruct as well as please.

A consideration of the didactic aspect leads to the moral dilemmas which are sometimes posed. Tutuola poses two of these at the end of *The Drinkard*. The first, dealing with a professional debtor and a professional debt-collector is not, in my opinion, nearly as good as the second — the love-trial. According to the latter, three women and their husband are going on a journey when the husband suddenly stumbles and dies. The first wife instantly dies in order to keep him company in the other world ; the second sets off to discover a wizard who can revive the dead, while the third stays by the bodies to keep away wild beasts that would otherwise maul them. Later, the second wife brings a wizard who revives the bodies. Asked what the fee for his labour is, he demands to be given one of the wives. None agrees to be given away and the dilemma, therefore, is which one should be given to him ? Here, the audience recognizes, or is expected to recognize, that the three wives have each in her own way demonstrated their affection for their husband, one by dying with him, another by bringing his reviver and the third by protecting his body from harm. They have shown that they love him in life and in death and are prepared to make any sacrifice to be with him. He alone gives meaning to their sacrifice. To go with the wizard would mean being cut off physically and spiritually. Such a sacrifice no longer has any meaning : it is as if Christ would have allowed himself to be crucified only that Man may be claimed by the Devil — a case of stupid self-immolation and a repudiation of reason. The audience is made both judge and jury in the case but everyone knows that there cannot be a just and equitable decision.

It may be asked why « dilemma stories » form a considerable part of the African folk-tale corpus. One may be permitted to dismiss with impatience Alta Jablow's view that they abound in West Africa because West Africans are interested in legal problems (8). The image of the African as the incorrigible lit-

_____

(8) Introductory note to *Anthology of West African Folk-Lore*.

igant who spends most of his time talking « palavers » is one of those annoying *clichés* which have no basis in fact. It is absolutely naïve to imagine that indigenous African societies, not having the literate facilities for drawing up deeds and agreements, must have been in a chronic state of disorder. Every society evolves ways and means of reducing potential conflicts among its members and in ours there are well-established sanctions, apart from the purely legalistic ones, for preventing anti-social tendencies and the possibility of people having their rights trampled underfoot. At all events, the idea of the dilemma being used to inculcate legal expertise is a ridiculous one. The problems are very often not legalistic in nature but are always part of human life. People are constantly faced with choices, the making of which may not only be difficult but often tragic. The Kantian differentiation between the absolute and the categorical imperatives as the basis of the tragic dilemma has no doubt a universal application, but many dilemmas of the African folk-tale have no immediate divine or ethical bases which could help to arbitrate in making a choice or at least point a way to a final resolution. They are not always as clear-cut as (for example) Antigone's choice between a religious duty to a dead brother and her duty to the State. Tutuola asks which of these wives, whose loyalty and affection to their husband have been proved, ought to be sacrificed to the wizard ? In my view, dilemmas of this nature are posed here to remind the audience that life contains many moral imponderables that cannot be resolved by the making of a facile or an apparently clever judgment. The question transcends mere intellectual juggling : it touches the very bottom of our emotional being. In short, many of these dilemmas cannot be resolved and are not meant to be. Whereas the literary artist attempts to explore the complicated implications of a particular moral dilemma with the purpose of revealing his own individual insight, the duty of the traditional story-teller is to enunciate it in the clearest way possible and to leave each individual to reach his own solution if he can. This is exactly what Tutuola has done.

*
* *

The folk-tale as a well-developed narrative can be examined not only on the basis of its structure and content but also on the basis of style. Its stylistic form derives essentially from the fact that it is spoken rather than written and is therefore more akin to drama. The competent raconteur uses the possibilities offered by the oral nature of his narrative to immense advantage. By the modulation of his voice, facial expressions and gestures he can express varied emotional nuances that are difficult to recapture in written form. The use of songs and ditties does not only heighten and vivify the narrative ; it establishes a rapport between the story-teller and his audience. It will be expected that the loss of these dramatic devices and songs, as a result of committing what is essentially an oral form to writing, will weaken Tutuola's stories. Anyone who is brought up within the oral tradition cannot fail to notice some gaps in the plot of a written version. In *Simbi*, for instance, the absence of song is often felt because Tutuola tells us from the beginning that Simbi is an expert singer who has delighted the people of her village. However, he goes some way towards capturing the effect of song by the simple colloquial rhythm of the speeches. This effect comes out in the scene when Simbi narrowly escapes being sacrificed to the wicked gods of the people of the Sinners' Town. Several of Simbi's companions have already been sacrificed and now that it is her turn, she bursts into a long sorrowful song, part of which is an appeal to the people to save her life and the lives of her surviving colleagues. She sings and the King responds in song also :

> « *Please, the King, set the rest of us free* ».
> « *Ha ! — a ! — a ! don't you know you have become the slave of these gods this midnight !* »
> « *Please, the chiefs deliver us from these gods !* »
> « *Ha ! — a ! — a ! you chiefs, don't you hear her plead now...* »

> « *Then the King, the chiefs, the prominent people and with the whole of the common people who were at the outside of the shrine replied to Simbi's request with song, loudly : 'Don't you hear, she asks the chiefs to deliver her. But she is not aware that she has become the slave of the gods this midnight who are going to drink her (Simbi's) blood in just one or two minutes time'.*

> « *Having heard like that... she changed that song to a kind of melodious song* ».

She soon has the whole congregation swaying and dancing. One may say that the reporting of the singing here, like the reporting of an action in the theatre, is no adequate substitute for the real thing and that in a story-telling session the alternate singing by the victim and the congregation would have produced an operatic effect which cannot be adequately recaptured in writing. Nevertheless, it must also be said that the colloquial rhythm of the speeches, especially the interjected remarks and repetitions, does give the feel not so much of traditional folk-tale singing which can be extremely lively, but of the kind of irregular incantatory singing which one sometimes hears at a place of ritual sacrifice, a general stirring within the taut sacrificial atmosphere like the rustling of dry leaves under a dark overcast sky.

Tutuola achieves his best story-telling effect by a simple, direct and almost bald narrative method. He goes straight to the story without any preambles or circumlocutions. In four brief opening paragraphs, he sets the stage for the long adventure in *The Drinkard*.

« *I was a palm-wine drinkard since I was a boy of ten years of age. I had no other work than to drink palm-wine in my life. In those days we did not know other money, except COWRIES, so that everything was very cheap, and my father was the richest man in our town.*

« *My father got eight children and I was the eldest among them, all of the rest were hard-workers, but myself was an expert palm-wine drinkard. I was drinking palm-wine from night till morning. By that time I could not drink ordinary water at all except palm-wine.*

« *But when my father noticed that I could not do any work more than to drink, he engaged an expert palm-wine tapster for me ; he had no other work than to tap palm-wine every day.*

« *So my father gave me a palm-tree farm which was nine miles square and it contained 560,000 palm-trees, and this palm-wine tapster was tapping one hundred and fifty kegs of palm-wine every morning, but before 2 o'clock p.m., I would have drunk all of it ; after that he would go and tap another 75 kegs in the evening which I would drink till morning. So my friends were uncountable by that time and they were drinking palm-wine with me from morning till a late hour in the night. But when my palm-wine tapster completed the period of 15 years that he was tapping the palm-wine for me, then my father died suddenly, and when it was the 6th month after my father had died, the tapster went to the palm-tree farm on a Sunday evening to tap palm-wine for me. When he reached the farm, he climbed one of the tallest palm-trees in the farm to tap palm-wine but as he was tapping on, he fell down unexpectedly and died at the foot of the palm-tree as a result of injuries* ».

In these few paragraphs we are given in a graphic way the time-setting of the story. This, as has been stated earlier, is one of the few stylistic requirements of folk-tale narrative, the temporal remove which helps to give plausibility to incidents which would otherwise seem incredible in a contemporary setting. Then we are given a brief insight into the character of the Drinkard. He is obviously utterly spoilt by his father. We are shown by facts and figures his obsessive addiction to palm-wine and then, of course, we are told of the death of the Tapster which necessitates the quest.

••

Tutuola's humour and a sensitive nose for the kind of detail which gives beauty, power and immediacy to writing is illustrated in almost every page of his books. Simbi's conversation with Dogo the slave-raider along the Path of Death and with the Satyr of the Dark Jungle at the first encounter, are handled with delicate humour which is greatly reinforced by the deadly menace lurking behind the apparent innocuity of the situations. Tutuola's imaginative inventiveness is at its best in the description of the masque cunningly staged by the Satyr of the Dark Jungle as a trap for capturing Simbi. The magic hall within which the masque is staged, the phantom orchestra and the ultra-beautiful ladies are all described with engaging ease and ample imaginative detail. The last arrivals at this colourful pageant are the six fearful ostriches who wear white shoes on their hooves and cover their faces with masks. The image conjured up by the entire masque is of a great variety of colour and ornament and a sort of fairy-tale ballet whose serial effect is increased by the knowledge that hidden in an obscure corner, ready to pounce at any moment and dissolve the whole scene, is the implacable Satyr. The ability to produce a fascinated response behind which there is a background of dread and horror is one of the most outstanding qualities of Tutuola's genius as a story-teller.

Finally, an aspect of his writing which has intrigued many readers is the incorporation of several elements from modern culture. In the dark jungle, time is measured in hours and minutes as if the protagonists are carrying their pocket watches, distance is gauged in miles and business is conducted in £.s.d. The skulls chasing after the Drinkard are likened to a thousand petrol-drums pushing themselves along a hard road. Bombers, buoys, technicolour, telephones, electric switches, and the other paraphernalia of modern civilization, all find their way into these stories. A bewildered German reader asked me why this is so and even compared Tutuola's stories with those of the Brothers Grimm to show that « pure » examples cannot incorporate « foreign » culture elements.

An explanation of this phenomenon must be sought in the nature of the traditional African folk-tale. As has already been stated, the latter is a very free narrative form and the narrator has ample scope to incorporate whatever elements within the experience of the community he thinks will make his story effective, especially since these elements do not alter plot, setting or moral purpose. Even though Tutuola's stories (like all traditional folk-tales) refer to a remote age, the fact that he was writing in the second half of the twentieth century meant that he would have to incorporate some modern elements which have become a part of the every-day reality of Nigerian life. Even an illiterate person in the streets of Lagos has seen a clock, a petrol-drum and a torch, and may have heard of bombers, telephones and technicolour. Tutuola's life in the capital must have made him aware of the buoys in the harbour and his Christian education must have familiarized him with angels, etc.

These things cannot correctly be regarded as « foreign » and are as essentially a part of the composite culture of modern Africa as are the purely traditional elements. In the words of Professor Busia : « Survivals of extremely old cultures can be found alongside recently borrowed intentions and ideas. The old and the new are both a part of Africa as it is today. The talking drum belongs as much to contemporary African cultures as does the telegraph or the jazz band ; the baby at its mother's back as much as the baby in the pram ; the lineage or clan as much as the trade-union or the political party ; the chief as much as the president. All have been accepted and incorporated into the ever-changing and growing cultures that constitute Africa's way of life » (9). Because the folk-tale narrator builds his story essentially from contemporary material even while asserting that his story refers to a remote past, it must be conceded that Tutuola is perfectly justified in incorporating such elements of modern industrial civilization that have become part of neo-African culture. The analogy with the stories of the Brothers Grimm does not therefore apply. In that Tutuola's education has not gone beyond the elementary school, it is something of an advantage because he is much nearer to traditional society than if he were better educated ; culture contact operates mostly through education and the more highly educated are likely to be the more acculturated.

Reading his stories, anyone who has grown up within the oral tradition cannot but be impressed by the nearness of his

(9) K.A. BUSIA : *The Challenge of Africa*, p. 39.

effort towards capturing the real folk-tale effect. One can almost hear the speaking voice and discern the emotional nuances as one is carried along from one adventure to another. He thinks his stories in the vernacular and writes them in English much as he would have told them in the vernacular to a group of listeners. We can therefore appreciate them if we see them within this context. But this is not all. We should note, also, that though he has drawn his material largely from oral tradition, he has also succeeded in using the immense possibilities offered by writing to build his stories on a scale which would have been impossible for an illiterate narrator to do.

Non-West African readers who do not understand the chief influences in his writing tend to invest him with qualities of excellence which he has largely obtained from the living tradition of village story-telling. His West African readers, on the other hand, recognising his close identification with this tradition, have all too frequently refused to acknowledge his real imaginative merits (by utilising the facilities offered by the alphabetic script) to produce works whose scope, beauty and variety would have been impossible within the narrow formal potentiality of the former.

The typical traditional narrative form is built around a single theme and is self-sufficient in all its relevant details of structure, style and didactic purpose. For instance, the theme of the obdurate daughter who marries a demon-lover, is by itself enough to make a full story. The story of Ogilisi Akwalaka in C.O.D. Ekwensi's *Ikolo the Wrestler and Other Ibo Tales* (pages 65-68) which is a true folk-tale form, and the story of the girl who marries a skull in *The Drinkard* which is just an episode in a long chain of adventures, simply illustrate this. Whereas Ekwensi's story is sufficient unto itself, Tutuola's is just an episode which is strung on to many others to make a bigger, more complex story.

The uniqueness of Tutuola's work rests on his ability to assimilate elements peculiar to the oral tradition to elements peculiar to the literary tradition : in other words, to impose a literary organization over essentially oral narrative material. He thus represents an example of a transitional stage in the formal artistic evolution from a purely oral narrative tradition to a purely literary narrative tradition.

The Palm-Wine Drinkard:
A Reassessment of Amos Tutuola

OMOLARA OGUNDIPE-LESLIE

The controversy around Tutuola flickers on. The Nigerian critics are unmoved from their initial positions of contempt and indignation at the esteem accorded Tutuola in European circles, while Anglo-American critics stubbornly maintain that he is undoubtedly a writer of 'unique and prolific genius'.

The reservations of the Nigerians about Tutuola are summarized fairly completely by John V. Murra.[1] The Nigerians deplore Tutuola's crudities,

... his lack of inhibitions, and the folk-tale basis of his stories. They accuse him of plagiarizing from the traditional folk-tales, of encouraging a useless, impractical mythical way of thinking, of leading West African literature up a blind alley, and of providing the supercilious Westerner with an excuse for continuing to patronize the allegedly superstitious Nigerian.

On the non-Nigerian side of the field, two identifiable divisions are grouped. One views Tutuola's writing with wonder and amazement, as something fascinating and foreign, yet not so foreign because it resembles surrealistic products of the twentieth century. The other group, admitting the foreignness of Tutuola's writing, are willing to step into Tutuola's world in order to understand the character of the work. These critics try to judge his achievement by some universal (really European) literary standards. Both Dylan Thomas and the

[1] John V. Murra, 'The Unconscious of a Race', *Nation*, CLXXIX (1954), pp. 261–2.

Reprinted from *The Journal of Commonwealth Literature*, No. 9 (1970), 48-56. The same article appeared in *Présence Africaine*, 71 (1969), 99-108, and in *Ibadan*, 28 (1970), 22-26.

reviewer of *The Palm-Wine Drinkard* in the *Listener* belong with the first group. *The Palm-Wine Drinkard* is described in the *Listener* as 'a strange poetic nightmare . . . a very curious work, with an auroral quality of half-light . . .' Dylan Thomas who might have been describing his own work calls *The Palm-Wine Drinkard* . . . 'the brief, thronged grisly and bewitching story . . .' He says 'nothing is too prodigious or too trivial to put down in this tall, devilish story'.

Gerald Moore[2] and Harold V. Collins[3] belong with the second group of non-Nigerian critics. Collins evaluates the actual literary merits of Tutuola's 'ghost novels', as he named them, and comes to the conclusion that 'for the verve, the assurance, the creativity, the human values sustained, and the gay humour of the work, Amos Tutuola of Abeokuta deserves to be called the founder of Nigerian literature'. Gerald Moore argues two main points: that Tutuola is a writer of undoubted and unique genius, albeit of declining power, and that his novels are not to be judged as novels 'for the novel as we know it deals with man in society while Tutuola is concerned with man alone, suffering and growing amid the images thrown forth by his own mind and by the imagination of his race'. Emphasizing the visionary quality of Tutuola's writing, Moore affirms that Tutuola is something rarer and more interesting than another novelist, and in an earlier version of the same essay, went on to characterize Tutuola's writings as 'prose-epics'.

It is difficult to see how *The Palm-Wine Drinkard* is an epic, except in the very slackest sense. The novel does not embody the Yoruba nation's conception of its own history as the Greek and the Roman are embodied in the *Iliad* or the *Aeneid*; nor is it intended to express the collective consciousness of a group by allegorizing through one or more persons what the particular group accepts as its collective will and destiny, in the way *The Pilgrim's Progress* expresses the Protestant consciousness, and *The Divine Comedy* the medieval Roman Catholic.

What is the achievement of Tutuola? Does he deserve the odium in which his work is frequently held in middle-class English-educated Nigerian circles? Is Tutuola true genius but untutored bard? To find

[2] Gerald Moore, *Seven African Writers*, O.U.P., 1962, revised version of essay on Tutuola that appeared in *Black Orpheus*, republished in *Introduction to African Literature*, ed. Ulli Beier, Longmans, 1967.
[3] Harold R. Collins, 'Founding a New National Literature: the Ghost Novels of Amos Tutuola,' *Critique*, IV (Fall–Winter, 1960–61), pp. 17–28.

answers to these questions, it will be sufficient to look in detail at *The Palm-Wine Drinkard* because it is his first work (which probably emerged less influenced than the others by outside reaction) and because, in my view, it contains the basic ingredients of his art.

In *The Palm-Wine Drinkard*, Tutuola has used the simple literary form of the Quest. It does not surprise one that he uses this form since it is a frequent one in folk-tale.[4] It is the simplest of all artistic patterns.[5] The Quest is a well-worn motif in the genre of the folk-tale. Tutuola has come to the pattern naturally and not through an intellectual choice conceived as 'structure'. Tutuola is certainly not aware of such monsters as 'monomyths' and 'archetypes' or of such texts as Campbell's *Hero with a Thousand Faces*. The argument here is not that Tutuola's use of the Quest motif is completely intuitive or self-derived; it is that certain literary forms are the property of a culture, and that the kinds of literary forms present in a culture depend on what the experience of the culture has been. It is not then surprising that Tutuola exploits one of the commonest forms in the folk repertoire.

So, admitting that it was not by any stroke of genius that Tutuola hit on the motif of the 'cycle of the heroic monomyth . . . made up of Departure, Initiation and Return', one may go on to admit, however, how well he has used this simple and prevalent form. He has given the motif in *The Palm-Wine Drinkard* an asymmetric form, thereby increasing the dramatic impact of his tale. Roughly twenty-one episodes made up the Departure, that is, the journey to Deads' Town; five bring him back to the river which all too frequently in folk imagination demarcates the land of the dead from the land of the living; and about four episodes comprise the events taking place after his return from his Quest. Twenty-one episodes lead us suspensefully to Deads' Town, thrilling us with fear and dread, forcing emotional participation; nine bring us back hurriedly, as they should, to the original scene. We would not have had the patience to go through too many episodes

---

[4] For a wider discussion of the folk-tale material in Tutuola, see E. N. Obiechina, 'Amos Tutuola and the Oral Tradition', *Présence Africaine*, 65 (1968), pp. 85–106.

[5] Without necessarily agreeing with the view, it can be observed that it has ever been argued that the quest myth lies deep in the subconscious of man and harks back to early man's first reactions to natural phenomena. See for instance the famous Northrop Frye categories in 'The Archetypes of Literature', *Kenyon Review* (Winter, 1951).

on the return journey. The overall structure of *The Palm-Wine Drinkard* is therefore pleasing.

The novel is picaresque hence episodic, comprising events of 'derring-do' and suffering. Tutuola's handling of his material is probably more commendable than the material itself. He has often been praised for his inventiveness and his creative energy, though many of the incidents in *The Palm-Wine Drinkard* are derived. Of the twenty-nine episodes in the book, sixteen are unoriginal, taken from folklore, or from Fagunwa, or from popular wit and imagination (for instance, the cases the Drinkard has to judge in 'the mixt town'). Admittedly, Tutuola, like any artist, has the right to plunder all sources of his choice (Fagunwa himself went unashamedly of folk imagination to *A Thousand and One Nights* and to Shakespeare) but one cannot then go on to exclaim over the inventiveness of such a borrower. Tutuola did not invent very much of the material in *The Palm-Wine Drinkard*.

What commands acclaim is Tutuola's use of his material, chosen from all and sundry, and minted to make something beautiful, new and undeniably his own. He has handled his material with all of the skill of the good story-teller and he has been able to endow it with the qualities of a 'well-told tale'. His denigrators who think it devastating to name him a mere folktale-teller must realize that not all folktale-tellers are necessarily good. In *The Palm-Wine Drinkard*, Tutuola has infused the life of his hybrid with the energies of a well-wrought tale. There is the urgency in the telling, the rapidity, indispensable to the Quest-motif, with which life unrolls itself; the fertility of incidents; the successful maintenance of our interest through the varying scenes. And the good-story teller is ever present in *The Palm-Wine Drinkard*, speaking to us in warm human tones, genial, good-natured and unpretentious. Yet the Drinkard is not a simple person, for at one time he is humble because he is a mere mortal, inferior and lost in a dreadful world of spirits, at another time, he is arrogant and vaunting because he is Man whose spirits will not be put down. He is lovable for his sense of humour, intelligent for his ability to see himself and humanity, and worthy of respect for his ability to satirize himself and man. The Drinkard has no illusions about human nature. He is aware of men's selfishness (men fleeing danger and abandoning the young and the old), of their gratuitous and conscious cruelty, of their preoccupation with themselves over and above everything else. Even he and his wife betray each other once in a moment of danger. But his view of the world is not at all cynical or myopic. Men can and do love each other; they can be generous. Tutuola's 'persona' in *The Palm-Wine Drinkard* is an endearing character who has no unhealthy need to strike attitudes like his middle-class counterparts. He is able, in Afro-American idiom, to 'tell it as it is'.

This then is Tutuola's achievement, that in spite of his handicaps, he is able 'to tell it as it is'. He writes genuinely about a real world, about a world which has validity for some men. The consciousness of the Drinkard is probably an African Consciousness and certainly a Yoruba one. Death is not a thing of horror and the worlds of the living and the dead are co-extensive, yet different, as Tutuola poignantly shows in the scenes of the Drinkard with his dead Tapster. There is awareness and acceptance of the difference but no revulsion, no shuddering fear of the dead as you would find in a Western consciousness. To the Yoruba dead babies are the most cruel of all the dead; because of the high infant death-rate the Yorubas, like other people in Africa, suffer emotionally from what they see as the cruelty of children who die. The human communities through which the Drinkard passes behave in a recognizably real way. They are neither idyllic nor hell-like. Sometimes generous and hospitable, the people can also be cruel. The collectivity tyrannizes over the individual. The child-prodigy considered 'evil' by the community is killed off without any sense of guilt by the father. The individual is sacrificed to ensure the well-being of the collectivity. These patterns of behaviour are allowed to come through without justification or defensiveness. The world of *The Palm-Wine Drinkard* is also truly African. It is a world populated by spirits and controllable by magic.[6] The adventures of the Drinkard are not allegorical nor do they represent a delving into the sub-conscious. The details of the journey could be imaginary for some readers and literally true for many others. For the Western critic, such

---

[6] It is amusing how the Drinkard's character recalls Frazer's description of the personality of the magician: '. . . the haughty self-sufficiency of the magician, his arrogant demeanour towards the high powers and his unabashed claim to exercise a way like theirs . . .' (*The Golden Bough*, Macmillan abridged edition, p. 68. In a less satirical vein, Obiechina rightly points out the 'essential humanism of the world of the folk-tale where *homo sapiens* is the pivot around which the drama revolves. The humanism of the world of the folk-tale, the belief by man in his own infinite possibilities comes from the magical conception of the world – a conception which posits an order and uniformity in nature, influencable by the proper practice of the arts of magic.'

a work may *have* to be symbolic to be understandable but for some Africans, including the sophisticated and Westernized, these 'images' could have independent and real life.

Though unable to use the Queen's English, Tutuola is able to tell of life as it is felt by some portion of humanity. A great deal has been said about the language in which Tutuola chooses to express himself. For some readers, the appeal of his language lies in its quaintness. Such an attitude is essentially patronizing. Others are irritated by the patronizing attitude implicit in the enthusiasm over what they consider such 'imperfect' English. Middle-class Nigerians are ashamed of his language since oddly enough, among both the British and the Nigerians, inability to use the English language indicates some mental deficiency. However, it is more interesting to consider the comments of critics who have striven to analyse and discover the components of Tutuola's style, Parrinder says it is 'English as it is spoken in West Africa'.[7] Paul Bohannan thinks it is 'a combination of schoolboy English, officialese and West African pidgin'.[8] For John V. Murra, Tutuola's language is a 'terse, graphic and personal kind of young English', Harold V. Collins thinks that:

For all the crudity of language, we are as much struck by the clarity, directness, vigor and felicity of this Anglo-Nigerian language of Tutuola's as we are by its unconventionality.

None of these views is totally true. Tutuola's English is not English as it is spoken in West Africa, though English could conceivably be spoken in his way by some groups in specific social classes. The English language spoken in West Africa is complex, varying according to social position and the formal educational experience of the speaker. Schoolboy English (something which affronts Nigerian teachers of English who have read Tutuola) exists in Tutuola's language and so does officialese. But there is hardly any incidence of pidgin in Tutuola. To speak of a West African pidgin is to be typically reckless – as pidgin varies from one West African country to another and from one part of one country to another. John V. Murra touches on an important point when he speaks of the 'terse, graphic and personal' nature of Tutuola's language. Without a doubt, Tutuola's language is personal. It is something of his own making, forged from scraps of language such as officialese, journalese, ungrammatical English formations super-

[7] H. R. Collins, *op. cit.*   [8] P. Bohannan, *Listener,* May 13, 1954.

imposed on his own rendition in English words of the Yoruba language.

The authentic tone to be found in *The Palm-Wine Drinkard* derives not only from the 'intensely oral quality of his writing'[9] (though this is an important and related element) but also from the use to which Tutuola has put the genius of the Yoruba language. He has simply and boldly (or perhaps innocently) carried across into his English prose the linguistic patterns and literary habits of his Yoruba language using English words as counters. He is basically speaking Yoruba but using English words. The characteristic literary qualities and linguistic habits in Yoruba abound: the incantatory quality (sometimes responsible for Tutuola's breathless paragraph and sentence formations and punctuation):

When I felt that these strings did not allow me to breathe and again every part of my body was bleeding too much, then I myself commanded the ropes of the yams in his garden to tight him there, and the yams in his garden to tight him there [sic], and the yam stakes should begin to beat him also. After I had said so and at the same time, all the ropes of the yams in his garden tighted him hardly, and all the yam stakes were beating him repeatedly, so when he (Death) saw that these stakes were beating him repeatedly, then he commanded the strings of the drum which tighted me to release me, and I was released at the same time. But when I saw that I was released, then I myself commanded the ropes of the yams to release him and the yam stakes . . .[10]

Tutuola's language gets its peculiar ring from the use of Yoruba rhetoric and word-play; from the love of the word, the proverb and the gnomic saying characteristic of Yoruba. Of rhetoric and word-play, two examples will be given:

My wife had said of the woman we met: 'She was not a human-being and she was not a spirit, but what was she?' She was the Red-smaller-tree who was at the front of the bigger Red-tree, and the bigger Red-tree was the Red-king of the Red-people of Red-town and the Red-bush and also the Red-leaves on the bigger Red-tree were the Red-people of the Red-town in the Red-bush.[11]

Here the passage begins with a paradox, a form which pleases the Yoruba very much (note Tutuola's use of paradoxes as section head-

[9] G. Moore, *Seven African Writers.*
[10] *The Palm-Wine Drinkard*, Faber, 1952, p. 13.
[11] ibid., p. 83.

151

ings) and the explication of the seemingly absurd is given while playing upon the word 'Red'. Such rhetorical tricks, which succeed enormously in Fagunwa's Yoruba novels, do not come off in Tutuola owing to the differences between Yoruba and English. Tutuola's lack of adroitness in the handling of English is also partly responsible. Failure at points such as these is probably responsible for the unintended effects of quaintness and naivete he frequently achieves.

In another passage, we have a sheer love of words, a revelling in the richness of their meaning:

. . . and knew 'Laugh' personally on that night, because as every one of them stopped laughing at us, 'Laugh' did not stop for two hours. As 'Laugh' was laughing at us on that night, my wife and myself forgot our pains and laughed with him, because he was laughing with curious voices that we never heard before in our life. We did not know the time that we fell into his laugh, but we were only laughing at 'Laugh's' laugh and nobody heard him when laughing would not laugh, so if somebody continue to laugh with 'Laugh' himself, he or she would die or faint at once for long laughing, because laugh was his profession and he was feeding on it.[12]

Yoruba syntactical structures also appear frequently in Tutuola's English; for instance, in the posing of questions:

He (Death) asked me from where did I come? . . . Then he asked me what did I come to do?[13]

and in the use of the adverbial:

Whenever I reached a town or village, I would spend almost four months *there*, to find out my palm-wine tapster from the inhabitants of that town or village and if he did not reach *there*, then I would leave *there* and continue my journey to another town or village.[14]

'There' is being used to express three senses in the adverbial. In English, one would not use 'there' in each case; in Yoruba, the same word 'ibe' would be used.

Tutuola's use of the conjunctive is a very important aspect of his language, as is his use of time adverbials. So foreign to English is his use of time adverbials that to try to apprehend it without the background of an African language is to render oneself dazed. (Is this why

[12] ibid., p. 45.
[13] ibid., p. 13.
[14] ibid., pp. 9–10; my italics.

European critics feel it is set in a 'timeless' situation and judge it in the light, or in the chiaroscuro of modern abstract art?) Tutuola also uses conjunctives ('and', 'if', 'but', 'although', 'since', 'then') in a way they are not used in English. These two usages, I feel, give his prose style its distinctive and peculiar quality because they affect not only the way his prose sounds, but also the way he discharges his fictive material. Here are some random examples:

1. When he wanted me to go, I asked for his name, *then* he told me that his name was 'GIVE AND TAKE'.[15]

2. I told him that my name was called 'Father of gods who could do anything in this world'. *As* he heard this from me, he was soon faint with fear.[16]

3. By and by the market closed for that day *then* the whole people in the market were returning to their destinations etc., and the complete gentleman was returning to his own too, *but as* this lady was following him about in the market all the while, she saw him when he was returning to his destination as others did, *then* she was following him (complete gentleman) to an unknown place. *But* as she was following the complete gentleman along the road, he was telling her to go back or not to follow him, *but* the lady did not listen to what he was telling her, and when the complete gentleman had tired of telling her not to follow him or to go back to her town, he left her to follow him.[17]

In using the habits of a language familiar to him, Tutuola overcomes the problem of linguistic alienation which plagues other Nigerian writers, some of whom have at first to wrestle with the English language, before they can begin to try to say what they mean. Tutuola could never have been articulate in the Queen's English, but he becomes fluent, even eloquent, in a language of his own making. Unwittingly (for Tutuola is not like James Joyce, a conscious inventor) he has created a language which enables him to express himself. He has successfully explored areas of human experience, using an appropriate dramatic metaphor and language which permit him to tell of life as it is. One is not simply praising him for verisimilitude. He is being praised for doing what all good artists aim at doing – recording human experience in form and matter which do not ultimately falsify life.

[15] ibid., p. 86; my italics.
[16] ibid., p. 17; my italics.
[17] ibid., p. 19; my italics.

Tutuola's Literary Powers

IT is now time to tally up and consider some of Tutuola's powers and graces, which will make or have already made him a classic in Afro-English literature. In doing so, we might well remind ourselves that several centuries of the dominance of the realistic tradition in the English novel have tended to deprive readers of the pleasure available in fantastic fiction like Tutuola's. In Tutuola's fiction the imaginatively conceived monsters, the fanciful transformations, and other marvels of oral literature are somehow intellectually refreshing, like brainstorming sessions, utopian thinking, and the wild absurdities of *risqué* jokes. It would seem that our minds are in danger of getting petty and stuffy if we feed too regularly on commonplace reality (perhaps the "fairy tales" of science also keep minds less stodgy).

I *The Marvelous*

Tutuola's work is of course jampacked with monsters and marvels to give us this sort of mental fillip. What reader, no matter how badly given over to the "mimetic fallacy," could fail to be stimulated by such matters as the self-beating drum that sounds like the efforts of fifty drummers, the free-loaders' hostelry-cum-mission-hospital in the huge white tree, the exhibition of smells, the woman-hill with noisy hydra heads and fire-flashing eyes, the stumpy, weepy-eyed, ulcerous Television-handed Lady, and the concert hall of birds with a guard company of white-shoed ostriches?[1]

And the transformations! There is somehow a pleasure in the very idea of a metamorphosis, as the continuing popularity of the Greek myths and of Ovid's classic on transformations attest. Like many of the transformations in the traditional tales (and some of those in the

---

Reprinted from Harold Collins, *Amos Tutuola* (New York, 1969), pp. 117-128, 135-136.

Grimms' collection), Tutuola's changes are good fun; for instance, Drinkard's changing himself into a canoe by which his plucky little wife earns ferrying charges, his changing himself into a pebble and throwing himself ahead of the pursuing mountain creatures (an improvement over a traditional motif), Simbi's changing herself into a water insect so she can crawl up the Satyr's nostril and sting him to death, and Feather Woman's changing her victims into mud statues which (or who) can still feel and suffer.[2]

The appeal of these monsters and marvels is not escapist—that is, psychologically harmful. Tutuola's dream world is every bit as difficult for human intelligence and courage as our real world. The difficulties are often different in kind from those in the real world and so are many of the means of opposing the difficulties, but the human qualities are much the same. And, in a sense, modern science and technology—and their own ingenuity—will one day provide the Nigerians with marvels almost as incredible as those in Tutuola's novels.

II Self-Assurance

Even those critics and readers who do not care for Tutuola's work are likely to admit that he has one characteristic strength—his self-assurance, his literary aplomb, or composure. In spite of the junior clerk English with its distracting nonstandard syntax and vocabulary, in spite of the oddities of typography, in spite of the wildly mythical mode of fiction, Tutuola's authorial voice is magnificently composed, compellingly assured, like some oracle in the heyday of oracles, or like the passionate speech of a man speaking from lifetime convictions. We can note this quality, together with the accompanying oddities, in some of the opening passages of his romances:

I was a palm-wine drinkard since I was a boy of ten years of age. I had no other work more than to drink palm-wine in my life.

Simbi was the daughter of a wealthy woman, and she was an only issue of her mother.

She was not working at all, except to eat and after that to bathe and then to wear several kinds of the costliest garments.

I, Adebesi, the African huntress, will first relate the adventure of my late father, one of the ancient brave hunters, in brief:

My father was a brave hunter in his town. He had hunted in several dangerous jungles which the rest hunters had rejected to enter and even to approach because of fear of being killed by the wild animals and harmful creatures of the jungle.[3]

It is intriguing to try to account for this Tutuolan self-assurance.

Apparently Tutuola is one of those writers who "believe" their own stories. The *West Africa* correspondent who interviewed Tutuola reports that he "more than half-believes the tales he writes and he can, without mental trauma, reconcile this quasi-belief with his strong Christian views." [4] Perhaps the uncomplicated syntax without elaborate qualifications helps produce the effect—that, and the uncomplicated emotions felt by the main characters. But however we explain it, there it is, a monumental self-assurance, a steadfast, steady-as-she-goes self-assurance.

III   *Memorability of Incidents*

Another of Tutuola's distinctive literary qualities, the memorability of his incidents, may be partly due to this verve and assurance, this sort of impetuous aplomb, and to his downright, no-nonsense style. Many of his incidents lodge fast in our consciousness; they stick like burrs in the memory. This writer drives by a limestone supply company and thinks of the nasty citizens of the "7th Town of Ghosts" who drink a urine and limestone mixture because water is "too clean for them." Driving across a long narrow bridge he thinks of the stick bridge over Lost or Gain Valley which is so fragile that travelers have to leave their clothes on the near side and take in exchange those they find left on the far side. In the midst of an acrimonious argument with a bigot, his mind is refreshed with the memory of the town of the "multi-coloured people" who hate the "mono-colour" of Simbi and her friends. A glance at the hideous expanse of paunchy male torsos at a beach calls up the grotesque scene in which the huge stern pigmy pushes the Brave Huntress along the road toward the pigmies' town—with his outsized navel. A row of statues in a museum brings back Feather Woman lashing her enchanted mud images until her fistful of switches are all broken.[5]

Although Tutuola is devoted to the mythical mode of thought, his works are full of graphic touches, clear and lively descriptions showing striking imaginative power, that should make the most inveterate partisans of realism lend momentary belief to his magical world. Telling detail of this sort is so commonplace that we have an embarrassment of riches from which to illustrate.

We can only offer a random sampling, reminding the reader that the illustrations will suffer considerable loss from being taken out of context. The king of the "field creatures," who menaces Drinkard and his wife, has a "hot steam . . . rushing out of his nose and mouth as a big boiler" and he is breathing "at five minute intervals." When some person or creature in Faithful-Mother's huge white tree motions with his hands that Drinkard and his wife should approach, each of them wishes the other to go first: ". . . I myself pointed her to the hands too; after that, my wife forced me to go first and I pushed her to go first." [6]

During the first marriage of the wanderer in the Bush of Ghosts Evil-of-evils shakes hands with him and gives him a shock like that from a "live electric wire"; his friend has signaled him "with his eyes not to shake hands with him to avoid the shock," but the wanderer-bridegroom has not understood. When the same hero notices a very short ghost at the foot of the tree in which he has been sleeping he sees that she is "very corpulent as a pregnant woman who would deliver either today or tomorrow." When Simbi and her adversary, the satyr, are locked in deadly struggle, they hold each other very tightly, and their eyes are open so wide with the strain that they are almost ready ("nearly") "to tear like cloth." When the hollow tree inside of which she has fallen catches fire from lightning, the birds which have been nesting in the tree are frantic: "the eagles, parrots, hawks, etc." are driven away by the smoke and the flame; they "scatter" in the sky, then fly "round the top of the tree . . . trying to take their young ones away from the smoke. . . ." [7]

In her fight with the pigmy guard with the "half fall goitre," the Brave African Huntress and her enemy have "within a few minutes . . . scattered away the dried leaves and refuses of that spot with [their] feet." When the Chief Keeper of the "custody" brands the Huntress on the forehead with three X's, the "rest of the two pigmies" have to bend her head down first, because they are all so short. The Feather Woman's teeth have fallen out, so that her mouth is "moving up and down always as if she was eating something in the mouth." The jaws of the starved villagers described in the fifth "entertainment" of *Feather Woman of the Jungle* have already "dried up like roasted meat." The excited reaction to the earthquake produced by the warriors of the Goddess of Diamonds in the seventh "entertainment" is reminiscent of the flurry caused by the fox in Chaucer's "Nun's Priest's Tale"; it is a mad scene with the "dumps" (dumb) murmuring, the "deafs" raising their "heads up to their Creator and . . . expecting help from Him although they could not hear," the cocks crowing, the elephants trumpeting, the "lames" creeping, the dogs barking, the horses neighing, the cats jumping, the goats butting the ewes, the rams scratching the ground "to escape into it," the bats flying "all over the sky with fear." [8]

IV Evocation of Terror

Tutuola is a master in the evocation of the simple, uncomplicated emotion of fear. If in some romances terror is transmuted to delicious thrill, in Tutuola's romances it is terror pure—of course a vicarious literary version of it—much like the intense fear of nightmares. It is the fear of trapped, helpless humanity in the presence of, or in the grip of, bestiality and malignancy. Simbi inside the great hollow tree with the boa gliding toward her is typical; or the chief, treed by the "night woman" and her men, seeing his pursuers prepare to cut down the tree and tear him to pieces.[9] The fact that the incidents are hardly ever realistic does not keep them from giving the reader the vicarious terror: the vigor of the style, the graphic details, and the force and economy of the storytelling see to that.

Some critics have complained that Tutuola's horrors piled upon horrors become tedious, that his too closely packed episodes pall upon the reader. To a certain extent this is true, but these crowded, endless reels of frights and pursuits produce the nightmare atmosphere. For instance, a thinning out of the episodes in the short chapter "In the Spider's Web Bush" in *My Life in the Bush of Ghosts* would probably make the chapter a little less nightmarish. In the six and a half pages of the chapter, the wanderer is (1) chased by ghosts in an "alarm bush" (2) wound up in a spider web, as in a chrysalis (3) thus trapped, soaked by rain for three days (4) mistakenly buried as the body of the dead father of one of the spider-eating ghosts (5) dug up by a "resurrectionist" ghost and about to be eaten (6) burned in a fire while he effects his escape from three ghoulish ghosts about to eat him (7) while seeking shelter in a storm, carried off by a huge animal in whose pouch he has inadvertently taken refuge. Are not our own nightmares thus crowded? [10]

In Tutuola's episodes there is usually terror, and where there is no terror there is often anxiety. In his honeymoon with Super Lady, the wanderer in the Bush of Ghosts—feeling that the lady's bedroom is too grand for him and fearing her—is loath to lie down on her luxurious clean bed, so that she has to push him down on it "very gently as a breakable object." Tutuola's characters are hardly ever calm and at ease. In his nightmare world even the oddest-looking creatures are menacing, like the "half-bodied baby" with the "lower voice like a telephone," Faithful-Mother's White Tree, which "focuses" Drinkard and his wife, shouts at them in a voice that sounds as if it came from a tank, and flashes a stop sign, the "huge stern pigmy" with the herniated navel, the equestrian cudgel-bearer serving the Goddess of Diamonds, the Hairy Giant and Giantess of the underworld, the camel-riding archer. Funny-looking things and creatures in Tutuola's world are usually no joke.[11]

V Economy

A more sophisticated literary power of Tutuola's produces the dramatic impact of many of his incidents, especially in the last four romances. The actions and gestures in his later romances are as expressive as those in the first two romances, and in addition rather fewer episodes are more fully developed, with improved suspense, more conversation (delightful in itself but also sharply defining the conflict of characters), more exciting unexpected events, and more striking denouements. The other romances all contain about twenty episodes, but *My Life in the Bush of Ghosts* and all the later romances seem less crowded with episodes than *The Palm-Wine Drinkard*, without their losing the nightmare atmosphere. The romance with the fewest and best developed episodes is the next to the last: almost every one of the "entertainments" is restricted to one episode, and there are only ten "entertainments."

VI Surprise and Suspense

As we have observed, the conversational exchanges between Dogo the kidnapper and Simbi and between Satyr and Simbi are memorable; these battle dialogues are very spirited, and they serve admirably to characterize and to heighten the dramatic effect.[12] Delightful dramatic surprises would include Simbi's unwittingly killing her master by her singing, the Satyr's provision of an "illusive" concert hall complete with partially invisible orchestra and ostrich guards, the bugle speaking and "leaking out" the news of the King of Ibembe's horns while the African Huntress "winks her eyes" to warn the bugler, the chief keeper of the "custody" returning unexpectedly and finding the African Huntress drinking up his liquor, and the King of the Bush of Quietness confronting his wife and her lover's dead body (and her keeping the flies off the body).[13]

The suspense is well developed, among other instances, in Simbi's narrow escape from being sacrificed to the "spirit of the head" of the King of Sinners' town and from being executed as a thief by the King of the town of multi-coloured people, the terrified silence and the frenzied hiding of the people of Ibembe town, preyed on by the half-human bird, and the ominous hush of the Bush of Quietness entered by the chief-narrator.[14] Simbi's elaborate ruse for destroying her chief opponent, the Satyr, by flying up his nostril as a water insect, the African Huntress' escape from the "custody" by playing dead and being carried by the "pesters" out to the "place that they used to throw their deads," and the same heroine's escape from the ruined pigmy town by being hauled out by the "kind gorilla" would be fairly representative striking denouements.[15]

VII *Humor*

Tutuola's humor is one of his most ingratiating qualities, both the humor he draws from his traditional sources and that due to his own creativity. Although soliciting praise for one's own examples of a writer's humor is not a very promising business, humor is one of Tutuola's fortes and one likely to help him gain popularity, so we owe it to him to make the attempt. Sometimes it is the wild fancy that charms (a traditional Yoruba quality). In *The Palm-Wine Drinkard* the "complete gentleman," having won the affections of a lady "beautiful as an angel," returns his rented parts, limbs, "belly, ribs, chest, etc.," and is then reduced to a skull. (The episode is a very fine adaptation from traditional sources.) Drinkard, who modestly calls himself "father of gods who can do everything in the world," earns badly needed funds, as we have noted, by changing himself into a canoe ferrying passengers across a river; when his wife is swallowed by a "hungry-creature" he gets himself swallowed and fires his gun off in the creature's stomach. He escapes from the "mountain creatures," we remember, by changing himself into a pebble and throwing himself over the river (a bold improvement of his sources).[16]

As a sampling may indicate, the very fanciful variety and originality of the ghosts in the Bush of Ghosts are amusing: a copperish ghost, a silverish ghost, a golden ghost, handless, footless, and armless ghosts, naked ghosts, a smelling ghost, a "lower-rank" ghost, prominent ghosts, a homeless ghost, a famous ghost, "burglar" ghosts, a rich ghost, a "very beautiful young ghostess," a "jocose-ghostess," "triplet" ghosts, a very short ghost, ghost children, river ghosts (sometimes called aquatic ghosts or skeptical ghosts), the Super Lady Ghostess, the Rev. Devil Ghost, and the Television-handed Ghostess.[17] Odara in *The Brave African Huntress* keeps throwing his poisonous cudgels at the hunters though he is drowning. The pigmy gatekeeper quietly tells the huntress, "All right, come and lay your head on this rock and let me cut it off. I do not need yourself or rest part of your body but your head." The huntress, the junior keeper, and the stern pigmy all stand patiently at attention and in silence for two hours while the chief keeper finishes his drinking.

In *Feather Woman of the Jungle* the king of the savage people shouts so "terribly and loudly" that his voice shakes "the hills, rocks and trees. . . ." All the animals are so frightened that they become "mutes"; all the birds wake in their nests, and "all the rest living creatures" are so frightened that they are "unable to move their bodies" and they stand "still as if they [have] died." When this king, who walks with a walking stick made of human bones and rests his feet on a skull footstool, shouts a second time, his voice shakes the tree "so heavily" that the narrator falls out of the tree and on to the king. When a chief of this same savage people is tormenting the narrator by riding him horseback in a cave, the narrator tries to placate his tormentor by singing him a song, but the chief sings along with the narrator, singing a bass or a soprano (!) part; the chief enjoys himself so much that he jumps up and down in crazy joy, hitting his head on the roof of the cave. Tutuolan battle boasts come from the Hairy Giant in this romance: "Who are you? Who are you eating my mangoes: Stop in one place and let your death meets [sic] you or be running away and let your death chase you!" [18]

Much of Tutuola's humor is, of course, humor of hyperbole, which is also a traditional quality. A certain bush that Drinkard passes through is so thick that "a snake could not pass through it without hurt." A road he encounters is very lonely; no one passes on it, "even a fly did not fly on it." When the Red-king's subjects do not eagerly volunteer to be human (or should we say ghostly?) sacrifices to the local monsters, he offers the opportunity to Drinkard and his wife, and ". . . wanted to hear from [them] as soon as possible." In *My Life in the Bush of Ghosts*, when the hero screams during his baptism by fire and hot water, the ghosts answer unsympathetically, "You may die if you like, nobody knows you here." The hero's best man in his wedding to the beautiful ghostess is so bad that he has been "expelled from hell." In *Simbi and the Satyr of the Dark Jungle* the Satyr delivers himself of some pretty extravagant battle boasts, for instance, "Come along, my meat, I am ready to eat both of you now! Come along, and don't waste my time!" and "Certainly you have put yourselves into the mouth of 'death'! You have climbed the trees above the leaves!" *The Brave African Huntress* has an amusing summary of the quality of justice in the "custody": "Every mistake was a great offense and the penalty was to beat the offender to death at once." When required to choose a husband in Bachelors' town the huntress chooses a man she describes as "so old and weary that he could not even distinguish man from woman." [19]

But perhaps Tutuola's best humor is humor of situation. When Drinkard lets Death escape from the net in front of the house of the old man who has sent him to get Death, the old man and his wife make their getaway through the windows, and "the whole people in that town" run for dear life, leaving "their properties" behind. Drinkard has to judge a law case involving a "debiter" who has "never paid any of his debts since he was born," a bill collector who has "never failed to collect debts since he has begun the work," and a curious bystander who lingers on the scene to see the outcome of the encounter of the first two; the denouement of this little drama is alone worth the price of the book. For all the terror of the Bush of Ghosts humorous situations abound there. The golden, copperish, and silverish Ghosts have a ghostly brawl which only the superior dignity of Smelling-Ghost can put a halt to. Later the hero, transmogrified into the shape of a cow, shakes his head in agreement and disagreement with human arguments, talks cow talk which is "fearful" to his captors, and "also not clear to them." On another occasion his screams from a hollow log in which he is "corked tightly" seem delightful "lofty music" to the "homeless ghost" and his convivial friends. When Invisible Pawn puts a ghost head on the hero's shoulders, after the Ghost War, the hero is troubled by a compulsion to say things he does not mean to say, especially his "secret aims." In Hopeless-town he does poorly trying to talk in the shoulder-shrugging language that is locally current: he shrugs to the monarch of the place the tactless remark, "You are a bastard king." [20]

The humorous situations in *Simbi and the Satyr of the Dark Jungle* are less frequent, but choice. When Simbi's friend the snake-gnome removes the multi-coloured king's treasure, that autocrat's court is in a fine panic: a terrified bell-ringer lies prostrate, momentarily expecting the king to "behead him or send him to somewhere." Obsequious courtiers (and no courtiers are more obsequious than old-time African ones) scramble for the privilege of blowing the smoke out of the ceremonial pipe, and hold it while the king smokes, the bell-ringer being prostrate all the while. A later humorous situation concerns the tyranny of beauty. Two love-stricken young men carry Simbi and her friend Rali through the hostile Sinners' town; she has asked them "sharply with her attractive voice," and they have, in charming Tutuolan officialese, "lost all their senses in respect of the two ladies." When the Brave African Huntress Adebesi challenges her, the "bad semi-bird," in a burst of outraged self-esteem, shrieks (somewhat immodestly) that she is a wonderful bad creature who is half-human and half-bird and that she is so "bad that she is customarily eating together with witches." Before the stern pigmy can accost Adebesi she gets in the first word, "By the way, you this stern pigmy, what are you shouting for? You hopeless thing!" The king of the pigmies, who is old and half-blind, tries to shake hands with her captor, congratulating him, and shakes hands with Adebesi herself. But perhaps the funniest situation in the romance is Adebesi's drinking the chief-keeper's liquor while he is out on inspection and her being caught at it. Adebesi's sneaking the drinks, the keeper's incredulous astonishment at such boldness, and his throwing her "from the room to the outside of the office" and ordering his subordinates to beat her to death "at once"—it's all very fine humor of situation.[21]

The next romance has as many humorous situations as the others. Consider, for instance, the ludicrous aspect of the narrator's painful position when the Feather Woman has changed him into a mud image: his sister's suitor, a prince, ties his horse to the image and the horse kicks the narrator, bites him, "snorts" on his body, and scratches the image's head with his "snout." Before the narrator answers the Goddess of Diamond's questions about him, he gives himself the satisfaction of sitting down in one of her diamond chairs. When he seems covetous of her diamonds, she complains, "I wonder, why every human being never satisfy with whatever his Creator had provided for him," and the narrator replies, pertly but pertinently, "That was how our Creator had created all human beings." As the Hairy Giant and his hairy wife run out of their cottage in hot pursuit of the narrator, they collide in the narrow doorway—as in a movie cartoon comedy—and knock their heads together. The narrator and his wife Sela return to the domain of her mother, the Goddess of Diamonds; the old lady is so blind that she hires the couple as cleaners.[22]

VIII *Humanity*

But Tutuola's most important literary virtue is what we must call, for lack of a better term, his humanity—his compassionate view of human beings and his dramatizing and offering for his readers' admiration some of the saving traits of humanity: courage, resolution, persistence, ingenuity, resourcefulness, tolerance, kindness, and forbearance. His main characters, untrammeled by the usual human modes of moral bondage, are free from such idolatries as the devotion to slogans and fanatical ideals, to a domineering god or gods, to social standards, to war, to tribal traditions, to class mores, to sexual demands. They exhibit, after their own fashion, not a few of the cardinal virtues ascribed to the heroes and heroines of *Pilgrim's Progress* or *The Faerie Queene*—works in which, it might be added, monstrous elements exist in great abundance. It is impossible to illustrate by quotations these traits of Tutuola's heroes and heroines —Drinkard and his wife, the nameless wanderer in the Bush of Ghosts, Simbi and her friends, the African Huntress, and the storytelling chief—but by this time the reader will have noticed the traits in materials illustrating other matters.

It might be objected that these simple, uncomplicated virtues of Tutuola's characters are more admirable and pertinent in Tutuola's mythical world of physical and magical conflict with demons and ghosts than they are in our real world with its painfully complex moral conditions and its conflicts on so many different planes and in so many different relations. But surely simple virtues may have complicated applications, and just as surely in our day we are continually in danger of sophisticating our virtues into outright vices.

It might also be objected that a paralyzing fear in Tutuola's characters makes the moral atmosphere of Tutuola's mythical world unwholesome. It is true that fear is almost constantly in the minds of Tutuola's heroes and heroines and that this fear inspires in them some very rough combat tactics. On the other hand, this fear does not debase or brutalize the characters, or make them mean, suspicious, and cruel. Toward human beings, Tutuolan heroes and heroines are almost always generous, open, and kindly. Toward demons and hostile ghosts, they are at least open and aboveboard in their hostility.

One of the most striking peculiarities of Tutuola's protagonists is that they are wonderfully free from rancor and the desire for revenge. Drinkard does not harbor a grudge toward the old man who sends him to capture Death, and he does not brood over the incredible troubles brought on him by his monstrous "half-bodied baby." The wanderer in the Bush of Ghosts does not cherish his resentment of Smelling-Ghost, who mistreats him badly, or of the "homeless ghost" who "corks" him in a hollow log, or of Rev. Devil, who baptizes him with fire and hot water, or even of his wife, who displays a "rude attitude" to him and drives him out of town. Simbi shows no rancor for those who send her down a river nailed in a coffin, or for her mad friend who knocks out several of her teeth, or even for the Satyr himself, who has tortured her horribly.[23] The Brave African Huntress does not deeply resent the deadly pursuit of the outraged supporters of the King of Ibembe; she is very cool about the cruelty of the guards at the "custody" and she blames only herself for her sad fall from the good fortune of Bachelors' town. Similarly the storytelling chief does not think of revenge against the Feather Woman, a witch who has practiced several sorts of deviltry against him; he does not bother to entertain rancorous thoughts about the Goddess of Diamonds, who shakes up his property with an earthquake and has his wife abducted.[24] In spite of the superficial paganism of Tutuola's romances, there are clear reflections of his Christian beliefs and his personal gentleness.

What then is the significance of Tutuola's work? He has made available to the world the human values of the Yoruba folk tales, in the way the folk tale collectors could never do. He is in the true Yoruba tradition of the professional storytellers, the *akpalo kpatita*, but he performs in every place in the world where there are readers.

This fairly catholic reader believes Tutuola's work will endure for the vigor and interest of his language (never mind the errors and hardly ever mend them!), the force and economy and dramatic effect of his storytelling, his fertile imagination, his graphic descriptions, his wild humor, the compelling power of his nightmare flights, tortures, horrors, ogres, and transformations, and the great humanity of his gentle Christian soul, unembarrassed by the African past, Western technology, or indeed anything else. Surely one day Amos Tutuola will be recognized as West Africa's first classic in world literature.

Notes and References

1. *PWD*, pp. 58, 68–73; *MLBG*, pp. 35, 96–104, 161–163; *SSDJ*, pp. 109–114.

2. *PWD*, pp. 39, 117; *SSDJ*, p. 124; *FWJ*, p. 19.

3. *PWD*, p. 7; *SSDJ*, p. 7; *BAH*, p. 9.

4. *West Africa*, XXXVIII (May 1, 1954), 389.

5. *MLBG*, pp. 39, 131; *SSDJ*, p. 52; *BAH*, p. 77; *FWJ*, p. 20.

6. *PWD*, pp. 46, 66.

7. *MLBG*, pp. 61, 63; *SSDJ*, pp. 79, 88.

8. *BAH*, pp. 63, 84; *FWJ*, pp. 15, 68, 99.

9. *SSDJ*, pp. 83, 86; *FWJ*, p. 57.

10. *MLBG*, pp. 89–95.

11. *Ibid.*, p. 120; *PWD*, pp. 35, 66; *BAH*, p. 77; *FWJ*, pp. 99–100, 114–122.

12. *SSDJ*, pp. 16–20, 73, 75, 122.

13. *Ibid.*, pp. 27, 109–114; *BAH*, pp. 44, 93; *FWJ*, p. 45.

14. *SSDJ*, pp. 39, 54–63; *BAH*, pp. 34–37; *FWJ*, p. 38.

15. *SSDJ*, p. 124; *BAH*, pp. 93, 105–106.

16. *PWD*, pp. 17–21, 39, 109–110, 117.

17. *MLBG*, pp. 24–25, 27, 29, 32, 39, 49, 52, 55, 56, 57, 59, 63, 65, 72, 83, 112, 129, 161.

18. *BAH*, pp. 31, 50, 82; *FWJ*, pp. 60, 63, 99, 116.

19. *PWD*, pp. 41, 56, 71; *MLBG*, pp. 60, 59; *SSDJ*, pp. 73, 75; *BAH*, pp. 89, 114.

20. *PWD*, pp. 15, 111–112; *MLBG*, pp. 28, 44, 47, 50, 109, 126–127.

21. *SSDJ*, pp. 58–59, 131; *BAH*, pp. 38, 75, 81, 93.

22. *FWJ*, pp. 31, 82, 90, 121, 131. The story "Ajayi and the Witchdoctor" has a grotesquely humorous situation: Ajayi is prepared to behead his own dead father as he comes out of his grave (*Black Orpheus*, No. 19 [March, 1966], 10–14).

23. *PWD*, pp. 16, 35–58; *MLBG*, pp. 29, 42, 49, 59–63, 135; *SSDJ*, pp. 29, 49–50, 122.

24. *BAH*, pp. 46, 85–94, 119; *FWJ*, pp. 33–34, 97–103.

RECENT CRITICISM

Recent Criticism

All the essays in this section were originally published in the early nineteen-seventies, and together they represent a new era in Tutuolan criticism. Each critic views Tutuola's writing from a different disciplinary perspective, applying textual, psychoanalytic, linguistic, esthetic, structural, archetypal, rhetorical or historical modes of literary analysis to his works. The impressive diversity and rigor of these approaches reveal that Tutuola's writing repays serious academic study of many types, a fact which virtually guarantees that his books will continue to be the subject of much stimulating research in the years to come.

Time, Space, and Description:

The Tutuolan World

It is in his use of time that Tutuola differs so widely from the Western writers with whom he has often been compared and even from some of his African contemporaries. In *The Palm-Wine Drinkard*, the reader is always conscious of time, because Tutuola constantly makes references to hours, days, weeks and months, even years; * still there is the impression that many of the events that the Drinkard encounters are beyond the control of the normal dictates of time. One is reminded that many years ago Spengler maintained that interest in time is peculiar to Western civilization. If lack of interest in time may often be more typical of non-Western cultures, Tutuola is in many ways a perfect example.

The narrated time of *The Palm-Wine Drinkard* is a little more than eleven years. The Drinkard himself is approximately twenty-five years old at the beginning of the story (after being a palm-wine drinkard for fifteen years.) Although Tutuola's references to specific periods of time are somewhat inconsistent, he does inform his reader that ten years have passed from the time the Drinkard begins his search for his Tapster until the time when he locates him; and the references to blocks of

---

* Numbers tend to be whole units instead of fractions. Time is usually referred to in complete hours (such as eight o'clock p.m.) rather than by minutes or portions of hours, as if Tutuola is not quite used to having to pinpoint exact periods of time.

Reprinted from Charles R. Larson, *The Emergence of African Fiction* (Bloomington, 1972), pp. 102-112.

time add up to a little more than a year for the return journey. Here alone there appears to be an inconsistency; if the trip to the Deads' Town takes ten years, why is barely more than a year involved for the return? The answer, however, has nothing to do with space or the actual distance between the Drinkard's own village and the Deads' Town. Rather, time is related to the incidents involved in the Drinkard's going and coming from the Deads' Town and in the relative value of these incidents; and the return, even though it involves only a few pages of the text, seems overdrawn simply because the quest has been for the most part fulfilled.

It may be easier to understand Tutuola's presentation of time by considering his references to temporal factors and their relationship to a more traditional value system. Such an interpretation gives us "evil time" and "good time" and in both categories time may be speeded up or slowed down. Many of the terrible creatures in the *The Palm-Wine Drinkard* exist in a time that is proportional to their function in the novel. Their evil doings are successful because they may be accomplished almost instantaneously. The "Skull" who keeps the Drinkard's future wife as prisoner, for example, "could jump a mile to the second before coming down. He caught the lady in this way: so when the lady was running away for her life, he hastily ran to her front and stopped her as a log of wood" (p.22). Clearly, the Skull catches his victims because he operates in a time different from theirs. The evil child born from the Drinkard's wife's thumb is also at an advantage because of a differing time system. Tutuola tells us,

> . . . the thumb bust out suddenly and there we saw a male child came out of it and at the same time that the child came out from the thumb, he began to talk to us as if he was ten years of age.
> Within the hour that he came down from the thumb he grew up to the height of about three feet and some inches and his voice by that time was as plain as if somebody strikes an anvil with a steel hammer. (pp.31–32)

The Thumb Child's obnoxiousness is indeed related to his rather abrupt growth. Another evil creature encountered in the story is capable of destroying a freshly cleared field in a few minutes: "but before 30 minutes that he was watching the field, he saw a very tiny creature who was just a baby of one day of age and he commanded the weeds to rise up as he was commanding before" (p.50). Tutuola also describes a flock of evil birds whose havoc is due in large part to their suddenness:

> When these birds started to eat the flesh of those animals, within a second there we saw about 50 holes on the bodies of those animals and within a second the animals fell down and died, but when they began to eat the dead bodies it did not last them more than 2 minutes before they finished them (bodies) and as soon as they had eaten that, they would start to chase others about. (p.53)

Closely related to the terrible birds is a creature called "Spirit of Prey" who is capable of eating "off the dead body of [a] buffalo within four minutes . . ." (p.55). In all of these cases, the havoc or evil these creatures are capable of causing is directly proportional to the speed with which they are able to carry out their deeds.

On occasion—and it depends where the Drinkard and his wife are—speeded-up time operates to the advantage of the Drinkard too. In both of the substories of the novel where the Drinkard and his wife encounter no harmful creatures, good time operates quickly to their advantage. During the "Wraith-Island" incident where the Drinkard and his wife become farmers, time is definitely on their side. After the Drinkard plants his crops he tells us,

> to my surprise, these grains and the seeds germinated at once, before 5 minutes they became full grown crops and before 10 minutes again, they had produced fruits and ripened at the same moment too, so I plucked them and went back to the town (the Wraith-Island). (p.48)

Good time also operates in the Faithful Mother's kingdom in the white tree: "within a week that we were living with this

173

mother, we had forgotten all our past torments. . . ." (p.69). The hair on their heads, which had been so brutally scraped off in the Unreturnable-Heaven's town so that their heads were bleeding, returns within a week from the treatment in the Faithful-Mother's hospital. And the magical egg that the Drinkard takes back to his village "produced food and drinks for each of these people, so that everyone of them who had not eaten for a year, ate and drank to his or her satisfaction" (p.121), within a matter of a few brief moments.

It is easy to argue that in many literary works which are outside the bounds of realism—that in all tales and stories, and especially in folklore and mythology—time operates in no logical manner. Tutuola's world is not that simple, however, as his occasional references to time in his own life clearly indicate. In the five-page autobiographical account appended to *The Palm-Wine Drinkard,* Tutuola describes a youthful experience, by informing the reader:

> I was trekking this distance of 23¾ miles instead of joining a lorry, because I had no money to pay for transport which was then only 2d. If I left home at 6 o'clock in the morning, I would reach the village at about 8 o'clock in the same morning or when my people were just preparing to go to farm, and this was a great surprise to them, because they did not believe that I trekked the distance but joined a lorry. (p.128)

Twenty-three and three-fourths miles in two hours through African bush would indeed make Tutuola one of the fastest runners in the world! * When asked during an interview for National Educational Television how long it took him to write *The Palm-Wine Drinkard,* Tutuola replied "three days," later stating that most of his works take no more than two or three weeks.[1] If this is true, one wonders why Tutuola has

---

* The distance from the school where I taught in Eastern Nigeria and the Onitsha market was thirteen miles, yet I was rarely able to cover this distance (only in part over bush roads) on my motor scooter in less than an hour.

1. "Conversation with Amos Tutuola," *Africa Report*, 9 (July 1964), 11.

published only six works during his eighteen-year literary career.

The implication is certainly that Tutuola views time in some other way than we do in the West, as related to some definite system involving good (accomplishment) and evil (hindrance or stagnation); and, by extension, that time in an African sense has little to do with actual blocks of time as measured in a Western sense but rather with human values and human achievements. Certainly this is true of a number of other African novels far removed from the folkloristic domain. Yambo Ouologuem's *Le devoir de violence*, I have already noted, begins in the year 1202 and ends in the year 1947. Ouologuem's novel is a bloody chronicle of violence and brutality which he implies are basic factors in African tradition, and it is a fact that these atrocities perpetuate themselves down through the ages that Ouologuem records so sadistically in his novel. Even in a work such as Chinua Achebe's *Things Fall Apart*, time definitely appears to be related to human accomplishments rather than to clocks and Western measurements, for it is only during Okonkwo's seven years of exile that time plays any significance in the development of the story. For Okonkwo, time exists (in a Western sense) only when the conventional value system has been thrown out of balance. Much the same may be said for Chief Priest Ezeulu in Achebe's later novel, *Arrow of God*.

As a corollary, space and its treatment in *The Palm-Wine Drinkard* is also something frequently quite removed from the Western concept as shown in much Western fiction. Tutuola makes constant references to vast distances (to miles and miles and miles) that his hero and other characters are capable of covering in very limited periods of time in spite of the fact that in many cases there are no roads or pathways from one place to another, as for example on the way to the Deads' Town where "there was no road or path which to travel, because nobody was going there from that town at all" (p.41). At a later stage in their advance toward the Deads'

Town, the Drinkard and his wife illustrate that space, like time, is often regarded in a manner different from that of the West:

> Then we continued our journey as usual to the Deads' Town and when we had travelled for 10 days we were looking at the Deads' Town about 40 miles away and we were not delayed by anything on the way again. But as we were looking at the town from a long distance, we thought that we could reach there the same day, but not at all, we travelled for 6 more days, because as we nearly reached there, it would seem still to be very far away to us or as if it was running away from us. We did not know that anybody who had not died could not enter into that town by day time, but when my wife knew the secret, then she told me that we should stop and rest till night. When it was night, then she told me to get up and start our journey again. But soon after we started to go, we found that we need not travel more than one hour before we reached there. Of course we did not enter into it until the dawn, because it was an unknown town to us. (p.95)

The Drinkard's advance here is much like K's attempt to reach the castle in Kafka's novel, *The Castle;* time and space frequently repel one another. However, whereas K is unsuccessful, the Drinkard reaches his destination.

Also like Kafka, Tutuola's merging of time and space frequently leads to surrealistic passages, as the physical aspects of the environment divide, alter, and coalesce into new forms. On one occasion a termites' house changes into a market while the Drinkard and his wife are sleeping. Again:

> As we were going on in this bush, we saw a pond and we branched there, then we started to drink the water from it, but as the water dried away at our presence and also as we were thirsty all the time, and there we saw that there was not a single living creature. (p.52)

The most heightened example of the surreal, however, occurs when the Drinkard and his wife enter into the Faithful-Mother's tree. The tree itself, before they enter it, is described as being "about one thousand and fifty feet in length and about two hundred feet in diameter" (p.65). As soon as they enter it, they discover that it is large enough to contain a whole Alice-in-Wonderland-like world: "When we entered inside the white tree, there we found ourselves inside a big house which was in the centre of a big and beautiful town . . ." (p.67). Later, the Faithful-Mother takes them "to the largest dancing hall which was in the centre of that house, and there we saw that over 300 people were dancing all together. . . . This beautiful hall was full of all kinds of food and drinks, over twenty stages were in that hall with uncountable orchestras, musicians, dancers and tappers" (p.68). The exposition continues to describe the dining hall, the kitchen "in which we met about three hundred and forty cooks" (p.69) and the Faithful-Mother's hospital. The Drinkard and his wife remain with the Faithful-Mother for one year and two weeks; upon leaving, the Drinkard states that "what made us very surprised was that we saw the tree opened as a large door, and we simply found ourselves inside the bush unexpectedly, and the door closed at once and the tree seemed as an ordinary tree which could not open like that" (p.71).

As in Achebe's *Things Fall Apart* and in the works of the Onitsha writers, description in *The Palm-Wine Drinkard* tends to be functional, very rarely related to mood and atmosphere or landscaping in spite of the fact that landscape description would seem likely to occur in the many sections of the *Drinkard* that deal with the bush. Undoubtedly the most detailed descriptions are limited to the curious creatures themselves, such as Tutuola's picture of the Complete Gentleman:

> He was a beautiful "complete" gentleman, he dressed with the finest and most costly clothes, all the parts of his body were completed, he was a tall man but stout. As this gentleman came to the market on that day, if he had been an article or animal for sale, he would be sold at least for £2000 (two thousand pounds). (p.18)

The functional is obvious here: the Complete Gentleman would have to be described in rather complete detail.

On the "Wraith-Island," the Drinkard encounters the following creature:

> . . . I saw a terrible animal coming to the farm and eating the crops, but one morning I met him there, so I started to drive him away from the farm, of course I could not approach him as he was as big as an elephant. His fingernails were long to about two feet, his head was bigger than his body ten times. He had a large mouth which was full of long teeth, these teeth were about one foot long and as thick as a cow's horns, his body was almost covered with black long hair like a horse's tail hair. He was very dirty. There were five horns on his head and curved and levelled to the head, his four feet were as big as a log of wood. (p.47)

Still later, one of the terrible red creatures is described in this manner:

> At the same time that the red fish appeared out, its head was just like a tortoise's head, but it was as big as an elephant's head and it had over 30 horns and large eyes which surrounded the head. All these horns were spread out as an umbrella. It could not walk but was only gliding on the ground like a snake and its body was just like a bat's body and covered with long red hair like strings. It could only fly to a short distance, and if it shouted a person who was four miles away would hear. All the eyes which surrounded its head were closing and opening at the same time as if a man was pressing a switch on and off. (pp.79–80)

The eyes which switch on and off are an excellent example of the many Westernizations which creep into Tutuola's narrative.

Much more typical, for describing a person or creature, is the Tutuolan comparison, illustrating a power or a trait by relating it to another. The Drinkard's Thumb Child is characterized in this manner: "This was a wonderful child, because if a hundred men were to fight with him, he would flog them until they would run away" (p.33). At other times, Tutuola will use a series of comparisons to illustrate the consummate powers of a character. In such a way, the Drinkard describes the Complete Gentleman's beauty:

I could not blame the lady for following the Skull as a complete gentleman to his house at all. Because if I were a lady, no doubt I would follow him to wherever he would go, and still as I was a man I would jealous him more than that, because if this gentleman went to the battle field, surely, enemy would not kill him or capture him and if bombers saw him in a town which was to be bombed, they would not throw bombs on his presence, and if they did throw it, the bomb itself would not explode until this gentleman would leave that town, because of his beauty. (p.25)

It should be noted also that Tutuola makes extensive use of sounds and noises throughout his narrative to further illustrate character and quasi-superhuman powers, such as the Thumb Child who "was whistling as if he was forty persons" (p.36), or two red fish "making a noise as if it was a thousand persons. . . ." (p.79).

In spite of being established primarily by these types of comparison or limited physical description, characterization in *The Palm-Wine Drinkard* tends to be utilitarian. Characters are for the most part named because of their specific function or purpose. The Drinkard and his wife, of course, are the best examples of this. Only the Tapster and the Thumb-Child have actual names, and the Tapster's name (Baity) is not given until the Drinkard reaches the Deads' Town. Other characters Tutuola realizes are designated best by their actions and deeds, often again implying a value system comparable to that of Tutuola's conception of time and space: Faithful-Mother, Give and Take, the Wise King, the Hungry Creature. In the case of the Drinkard's wife, except for her tendency to speak in parables, we know little about her other than her early attempt to try to avoid an arranged marriage.

The Drinkard himself is, of course, best characterized by the many heroic challenges he accepts and overcomes. In spite of the fact that he narrates the entire novel, there are very few passages which could actually be referred to as introspection. The following is perhaps the closest example: "then I *thought within myself* how could we get money for our food

179

etc." (p.39. Italics mine). Nor does Tutuola use extended dialogue to develop the Drinkard's or any other character's personality. Instead, dialogue in *The Palm-Wine Drinkard*, too, appears to play a completely utilitarian purpose. The following passage is typical of Tutuola's sparse use of it:

> The questions that their king asked us went thus:—From where were you coming? I replied that we were coming from the earth. He asked again how did we manage to reach their town, I replied that it was their road brought us to the town and we did not want to come there at all. After that he asked us where were we going to? Then I replied that we were going to my palm-wine tapster's town who had died in my town sometime ago. As I had said already that these unknown creatures were very cruel to anybody that mistakenly entered their town, as I answered all the questions, he repeated the name of their town for us again—"Unreturnable-Heaven's town." He said:—a town in which are only enemies of God living, only cruel, greedy and merciless creatures. (pp.59–60)

It should also be noted that the Tutuolan world is replete with humor—often in the form of puns and curious anachronisms. There is a tendency, also, toward the didactic at the end of many of the incidents in the narrative and at many of the transitions from story to story. This didactic tendency, as we have already noted with other African writers, is in part a carry-over from traditional literary materials—in Tutuola's case the Yoruba oral tradition.

Storytelling is clearly at the heart of Tutuola's art, and Tutuola himself has said that even as a child he was admired by his playmates as a teller of tales. If this storytelling borders on the dreamlike, the surreal, the fantastic and the archetypal, we have only to note that Tutuola's tales are rooted in an oral tradition which is still very much alive in Yoruba society today—and the African reader often responds to these tales in a manner different from the non-African. In spite of the reshaping he often gives to his tales, Tutuola is for the African reader clearly a man whose work is grounded in the real world in which the African lives. When reading his work I am constantly reminded of the many essays I corrected when teaching English in Nigeria. Time and again, students related what to me appeared fantastic accounts of spirits and wild animals they had supposedly encountered in the bush. Tutuola's writing does just about the same thing. If Tutuola's imagination is frequently a bridge between the internal and the external world (the ontological gap), between the real and the surreal, between the realistic and the supernatural, we must at least point out in conclusion that passages of Tutuola's novels are rooted in a reality comparable to that of the more realistic works of his African contemporaries. The following is only one of dozens of possible examples:

> Then we left that town with gladness, we started our journey again, but after we had travelled about eighty miles away to that town, then we began to meet gangs of the "highway-men" on the road, and they were troubling us too much. But when I thought over that the danger of the road might result to the loss of our money or both money and our lives, then we entered into bush, but to travel in this bush was very dangerous too, because of the wild animals, and the boa constrictors were un-countable as sand. (p.40)

Yet how can we be certain that this passage may not be fantasy, and that all of the curious creatures may not represent reality to a mind that could create the writings of an Amos Tutuola?

Amos Tutuola: Emerging African Literature

Paul Neumarkt

In a study of Amos Tutuola, there are certain psychiatric categories, such as the syndromes of paranoia and lycanthropy which will have to be taken into consideration. When a man feels persecuted, he is subject to psychic disturbances whether he lives among Eskimos, African pygmies, or highly progressive members of modern civilization. The question is therefore whether the individual so afflicted can consciously or unconsciously take refuge within the secure limits of a collective frame that acts as an institutionalized prophylactic sphere. If his society provides a measure of prophylaxis, in terms of ritual for instance, he may escape the ordeal of psychic upheaval. However, if he has undergone a pronounced process of differentiation, as is the case in modern Western societies, he may have undercut his route of retreat into such a sphere of collective security. The result is alienation, concomitant with the gamut of pathogenic disturbances. The case of Amos Tutuola lies somewhere within these two areas of psychological delineation.

Comparatively little has been written on the work of this Nigerian author. The few published comments are inconclusive and confusing. Geoffrey Parrinder (of the University College of Ibadan, Nigeria) considers Tutuola's writings "a beginning of a new type of Afro-English literature."[1] This statement is off the mark. My thesis is that Tutuola is caught in a literary cul-de-sac, much against his own conscious intentions. Tutuola's significance in present day African writing reflects a thoroughly psychological antithesis which is far from representative for contemporary African literature. This antithetical streak is tied to a regressive proclivity which tends to thwart his conative powers.

The modern African scene is dominated by writers who are engaged in mythopoeic activity. Efua Sutherland, Chinua Achebe, Wole

---

1. Geoffrey Parrinder, "Foreword" to Amos Tutuola, *My Life in the Bush of Ghosts*. London: Faber and Faber, 1969, p. 10.

Reprinted from *American Imago*, 28 (1971), 129-45, with permission from Wayne State University Press.

Soyinka, Ezekiel Mphahlele, Abioseh Nicol, and others are all concerned, in one way or another with emergence by reconstructing some facet of the past. Hence, myth-making is the *raison d'être* in the African writer's rediscovery of his own cultural past. The phylogenetic memory of the black man, not that of his white master, is his innate storehouse from which his psyche must continue to draw sustenance. This is the pivotal point in our discussion. For, much as return to his own past is a *sine qua non*, and much as he yearns for the thrill to recreate the myth of his forefathers, he can never be oblivious of his encounter with the white man who, during the prolonged period of colonization, flaunted his "superiority" at every turn of the road. This, too, forms part of a past which is not easily repressed.

This then is the battlefield on which the African is engaged in the daily skirmishes for a meaningful existence, and it is in this context that the work of Amos Tutuola constitutes a psychological antithesis. At this point, I would like to refer to Slochower's *Mythopoesis* in which he posits that "myth addresses itself to the problem of identity, asking 'who am I?' And it proceeds to examine the questions that are organically related: 'Where do I come from?', 'Where am I bound?', and 'What must I do to get there?' In mythic language, the problems deal with Creation, with Destiny and with the Quest."[2] The problem of identity that occupies the contemporary African writers in terms of these postulates does not apply to Tutuola. True, he is thoroughly involved with his ethnic origin, but he does not go beyond the question "where do I come from"? In other words: Tutuola shares the commitment to the past, but does not ask the questions of "where am I bound" and "what must I do to get there"? It seems that the gravitational pull in the quest for identity through identification with his origin was so overwhelming that he could not extricate himself from the archaic powers. This is the reason why Tutuola does not find widespread appreciation among his countrymen, even though his work has created some stir in European literary circles. Gerald Moore implies that there is "a definite resistance on the part of many African readers, a refusal to enter the world which Tutuola inhabits, which is easily confused with all that they are trying to escape from."[3] The world which he inhabits and with which he identifies is one of fear. Parrinder states that "fear is present throughout. If anyone doubts that there is fear in African life, Tutuola's story should convince him of its reality.

2. Harry Slochower, *Mythopoesis*. Detroit: Wayne State University Press, 1970, p. 15.

3. Gerald Moore, *Seven African Writers*. London: Oxford University Press, 1970, p. 15.

The unknown bush with its frightful spirits stretching out their tentacles, like trees in an Arthur Reckham drawing, is a dreadful place. Fairy tales can scare, but this is more terrifying than Grimm as its matter is more serious and is believed in by millions of Africans today."[4] Parrinder's observation is correct in its assumption of a state of fear in Tutuola's work; but his generalization that this is characteristic of or "believed in by millions of Africans today" is doubtful. In fact, it betrays the dilemma of the missionary Parrinder. It must, of course, be admitted that fear is part of the white man's legacy by which he aimed to solidify his rule during the period of colonization. From this angle, Tutuola's work is a reflection on that particular part of African history. However, in the wider context of present day African writing, myth-making certainly transcends the narrow confines of Tutuola's literary premise. In fact, most modern authors on that continent are vitally interested in the direction and the purpose of their struggle for meaningful identity. A study of Tutuola's work reveals that his is an antithetical voice in the African chorus, and it is for this reason that one should look at his predicament as one of personal psychological dimensions. His work does not depict a social struggle or an involvement with the white man's culture *per se*. Even the Reverend Devil in his book *My Life in the Bush of Ghosts* with its Methodist Church and Sunday School instruction are marginal reflections which have no vital bearing on the development of the theme.

I propose to examine Tutuola's book *The Palm-Wine Drinkard* for a number of reasons. First, it stands at the beginning of his literary career and was hailed in the West as the product of a promising African writer. However, his subsequent publications did not live up to such expectations. This is connected with his particular psychological dilemma which I have mentioned. The Drinkard's adventure is, as Gerald Moore aptly states, "a journey into the eternal African Bush, but equally a journey into the racial imagination, into the subconscious, into that Spirit World that everywhere co-exists and even overlaps with the world of waking 'reality.' Or, to express it mythically, he is descending like Gilgamesh, Orpheus, Heracles or Aeneas before him, into the Underworld, there to confront death itself and attempt to carry off some trophy to the living as a symbol of his mastery over the two worlds."[5] The hero in *The Palm-Wine Drinkard* passes through all the stages that we find in the hero-myth. Having violated some basic tenet of his society, he must pass through a gamut of ordeals, according to the severity of the offence, until he has expiated his crime. In the

---

4. Parrinder, p. 11.

5. Moore, pp. 45-46.

end, he is usually elevated, as in Apuleius' *Cupid and Psyche*, or Goethe's *Faust* who ascends the highest spheres of heaven.

The Palm-Wine Drinkard's guilt is due to an act of omission: he hasn't done anything to earn a status in society. He is the African counterpart of Joseph von Eichendorff's "Taugenichts" (good-for-nothing), a parasitic, if pleasant type of happy-go-lucky who never earns his own means of subsistence and is turned out by his impatient father. Like his German counterpart, the Drinkard nevertheless remains a lovable creature throughout his meanderings, and both are rewarded in the end despite the fact that they dodged the responsibilities of the established order. The reason for this preferred treatment of the hero lies in the fact that there is no trace of evil or vindictiveness in Tutuola's Drinkard. While von Eichendorff's "Taugenichts" lives "happily ever after" in a fairy-tale setting, Tutuola's hero soon finds out that his beautiful reward, the magic egg that relieves him of material worries, can also bring about the horrors of pandemonium as well. The development of the Drinkard is a history of personal trials. At first, there appears the task-master from whom he must wrest the information concerning his "dead" tapster's whereabouts. Then, there is the Red Fish, a man-eating monster that he conquers to save an entire community from bondage and death. The hero shows his valor by rescuing a maiden from the "complete gentleman," a thoroughly polished sort of oppressor. The maiden follows the hero as his faithful wife through the horrors of life that are in store for him. The baby born of this union is a half-bodied, precocious creature that has sprung from the swollen left thumb of the hero's wife.

This incident throws light on the psychic condition of the hero. Freud claims that the syndrome of paranoia in the case of a male could initiate a process of *emasculation*. [6] The child is born from the "swollen thumb" of the mother, a phallic substitution projected upon her. Thus the offspring is a half-bodied monster.

The meeting with the Faithful-Mother in the White Tree suggests a process of regression. The tree sending its roots deep into the earth is, however, also the symbol of supreme knowledge, as in the case of the Biblical Tree of knowledge whose fruit is not eaten as long as man is not ready to challenge the *Magna Mater*. Goethe's Faust is sent to the "Realm of the Mothers" for the key that will unlock the door leading to Helen of Troy. The Chinese poet Lao-tze points to the "Mystic Female," the valley-spirit that must be overcome before the wanderer may attempt the ascent to the crest of the mountain. Tutuola's Drinkard does not challenge the Great Mother actively, but is rather the

---

6. Sigmund Freud, *St. Ed.*, vol. XII, "The Case of Schreber," pp. 12-58, passim.

passive bystander. This passivity proves fateful as the hero and his wife are swallowed by the Faithful-Mother who now turns into a "Hungry Creature." In the German "Nibelungenlied," where Siegfried slays the dragon guarding the treasure, the cave also represents the feminine pleroma and takes on monstrous dimensions. The slaying of the mother brings guilt upon the hero which he must expiate with his life. An outstanding example in modern literature is Heinrich Böll's Lieutenant Greek in *Wo Warst Du Adam?* (Where Were You Adam?) who is violently drawn into the maternal womb of forgetfulness amidst the stench of exploding bombs and human feces. The main difference is that Böll, having experienced the horrors of World War II, lets his hero pass into the limbo of no return, while Tutuola's Drinkard emerges reborn. The escape from the womb of the "Hungry Creature" is fraught with psychological overtones. The Drinkard shoots the creature from inside with a musket, and then, little by little, hacks his way out with a cutlass. This suggests that the physical death of the creature does not necessarily spell redemption, for the monstrous mother may trap him in a different sphere of the psyche. By hacking it apart he is cutting himself loose from the many fangs by which the maternal womb blocks his emergence as hero. Likewise in D. H. Lawrence's short story "The Lovely Lady": Only after the son has literally hacked his way out of the pleromatic embrace can he emerge heroically and thereby neutralize the stymying shadows which the dead mother casts even beyond her grave (cf. the Babylonian myth of Marduk and Tiamat).

The concluding part of Tutuola's novel is surprisingly realistic. Gerald Moore writes that "the resolution of the Drinkard's individual development as hero is linked with the restoration of harmony between man and his gods, for it is the Drinkard's new understanding won by the hard way of adventure, which enables him to settle the cosmic quarrel through which man is suffering."[7] Moore's term "restoration" implies an untroubled psychic disposition on the part of the Drinkard, prior to embarking on his adventures. Such is not the case. The reference to "harmony between man and his gods" is equally ambiguous. The development of the Drinkard is, as I have pointed out a slow process of breaking away from the embrace of the Great Mother, and his subsequent emergence on the plane of conscious awareness. There is no semblance of harmony with the gods anywhere. His "new understanding won by the hard way of adventure" is simply an expression of projection of his repressed masculine psyche, rather than true insight. This is substantiated by the "magic egg" that works wonders as long as he does not question its inherent miraculous quality. No sooner has he

---

7. Moore, p. 49.

probed its secret than it whips the challenger to death. This is far from the harmony Moore posits; but it is the only piece of writing in which Tutuola attempts a more or less realistic appraisal of his setting.

Where the Drinkard emerges from the infernal shadows with the "magic egg," the prize for his trials, but also with the recognition of the dubious character of his hard-won booty, we can point to some social frame of Tutuola's message. Such, however, is not the case in his subsequent books. The time element is absent in the eternal darkness of Tutuola's ghost-ridden bush; the social background is no longer a condition of man's survival, and the struggle for existence is stripped of any human semblance, as brute force is pitted against itself. Thus Tutuola's books can hardly be classified as novels.

Tutuola is a trapped man, trapped in the maze of his own pathogenic disturbance. Gerald Moore is aware of this when he writes: "Tutuola's books are far more like a fascinating cul-de-sac than a beginning of anything directly useful to other writers. The cul-de-sac is full of wonders, but it is nonetheless a dead end."[8] This becomes apparent in Tutuola's *My Life in the Bush of Ghosts*. In it, the narrator is a boy of seven who is the victim of the jealousies among his father's wives. He flees from home and enters the Bush of Ghosts by way of a hole in a large mound. A series of transformations change him alternately into a cow, a ju-ju-stick, a horse, a camel, and a monkey, as he experiences life among the ghosts. He no longer yearns to escape from his predicament—an indication that he has succumbed to the sinister forces of the unconscious that are firmly entrenched in his psyche. But Tutuola evidently felt obliged to create some semblance of a social continuum by making a half-hearted concession to the demands of organized life. Thus, the Television-Handed Ghostess intervenes on his behalf and leads him back to normal existence. This artificial *deus ex machina* solution is unconvincing, and his final words: "this is what hatred did,"[9] is a lame attempt to introduce some morality and coax the reader into acceptance of a half-hearted literary solution.

A similar situation prevails in Tutuola's book *Simbi and the Satyr of the Dark Jungle*. Here, the psychological setting is reversed. A young girl, named Simbi, ignoring her mother's warnings experiences poverty and punishment. This time, the matriarchal sphere is replaced by that of the Satyr, a sexually perverted, dominating father figure, who clearly avows this brute sexuality: "I believe, the two ladies [Simbi and Rali] shall come back to this jungle, and I shall kill both of them at all costs,

---

8. Ibid., p. 57.

9. *My Life in the Bush of Ghosts,* p. 174.

at any day [sic] I meet them. It is certain, they are my meat."[10] Simbi, however, changes into a water fly, creeps up his nostrils, and chokes him to death. In ancient myths, air connotes wind as well as breath and spirit (cf. the Hebrew "ruach"—spirit—as used in Genesis). In the story by von Eichendorff, the Taugenicht's illicit desire for the virgin is also abruptly terminated by a fly that creeps up his nostrils causing a sneezing attack which frustrates his secret desires.[11] Tutuola feels here, as in the previous book, that he must add a message. Simbi's final statement: "My mother, I shall not disobey you again,"[12] is another feeble attempt to salvage some kind of social idea, which is conspicuously absent in Tutuola's writings.

If the author has up to now taken his readers deep into the African Bush to afford them some glimpse of the weird inferno and its ghost-like inhabitants, he has, at least, remained true to his own tortured self. In his subsequent book, *The Brave African Huntress*, the last vestige of his personal pride melts away, as he realizes that his fellow Africans have turned their backs on him. The concession to his European audience is now glaringly apparent. Gerald Moore points to this decline in Tutuola's integrity when he states that his "magic has all leaked away. The catalogue of creatures with their European names straight out of Grimm's Fairy-Tales—'gnomes,' 'goblins' and so forth—is a terrible letdown. Even the word 'jungle' reads like a concession to European taste, for it is seldom used by West Africans, who always speak of 'the bush,' as Tutuola did in his first books."[13]

When I set out to write this paper, it appeared to me that a certain paranoid propensity was prevalent in Tutuola's psyche and that, as a certain Canadian psychiatrist observed after five years in Kenya, "by and large the same illnesses are seen throughout the world in all races."[14] The question that is paramount in the analysis of Tutuola's work is why he succumbed to the lures of the bush and its concomitant lycanthropic representations. Was it that this type of existence afforded him a zone of security which shielded him from the world outside, a world in which he felt haunted and misplaced? We are aware that archaic contents, such as lycanthropic representations are foreboding

10. Amos Tutuola, *Simbi and the Satyr of the Dark Jungle.* London: Faber and Faber, 1955, p. 80.

11. Joseph von Eichendorff, "Aus dem Leben eines Taugenichts," *Gesammelte Werke.* München: Carl Hauser Verlag, p. 219, passim.

12. *Simbi and the Satyr of the Dark Jungle,* p. 136.

13. Moore, p. 55.

14. Leonard W. Doob, "Psychology," *The African World,* ed. Robert A. Lystad. New York: Frederick A. Praeger, 1965, p. 393.

signs of serious pathogenic regression which may destroy whatever is left of the ego-defences. What Janet calls "abaissement du niveau mental" reaches the lowest level in Amos Tutuola where lycanthropic representations are the inventory of a disturbed psyche. Lévy-Bruhl states that to "the primitive mentality it is neither unprecedented nor absurd that an animal should appear in human shape, just as it is neither surprising nor terrifying to see a man assuming the outward appearance of an animal."[15] Tutuola's exposure to the "thrill of the wild blood" of the forefathers was evidently more than he had bargained for.

When the first white settlers appeared in Bechuanaland, the native Hereros, a proud and warlike tribe, realized the futility of resistance and aborted their wives' pregnancies, thus committing racial suicide. The aborigines in the wild expanses of Australia are rapidly dying out. In Northern Borneo, the primitive Muruts who roam the jungles as hunters have only recently established contact with civilization. Clinical and anthropological investigations indicate that they are fast declining in numbers. Simeons claims that individuals as well as ethnic groups whose growth is strongly hampered by a ruling power wielding terror, may in time be forced into a state of regression.[16] This is corroborated by Freud who in his treatment of a paranoid patient states that "the strikingly prominent features in the causation of paranoia, especially among males, are social humiliations and slight."[17] In this context, Tutuola's dilemma becomes psychologically transparent. Among contemporary African writers, he represents that singular minority for whom encounter with the colonial powers has contributed to a state of psychic regression. In his novel *Things Fall Apart*, Chinua Achebe speaks about the social pressures connected with the coming of the white man. The hero Okonkwo, who supposedly lived at the end of the 19th century, is a man of personal integrity. Through a tragic concatenation of events, he loses face in his clan and is exiled for seven years. Upon his return, he is confronted with a new situation. Missionaries have won over many of his tribesmen to the new faith. Okonkwo's clan is divided. In a surge of fury and hatred, the church is burnt to the ground. This, in turn, leads the District Commissioner to extort a collective fine from the village. Okonkwo can no longer face the desecration of all he has held dear and ends his own life. Chinua Achebe's hero is depicted here not as a coward who withdraws to a

---

15. Lucien Lévy-Bruhl, *The Soul of the Primitive*. London: George Allen Unwin Ltd., 1928, p. 42.

16. A. T. W. Simeons, *Ärger und Aufregung als Krankheitsursachen*. München: Wilhelm Goldman Verlag, 1962, pp. 186-88, passim.

17. Sigmund Freud, "On the Mechanism of Paranoia," op. cit., vol. XII, p. 60.

protective limbo. True, he commits suicide, but he dies this side of the bush, and his suicide is an active symbol of resistance. M. D. Faber in his article "Self Destruction in Oedipus Rex" differentiates between suicide due to guilt, and suicide due to frustration.[18] Okonkwo's suicide is redirected aggression which projects the entire psychic setting of the black native in a culture superimposed by the white man. Achebe's novel has mythopoeic quality. It is precisely in this respect that Tutuola's work falls short. For him, the experience of the bush turned into a universal encounter. Bush existence has a *raison d'être* of its own, one which is sharply removed from our normal communication, removed from its place in the general order of things. Once the psyche has succumbed to this way of life, the initiate is submerged in the flow of mana that distorts the last vestige of humanity which is left in him. Whether man takes on an animal shape for self-protection, or turns himself into a hunter in search of prey, as happens on practically every page of Tutuola's work, is no longer relevant in a world in which the phenomena of daily life are inflated by the magic spell of mana which rules supreme among the archaic representations of the psyche. Suffice it to state that wherever such representations occur in the analytical process, they are indicative of a psychotic, i.e. predominantly regressive syndrome. The first set of drawings contained in the book of *Psychopathology and Pictorial Expression* (vol. I)[19] shows the various stages of a catatonic condition with concomitant lycanthropic representations. The badly functioning ego sphere is apparent everywhere; in fact, it is contaminated by weird, archaic patterns.

The voice of Amos Tutuola on the contemporary African scene is a muffled voice. It is also the antithetical expression of a gifted man who seems to be unable to weather the psychological impact of his political and social situation. As modern Africans yearn to experience the "thrill of the wild blood" of their forefathers, as they surge ahead towards true independence, this yearning will surely be transformed into myth-making activity on an ever growing scale, a postulate most African intellectuals have come to understand. It is in this respect that the work of Amos Tutuola has fallen short. Of course, we do not know what we might expect of this writer in the years to come. However, even as he has taken us far afield in his flight into the bush, he represents that literary and psychological antithesis which is indigenous to modern Africa. It may be too early to fit Tutuola into a literary frame,

18. M. D. Faber, "Self-Destruction in Oedipus Rex," *American Imago*, 27, 1, (1970), 50, passim.

19. *Psychopathology and Pictorial Expression,* an International Iconographical Collection, ed. Sandoz, Ltd. Basel-New York: S. Karger, vols. I and II.

as it is too early to predict the final shape which the encounter of the African with the white man will assume. The struggle for self-identity can only result from meaningful myth-making activity. It is, however, in this context that the dimension of Amos Tutuola's voice will constitute a crucial psychological antithesis.

Language and Sources of Amos Tutuola

▼▼▼▼▼▼▼▼▼▼▼▼▼▼▼▼▼▼▼▼▼▼▼▼▼▼▼▼▼▼▼▼▼▼▼

A. AFOLAYAN

General Introduction

THE language of Tutuola has been the source of what may be regarded as lively literary politics. The two sides of the argument are well summed up by Gerald Moore in his paper[1] on Amos Tutuola.

The purpose of this paper is to examine this controversy and to suggest a new way of looking at the language and, via language, the material of Tutuola. What will be attempted is the application of stylistic method (the linguistic study of literature) to the study of Tutuola. Since this technique implies detailed examination of the text we shall limit ourselves to Tutuola's earliest novel, *The Palm-Wine Drinkard*. It is hoped that the outcome will be valid as a general statement for all six novels:[2] any of the novels would serve for an illustration of Tutuola's style because all of them show the same general linguistic characteristics. It must be noted,

---

[1] Ulli Beier (editor), *Introduction to African Literature*, Longmans, 1967, pp. 186–7; 'Many educated Nigerians, however, are embarrassed by the "mistakes" they find in Tutuola's English, which some of them seem to regard as an undeserved reflection on the African race in general. Their ears (being less sensitive than those of an Englishman to all that has become jaded and feeble in our langage), are likewise less able to recognize the vigour and freshness that Tutuola brings to it by his urgency of expression and refusal to be merely correct. A similar stage to this had been gone through even by the American reading public, though to them English was their native language, and the racy American vernacular, as opposed to "polite" English, did not become respectable till the enormous popularity of Mark Twain had made it so.'

[2] Amos Tutuola, *The Palm-Wine Drinkard*, Faber and Faber, 1952, paperback edition, 1962. Other novels include *My Life in the Bush of Ghosts; Simbi and the Satyr of the Dark Jungle; The Brave African Huntress; Feather Woman of the Jungle; Ajaiyi and His Inherited Poverty.*

Reprinted from Christopher Heywood, ed., *Perspectives on African Literature* (London and New York, 1971), pp. 49-63.

however, that the earliest is chosen because from the point of view of those who object to his language it is likely to be the most objectionable. After all, it is reasonable to expect that he would improve, however slightly, in his use of language as he gathered experience in the art of writing. In fact he does improve.

One final introductory word. It is necessary to state what model of stylistics we are adopting since, as in the case of general linguistics, there may be several models. The one adopted here is that being developed by Dr Ruqaiya Hasan within the general linguistic theory (the Systemic Model, a special version of Firth's System-structure model) developed by Professor M. A. K. Halliday, both of University College, London.

The Controversy

What is at stake here is the status of Tutuola's language. On the one hand there are people such as the educated Nigerians who for self-pride, nationalistic reasons or pre-conceived linguistic ideas, consider it as deserving no place in the Nigerian use of English, particularly for creative writing. To such people the language of Tutuola is too idiosyncratic and aberrant to be regarded as something representative of 'Nigerian English': it is an idiolect rather than an example of a recognizable brand (dialect or sub-dialect) of 'Nigerian English'. On the other hand there are others (such as Gerald Moore) who would like to class it as representing a dialect (or sub-dialect) of English comparable to 'the racy American vernacular'.

The suggestion of this paper is that neither of the two views is adequate but that the view that sees it as representing a sort of dialect or sub-dialect of English as used in Nigeria is nearer the mark. It is suggested that Tutuola's English can be regarded as a brand of 'Yoruba English' that can be assigned with a considerable degree of accuracy to a point on the scale of Yoruba English bilingualism.

Tutuola's English as 'Yoruba English'

The characterization of Tutuola's English as 'Yoruba English' brings us to the first of the two meanings of 'sources' adopted for the topic of this paper: the source of Tutuola's language and the source of his material. And I would like to suggest that there are two general notions of 'Yoruba English' relevant to the discussion of the source of the language.

Tutuola's English is 'Yoruba English' in the sense that it represents the expression of either Yoruba deep grammar with English surface grammar, or Yoruba systems and/or structures in English words. Though there will be no attempt to distinguish these two variants systematically in the following discussion, two examples of each will be given. The first type can be illustrated with the *italicised* part of 'but when I entered the room, *I met a bed* . . .' (p. 13).[3] '. . . I wanted him to *lead* me a short distance,' (p. 15). *Met* (from Yoruba *ba* as an alternative to *pade*) in the first example stands for *found*; and *lead* (from Yoruba *sin*) stands for *see off*. In both examples the two items of Tutuola have syntactic and lexical features different from similar items in Standard English, though the structures in which they occur are normal English ones. The second type can be illustrated with: 'He (death) asked me from *where did I come*?' (p. 13); and '*To my surprise was that when it was two o'clock* in the midnight, there I saw . . .' (p. 14) where the structures are not English but Yoruba.

In this sense of 'Yoruba English' we find that the major syntactic and lexical differences between English and Yoruba are reflected in Tutuola's English. Examples with comments are:

WITHIN SYSTEMS:

1 *Tense and aspect*: /they *saw* me *lied* down (p. 11) /we saw a male child *came* out (p. 31) /it *was* that day that I *saw* that snakes *were dancing* more than human-beings or other creatures (p. 84) /Since that day nobody *could see* the three fellows personally, but we *are* only *hearing* their names about in the world (p. 85) /

Comments: In the first two examples we find Tutuola, influenced by the lack of morphological inflections in Yoruba, attempting to mark the inflection in English with a logical regularity not found in the language. In the other examples we find Tutuola's equation of the Yoruba *n* morphological marker of progressive and habitual markers with the English '-ing' form.

2 *Transitivity*: /I *was* seriously *sat* down (p. 8) /he himself and his wife *were* narrowly *escaped* from that town (p. 16) /

Comments: These two examples reflect differences between the two languages with respect to passive constructions. Again, the lack of morphological inflections in Yoruba is important, and Tutuola's English here does not reflect Yoruba but his attempt to form new constructions on the analogy of other constructions such as *was . . . stopped, was . . . killed..*

---

[3] Amos Tutuola, *The Palm-Wine Drinkard*. All page references are to the paperback edition, Faber and Faber, 1962.

3 *Modality*: /Then I began to treat my wife there. In the day time, I *would go* around the bush, I *should kill* bush animals, after that I *should pick* edible fruits and we were feeding on them as found (p. 64) /

Comments: Here again we find the influence of the lack of morphological inflection in Yoruba and the correspondence of Yoruba *yo* (a future as well as a narrative or descriptive succession morpheme) to the four morphemes *shall, will, should,* and *would* in English.

WITHIN STRUCTURE:

1 *Sentence*: /But when he said this, *I asked how much did he want to borrow?* (p. 86) /When we completed the period of three months there for treatment my wife was very well, but as I was roaming about in that bush in search of animals, there I discovered an old cutlass which had had its wooden handle eaten off by insects, then I took it and coiled it round with the string of a palm-tree, then I sharpened it on a hard ground, because there was no stone, and cut a strong and slender stick and then bent it in form of a bow and sharpened many small sticks as arrows, so I was defending ourselves with it (page 64) /

Comments: The first example is a faithful translation of the Yoruba reported interrogative clause counterpart. And the second results from the conventional orthography in Yoruba which allows the stringing together of several sentences as a single orthographic sentence.

2 *Clause*: /he would only say that he would come, but *I would not see him come* (p. 98) /We reached a river *which crossed our way to pass* (p. 65) /

Comments: Again, the two clauses cited are a faithful rendering of the counterpart Yoruba clause structures which are not paralleled in English. Note also that the two examples can be cited as illustrating a complex verbal group structural type found in Yoruba but not in English.

3 *Groups*
  (a) *Nominal*: /So the man was on *our front* (p. 92) /*his both arms* were at *his both thighs, these both arms* were longer than his feet (p. 56) /
  (b) *Adverbial*: /We were travelling *inside bush to bush* (p. 91) / they called him and told him that today's work was to cut firewood *from the farm to the house* (p. 87) /
  (c) *Prepositional*: /had a full-bag of load *on* his front (p. 91) / Then I loaded the gun and fired *into* his stomach (p. 110) /

Comments: These examples also reflect Yoruba groups correctly. In the nominal group structure, the ordering in the two languages is different;

in the adverbial groups, elements that are not found together with some classes of verbs in English are found in Yoruba; and in the prepositional groups, one form in Yoruba may correspond to more than one in English (*si = to, towards, into* and *ni = on, in, at*).

UNUSUAL LEXICAL ITEMS

/ Unreturnable Heaven's town (p. 64), from Yoruba *ilu orun aremabo* / mixed = half x + half y as in *a mixed people, a mixed town* (p. 110, from Yoruba *adalu* = adulterated) / branch (p. 102, from Yoruba *ya = leave the way*; compare *bent* in '*we bent to another way*', p. 73) / remember = remind (p. 90, from the Yoruba item *ranti* (remember) which has comparable form with the item *ran . . . leti* (remind) / reserve-bush = forest reserve (p. 95, from the Yoruba item *igbo risafu* formed from the native *igbo* = forest (Tutuola's *bush*) and the borrowed English item *risafu* from *reserve*) / wake = raise from the dead (p. 113, *wake deads* from the Yoruba *ji* which means both *wake up* and *raise from the dead*) /

YORUBA IDIOMS AND PROVERBS

/ When I put it on my head it was just *like a dead body of a man*, it was very heavy, but I could carry it easily (p. 92) / So when we thought that we had never seen a tree with hands and talking *in our life* (p. 66) /

WORDY AND REPETITIVE STYLE ARISING FROM THE TRANSLATION OF YORUBA INTO ENGLISH

The apparent wordy and repetitive style of original Yoruba seems to arise from the need to be clear, unambiguous, and explicit whereas the language lacks any morphological inflections and there is only one form of the third person singular pronoun in the language (Yoruba *o = he, she, it*) / This was how I brought out Death to the old man who told me to go and bring him before he (old man) would tell me whereabouts my palm-wine tapster was that I was looking for before I reached that town and went to the old man (p. 16) / So after he had jumped very far away (luckily, I was there when he was doing all these things, and I saw the place that he threw both leaves separately) then I changed myself to a man as before, I went to the place that he threw both leaves, then I picked them up and went home at once (p. 30).

197

In this sense of 'Yoruba English'[4] there are three other recognizable secondary sources of Tutuola's English. These are psycholinguistic, sociolinguistic, and pedagogical. The psycholinguistic problems relate to the psychological aspects of second language acquisition and usage, such as matters relating to translation and the use of analogy. These processes are at work in some of the examples already cited: for instance, *saw . . . lied* in he *saw me lied, meet* (= found), *a various bush* (from *Igbo oniruru* = forest various), *which crossed our way to pass* (from *ti o re ona was koja*). Other examples are *when the eyes of all the human-beings were on our knees* (p. 75), *a pig in a bag* (p. 92, which involves possibly a double process of translation, first of the idiom from English to Yoruba and then back to English), *patentees* (= patients p. 69, on the analogy of 'absent – absentees'), *barb* (= cut hair, p. 87, a back-formation from *barber*) and *deads* or *alives* (p. 101, on the analogy of English plurals such as *white - whites*. The sociolinguistic source subsumes two separate sub-sources: tradition of English usage in the community which accounts, for example, for the lexical item *palm-wine*; and the sociological basis of certain usages such as the use of *they* for only one person who is of a higher social status. The pedagogical source accounts for elementary grammatical mistakes in his English which a sounder education in English would have removed. Within the wider context of Nigerian English this source accounts for deviations arising from an inadequate teaching programme. Such are the deviations involving the use of the modals.

Tutuola's English is 'Yoruba English' in the sense that it is representative of the English of the Yoruba users at a point on the scale of bilingualism.

There are two main points to be made here. Judging from Yoruba secondary school (grammar and modern) pupils' texts examined and analysed, it appears that although Tutuola's language in many ways represents his own inimitable personal style (see, for example, p. 92), his English is that of the Yoruba user, not of the average educated user but of generally the user with post-primary education at approximately the level of present-day Secondary Class Four. More precisely, in the

[4] In passing it must be mentioned that this view of 'Yoruba English' makes Tutuola's English have a two-sided interest. Firstly it throws considerable light on areas of the linguistics of Yoruba still in need of attention; for example, the demarcation of linguistic units, particularly orthographic units of the sentence, the clause, and the word. Secondly it strongly suggests the sort of linguistic problems that Yoruba learners and users of English may have in the process of becoming Yoruba-English bilinguals.

earliest novel it is the English user with about Secondary Class Two education whereas, in the latest novel it is the user with about Secondary Class Four education. Examples of sentences taken at random from such texts[5] are:

/When I got home I had that one of my best brother at Ibadan had dead in the accident, then I said what a scornful was this morning and I wept, wept, wept and wept then he was buried and this morning I will never forget it till the end of my life / Some of my classmates began to ask that what is happening to me / He said that why couldn't I come / The riot started about nine of the clock to nearly eleven of clock / We were assembled at the hall for morning prayer / In this case women are specialized in the bath of babies / A morning at school was if we open in the school at morning we shall pray / I did not late to school / He did not proud / He said that we should let us go / I had no *amount* that day (= money) / The teacher we are suppose to teach by we are not hearing her words / When I reached our school I met our class girls / When I got home I met his absence[6] / Some carpenter they will be helping us to do our sits / He gave us bush which we can never finish in five minutes / The Principal said that 'Do not beg me' I will not hear your begging / They had *medicine* (= Tutuola's *juju*) of creating themselves into another form like – men, women, etc. / What a melodious morning that I have at school one morning ... Is melodious because I ate ... / We are preparing hardly for our qualifying examination / I stayed lonely because I did not know any girl /

Though the examples are given without any comments on any particular element, item, or structure, it seems fair to suggest that anyone familiar with Tutuola will feel on familiar ground as he reads through them.

Secondly, I would like to suggest that by virtue of being a type of 'Yoruba English' Tutuola's English is also a kind of 'Nigerian English'. Though there are factors that inevitably make for differences in English as found in various parts of Nigeria, there are some equally important and effective standardizing factors that make the English used in Nigeria approximate to a general type. The principal causes of divergence are threefold. There are many different Nigerian languages and each interferes in its own way with the English used within its own speech community.

[5] The texts from which these examples are taken were collected by H. L. B. Moody and were made available to the present writer by the English Teaching Information Centre of the British Council in London.

[6] *Met his absence* seems to be a common usage in Nigeria and may be seen as reflecting a common tradition in the use of English in the entire country.

Again, there are great differences in educational programmes and practices in the various parts of the country. For example, in the recent past the six states of the North had comparatively fewer schools than the West, but many of the learners in the Northern schools had contact with teachers who were native speakers of English; whereas learners in the West hardly ever had such contacts. Finally Nigerian linguistic situations vary from one area to another. For example the people of the West generally speak only one mother tongue, Yoruba, whereas there are many different mother tongues in the Mid-West. As a result English is more widely used as a lingua franca in the Mid-West than among the people of the West. Since proficiency in a language is proportionate to the speaker's practice in it, the degree of proficiency in the English language differs between the two states.

Nevertheless the factors of standardization and stability have been generally more powerful than those of divergence. There has been considerable interaction among the various peoples of Nigeria. As the different peoples joined the same political party or trading company, or the civil service, or sat together on committees and discussed or debated together, they have tended to acquire a common model of intelligible English. This tendency has been helped by the influence of national educational agencies – the earliest teacher-training colleges, national secondary schools, the West African Examinations Council, and the universities. All these have helped to build up a tradition of correctness in English usage throughout the country. Moreover, the many languages of the country are in fact not so many in terms of families. For example, most of those of the South belong to the Kwa group. The influence of the mother tongues on the second language (English) is therefore less divergent than may be supposed. As a result of all these stabilizing factors, it seems fair to say that the English of the Yoruba users is typical of 'Nigerian English'. And as long as Tutuola's English is 'Yoruba English', it is also 'Nigerian English'.

Implications for the Initial Argument

This brings us to the consideration of the controversy with which we began. From what has been said above it can be seen why neither of the two views is adequate. It is true that Tutuola's English represents a brand of 'Nigerian English'. But whether we call it 'Nigerian' or 'Yoruba' English, it is not an 'educated' usage. It may be that Tutuola's language is implicitly equated with a dialect or even more precisely, a register, of

English when Gerald Moore likens it to 'the racy American vernacular'. But in this case Tutuola's language is really a temporary intermediate point in the bilingual evolution of a dialect – the dialect being the rather undefined abstraction 'Nigerian English' or at the least 'Yoruba English'.

This leads us to the other side of this question of equating Tutuola's language with 'the racy American vernacular'. While the literary users of the latter such as Mark Twain are themselves proficient users of Standard American English and use the racy style for particular realistic documentary literary effects, Tutuola is using the only 'English language' he knows all the time and there is no doubt that the more he approximates to Standard English in his acquisition of the language, the more standard his language will be at a later stage. This strong evolutionary element in his language is what differentiates him from an American writer, if there were any, who speaks and writes only 'the racy American vernacular'. Such an American writer is using a dialect which is also a register of English, but Tutuola is not.

The Source of Tutuola's Material

In the study of literary texts with the stylistic approach adopted here, there are two possible routes in establishing an axis of verification of the meaning of the text: internal and external. The internal route involves the examination of the linguistic execution of the text, the reference of the language to the context, and then the reference of the context to the situation. A problem arises when the literary text, for example, has no historical background and consequently the situation is not directly obtainable. What is to be done in such a case where there is no transparent thesis is to abstract the literary context from the text in order to provide an inferred situation. And the external route involves the studying of a literary text by going through an examination of the writer and his social setting. Though either or both routes may be taken in the study of a literary text, depending on the conditions and circumstances of the text, in this discussion we shall concentrate more on the internal: this is consistent with the rest of the paper. And this means that we shall be concentrating on only the two-sided central concern of stylistics: linguistic execution and textual contextualization. In doing this we shall for the present limit ourselves to lexical items.

As the starting point we offer three sets of items:

(*a*) cowries (p. 7), palm-trees (p. 7), palm-wine tapping (p. 7), keg (p. 7), yam garden (p. 12), fuel woods (p. 13), bush animals (p. 13), bull-frog (p. 22), lizard (p. 26), termites (p. 44), owner of the market (p. 44), palace (p. 45), loads (p. 64), fruits (p. 64), net (p. 26), trap (p. 76), pawn (p. 85), bell-ringers (p. 123), fowls, kolas, palm-oil, bitter kolas, pot (p. 124).

(b) parlour (p. 8), two thousand pounds (p. 18), petrol drums (p. 22), miles (p. 26), travel by air (p. 40), bombs (p. 45), photographer (p. 65), hall, one million pounds, orchestra, musician, tappers, technicolour (p. 68), kitchen (p. 69), hospital (p. 69), waiter (p. 69), clock (p. 69), umbrella (p. 79), football field (p. 89), debit collector (p. 111), jack-knife (p. 112).

(c) juju (p. 9), wraith-island (p. 46), spirit of Prey (p. 54), God (p. 54), Unreturnable Heaven's Town (p. 57), Wizard (p. 113), Dead's Town (p. 118).

Following the internal route from the linguistic item to the context and then to the situation, we can suggest that the subject matter of Amos Tutuola's novels is Yoruba oral literature set in a contemporary Yoruba community. The first set of items points to an earlier, though partly contemporary, Yoruba rural agricultural economy where money is in the form of cowries, where palm-wine tapping is an industry for men, where gourds (kegs) serve as measurement standards, and where credit facilities could be based on a system of domestic and agricultural service (pawn). The second set of items points to the contemporary emergence of a more modern, though in this instance greatly exaggerated, economy of the Yoruba community which could be symbolized by the organizational set-up of the Faithful Mother's household. It is interesting to note that in the spirit of the exaggerated view of contemporary modernity, Tutuola tells us that the Faithful Mother decorated her hall with about one million pounds (the full value of which is generally lost to the average literate Nigerian who sees it only representing the figure one followed by six zeroes). It is also interesting to note that the hall itself in which 'there were many images and our own too were in the centre' reminds one of a modern Nigerian museum, or more precisely a place like Madame Tussaud's in London. Finally the third set of items which provide the dominant atmosphere of the novel represents the religious and magical sentiments and beliefs of the Yoruba world (real and imaginary) of gods and people with an all pervading belief in myths, mysteries, and spirits. Thus the lexical evidence points to the conclusion that the contemporary Yoruba community and its oral traditional literature constitute the source of Tutuola's material. Of course, there is no doubt that the material has elements of universal appeal; for example, the popularity of the rich man as contrasted with the friendlessness of the poor one (p. 8), and the attraction of the 'complete gentleman' (p. 25).

There are three questions concerning Tutuola's use of Yoruba oral traditional literature – what are the elements of traditional literature in his novels, how does he come by them, and how does he use them? These are questions which are central to the external route of our approach but it is necessary to show the direction of their answers here.

There are three different dimensions of the external route: the author, the reader, and time and space. On the first dimension the relevant importance of the author's biography is considered. Here care is taken not to over-emphasize the author's life: 'The style is the man' is only true in part and a distinction should be made between the author's opinion concerning a question and the opinion concerning the question found in the author's work. On the second dimension the particulars of the intended readership of the work are considered. In particular this dimension is important in assessing the language and the particular register of it adopted by the author. The third dimension subsumes all aspects of Abiola Irele's 'sociological approach' and more: it is more like what Daniel Izevbaye calls the 'approach of complementarity'. Here the aspects of the author as a human being in a society, as being conditioned by a certain language norm, and as being conditioned by a certain literary norm, are considered. And it is in the light of the consideration of these three dimensions that the following brief answers are given to the three questions earlier asked. In answer to the first question we say that the major stories of *The Palm-Wine Drinkard* belong to Yoruba folklore. Such are the stories of the 'Complete Gentleman' (pp. 18 ff), 'Not too small' (pp. 40 ff) and the 'Çause of the Famine' (pp. 118 ff). These three stories respectively represent[7] the common stories *Oloko sin lehin mi* (Hoe-seller get back), *Obalaran be we* (Obalaran asked for help), and *Ile ja oun Olorun* (Land and sky-dweller fought). Besides there is perhaps little doubt that the entire plot of the novel – the journey of the drinkard to heaven to see his palm-wine tapster, and his return to his town – is itself built round the common story of an aggrieved person going to heaven to seek the help of a beloved dead relation and returning with a valuable possession.

Turning to the second question we say that Tutuola came by his material through two channels. Like any other Yoruba man of his age,

7. See next page.

he would as a child have heard many of the stories as a traditional evening family pastime. It should be noted too that there has been a tradition of telling the stories over Radio Nigeria, first by the late D. O. Alabi, and more recently by Tunji Ojo. Besides, there is little doubt he read some of the stories. There are some local collections of such stories (one of which collected by S. A. Adebagbo is known to the present writer), published by the local press and circulated locally. Another source likely to have influenced Tutuola is Fagunwa in his novels. For example, the story of the half-bodied baby (*The Palm-Wine Drinkard*, pp. 35 ff) could have been influenced by Fagunwa's story of Ajantala[8] which has a similar type of

[7] Here is a summary of a version of the songs that usually form parts of the narration of the three stories: each gives the basic plot of the story:

(a)
Oloko			*sin*	*Oloko*		*sin*	*lehin*		*mi*
hoe-seller			get back	hoe-seller		get back	behind		me
Bi	*o*	*o*	*ba*	*sin*	*o*	*o*	*dodo*	*kan*	*aro*
If	you	do	not	get back	you	will	get	to an	indigo river
Bi	*o*	*o*	*ba*	*sin*	*o*	*o*	*dodo*	*kan*	*eje*
If	you	do	not	get back	you	will	get	to a blood	river

(b)
Obalaran	*be*		*we*	
Obalaran	asked		for help	
O	*be*	*kini*	*eye*	
He	begged	this-type	of bird	
O	*be*	*kini*	*eye*	
He	begged	that-type	of bird	
O	*doun*		*kinkin*	*si*
He	left out him the 'kinkin'			bird
Ki	*koriko*	*dide*		
Let	the weed	rise up		
Ki	*eruwa*	*dide*		
Let the	elephant-grass	rise up		
Ki	*a*	*rele*	*wa*	
Let	us	go to	our home	

(c)
Ile	*ja*	*oun*	*Olorun*		
Land and sky-owner			quarrelled		
Ni tori	*eku*	*emo*	*kan*		
Because	of an	emo	rat		
Olorun	*l'oun*	*l'egbon*			
Sky-owner	claimed	seniority			
Ile	*loun*	*le gbon*			
Land	claimed	seniority			
Olorun	*binu*	*o*	*rele*		
Sky-owner	angrily	returned home			
Ojo	*ko*	*ko*	*ro*	*mo*	...
Rain	refused	to	fall ... disasters leading to famine followed		

[8] D. O. Fagunwa, *Ogboju Ode ninu Igbo Irunmale*, Nelson, 1950, p. 75.

hero and episodes. Again there is little doubt that the plot of Fagunwa's novel may have influenced the plot of Tutuola's later novels, particularly *Feather Woman of the Jungle*. But this question of Tutuola's indebtedness to Fagunwa should not be carried too far: both draw from the same source which has a traditional plot. A comparison (in a table) of the plots of Tutuola's and Fagunwa's stories is revealing:

Tutuola's story of the half-bodied baby	*Fagunwa's story of Ajantala*
1 A child that rose from the ashes of a house burnt down by the hero as the hero's wife looked for her trinkets in the ashes	1 A child born by a woman whose story is narrated by a person other than the hero (the story-teller is Iragbeje but the hero is Akara-ogun)
2 A miraculous half-bodied child	2 A miraculous beautiful child
3 Performed miraculous acts ; talked immediately after appearance, ate up all food available, kept hero and hero's wife hungry and made them to carry him, carried to a part of the bush where music was playing	3 Performed miraculous acts ; talked immediately after birth, washed and fed himself, won game of skill six times consecutively, killed six chickens, surprised brother's mouth got torn, fought all sorts of people including the *babalawo*
4 Was left in the bush with drum, song and dance.	4 Was left in the forest by mother
	5 Disrupted the company of the goat, the hyena, the leopard, the lion and the elephant and dispersed them to their present natural habitat.
	6 Was recalled to heaven by God.

The answer to the third question has two parts. Tutuola not only tells the story in the traditional way but also does so in his own personal manner. It appears that the features of the monomyth in his plot pointed out by Gerald Moore derive from the traditional plot of the stories in Yoruba folklore. It should be noted, for example, that the story of the drinkard's wife is in the tradition of the cycle of the heroic monomyth and, as already stated, the basic plot of her going with an unknown handsome man, her sufferings and her final rescue is traditional. An illustration outside Tutuola is a story about a woman who is the second wife of a man. This woman had to go into the bed of an ocean to recover the wooden spoon of the elder wife carried away by a flood (the story in Yoruba is entitled *Igbako orogun mi da?* = Where is the wooden spoon of the other wife of my husband?). Similarly in telling his individual stories Tutuola always paints the traditional scenes in detail. But the way he links these individual stories together to form a single super-story derives from his own imaginative genius, as can be seen from the summary of the story of the half-bodied baby given earlier. Thus Tutuola is to be seen not only as a man with 'great visionary power and imaginative intensity' (Gerald Moore) but also as a very keen and perceptive listener and an excellent reporter. Perhaps he is more of the latter and that is why some people fail to see the former in him.

Final Remarks

When the material is related to the language it seems reasonable to suggest that Tutuola first organizes his Yoruba material in his Yoruba mother tongue and then expresses the organized, though not necessarily vocalized or visually expressed, material in English. This means that some sort of translation (at least psychic) of literature takes place in the process of producing Tutuola's novels. This means that a lot of the 'vigour and freshness' Gerald Moore and others see in Tutuola's language derives from his original Yoruba and the subsequent interplay between the two languages, Yoruba and English and not so much from Tutuola's 'refusal to be merely correct'. One may even suggest that Tutuola thinks that he is correct when he writes.

We have already noted that Tutuola's English largely represents the differences between the two languages, Yoruba and English. It remains for us to suggest that his English represents the similarity between the two languages too. The deep grammars of the two languages are generally similar and even their basic sentence patterns are very largely similar, particularly at the primary degree of delicacy.

Examples:

1 *Mo*	*lo*	*lana*
I	go/went	yesterday

2 | *Mo* | *rı* | *Ojo* |
| I | see/saw | Ojo |

3 a. *Ode*   *pa*   *kiniun*
      Hunter   kill   lion
   b. *Kiniun*   *pa*   *ode*
      Lion   kill   hunter

4 | *Nigbati* | *o* | *sore* | *tan* | *o* | *jade* |
| When | he | talks | finish | he | went out |

5 | *Tani* | *soro* | | *lana?* |
| Who | speak/spoke | | yesterday? |

6 | *Bawo* | *ni* | *e* | *wa* |
| How | is | you are | = How are you? |

7 | *Sare!* | *Fo!* |
| Run! | Jump! |

8 | *So* | *omi* | *di* | *tutu* |
| Turn | water | into | cold |

9 | *O* | *se* | *ise* | *keji* | *daradar* |
| He | did | work | second | well = He did the second work well |

10 | *Emi* | *ko* | *lo* |
| I | not | go = I do/did not go |

From the fact that Tutuola's language is based upon basic similarities between the two languages we may also suggest that the English language is a source of his language and that the language derives from his own degree of competence in English. But there is another side to this question of his competence in English. He has also learnt English. This means that the areas of similarity between the two languages are areas of facilitation and what he ultimately acquires and uses are properties of normal English. Thus we find normal English sentences or clauses on pages of his novels.

Examples:

(1) I was drinking palm-wine from morning till night and from night till morning (p. 7).

(2) Then I replied 'I am still alive and I am not a dead man' (p. 12).

207

One quick final word. As Sapir points out:

> Literature moves in language as a medium, but that medium comprises two layers, the latent content of language – our intuitive record of experience – and the particular conformation of a given language – the specific how of our record of experience. Literature that draws its sustenance mainly – never entirely – from the lower level . . . is translatable without too great a loss of character. If it moves in the upper rather than in the lower level . . . it is as good as untranslatable.[9]

This means that if our suggestion that the production of Tutuola's novels involves some sort of translation has any validity, then there must be not only some loss of character in the process but also some degree of lack of intelligibility for his non-Yoruba-speaking readers, largely because of the Yoruba features, elements, and structures in his English. And this means that Tutuola may not be fully comprehensible to any but a Yoruba-English bilingual, particularly the one who is a native speaker of Yoruba.

Postcript

It may be necessary to underscore the implications of this paper for African writing in English or even, more generally, the writing or the study of literature in an African second language situation. Three such implications may be pointed out. First, the paper emphasizes that ironically language has been not only what recommends Tutuola to the readers whose mother tongue is English but also a barrier to his acceptance by his own people. Secondly, it emphasizes that the Nigerian readers' failure to appreciate Tutuola largely arises from their own inadequate linguistic awareness and incompetent knowledge of the theory, principles, and practice of literary art. And finally, since the general failure on the part of the Nigerian students to perceive the literary significance of Tutuola may be seen as representative of the African students' failure to perceive literature in general, there is the implication that if the present situation of failure is to be changed for the better it is time the various language and literature courses were re-examined with the aim of redressing the balance in order to give the African students the opportunity to appreciate and enjoy literature at first hand. A well-balanced blend of the sociological, psychological, literary, and linguistic approaches is needed in an African situation.

[9] E. Sapir, *Language: an Introduction to the Study of Speech*, Harcourt, 1921, p. 223.

THE NARRATIVE AND INTENSIVE CONTINUITY: *THE PALM-WINE DRINKARD*

Robert P. Armstrong

INTRODUCTORY NOTE   The following is the greatest part of a chapter from my book *The Affecting Presence: An Essay in Humanistic Anthropology*, to be published by the University of Illinois Press. In this book I am concerned to establish feeling as a separate, coeval, and considerable part of human culture, a part whose expressed existence is in large part to be found in works of art, which I call affecting presences. I use the word "presence" because the work of art has as its critical and definitive features many of the same characteristics as a person. I assert what is patently true, that the existence of the affecting presence is to be perceived in terms of time and space *emotionally* executed through the media proper to them (thus, for example, volume for space and movement for time) and that these media are exploited to create discrete works in *forms,* and the forms are music, sculpture, narrative, and so forth.

The universe of time is to be conceived of as being asserted by means of either continuity or discontinuity, and that of space through either extension or intension. I develop the point that the traditional mode of affecting *being* for the Yoruba is by means of a space-time universe that is intensive and continuous. After showing how intension and continuity characterize a spatial art, sculpture, I proceed to the following discussion of narrative as a time art.

All the affecting forms in my view constitute a system in that they are related one to the other in the relationship of identity, since they all bring into concrete existence forms actualizing an affecting life common to the culture. The means by which physical works incarnate feeling I call

Reprinted from *Research in African Literatures*, 1, 1 (1970), 9-34. A slightly different version of the same essay appears in Armstrong's *The Affecting Presence: An Essay in Humanistic Anthropology* (Urbana, 1971) pp. 137-73.

metaphor, and the respects in which the identical affecting view of time and space are incorporated into works I view equivalents of one another. Thus the means Tutuola uses to achieve intensive continuity in his work are similetically equivalent to the means by which a carver achieves the incarnation of the same mode in his figures. The following is a detailed study of these means in Tutuola.

I have elected to work with *The Palm-Wine Drinkard*-kind of folk-fantasy by Amos Tutuola[1] rather than with the novels of Wole Soyinka or T. M. Aluko for the simple reason that the novel is an imported phenomenon. Its mere exercise interposes a certain distance between practitioner and tradition, such that it becomes the more difficult to see the traditional affecting principle at work in an alien form because that form is exotic and learned, and its very exercise implies a further degree of acculturation. At the very least one cannot perceive the principle's effects with the same sharpness of focus one can have in the case of the more traditional sub-forms (if narrative is the form, then "novel" and "short story" are to be seen as sub-forms).

Prior to analysis, however, it is necessary for us to consider the media which comprise narrative, discussing them in general, and indicating the respects in which we should expect continuity and discontinuity, intension and extension to be expressed in these media. The reader will recall that these media are situationality, language, relationality, and experience. Each of these media is to be seen as having both synchronic and diachronic dimensions existing both in instantaneity and in sequentiality.

Situationality
Situationality is the dimension of human activity which most readily comes to one's mind when he thinks of narrative, for when one is asked what a given narrative is "about" and proceeds to recount the plot he is giving a synopsis of that narrative medium. Situation is composed of actor, action, motivation, sense detail, and psychological detail, and it exists as readily in the internal world of the individual actor as it does interpersonally. The properties of situation are inextricably related one to the other in specific times and places and for specific reasons by virtue of the simple fact that there must be a logic—an entailment, a follow-through—about human action if it is not to be chaotic. There is a decreasing entropy of action with every action committed. Granting a situation where actor and action have no predictable or reasonable relationship one to the other, where motivation is irrelevant to action and to actor, and

where sense and psychological details are either not significant or counter-significant to each of the other properties, it is doubtful whether meaningful narrative could exist. I am bearing in mind here the fact that disjunctions among the properties may be used for special effect, and indeed that surrealistic works may exist in which other logics prevail, such as the hidden logic of relationships among dream symbols. But in the first instance, such disjuncture does not characterize the total work, and in the second *a* logic does prevail, even if it is not the daily logic of fully disclosed cause and effect.

Situation is divisible into *acts,* which are identifiable, synchronic units constituting in their totality the medium of situationality in a given work. More specifically, an act is defined in terms of all the properties of situation, insofar as they are to be found in the span of situation under consideration, which conspire together to constitute an identifiable phase in the diachronic progression of the narrative, An act is that bit about which it can be asserted that at a given time and in a given place such and such an event of dramatic import occurred.

Concerning the properties of situation, it is clear that there are, in narrative, instances in which the distinction between sense detail and psychological detail would appear to be less than clear. It is readily apparent that sense detail can be used for the purposes of providing psychological information, as when it is used to create mood or when it comes to have significant or symbolic value representing or conveying something of the state of mind of one of the actors. For the purposes of analysis, however, it would seem best to take such details as they are given rather than as they are intended. Sense and psychological details may be used to give extension to a synchronic act, or indeed to restrict it, thus making the act intensive, much as the variously voiced instruments of a symphony orchestra may be used in wide or narrow range in order to extend or to restrict the synchronic structures of a given musical composition. Sense detail and psychological detail also contribute to the establishment of the durational existence of a work by maintaining continuity of scene and mood.

The psychological detail which is used to create the emotional milieu of a work, as sense detail creates its physical world, is to be distinguished from the psychological elements of a character adduced to give depth—or not adduced, thus producing shallowness—and believability to the motivation which links together actor and action in any given act and indeed in any given sequence of acts. Motivation may be explicit or implicit, simple or complex, obvious or subtle, resident in present situation or in situations past or yet to come, and it may be rooted in one's self, in another, or in the interests of some event quite removed from either. Motivation is the seed of action, expressed or repressed, and as it constitutes the license for action, so, when it is believable, does it establish action's historicity and authenticity. Finally, for the properties of situation, there is little that need be said of actor and action since these properties would appear to be self-explanatory.

Language

Language is the second medium of narrative, and it has several properties —denotation, connotation, images, irony, wit, paradox, ambiguity, rhythm, contrast, alliteration, sound, and the whole range of rhetorical devices which may be used to give fabric, metre, balance, and affect to the narrative—all these, of course, in addition to the common properties of language: tense, mood, voice, and case. Primarily the affecting properties of language are useful in creating range of act, and thus they are chiefly of concern in the consideration of the problem of intensionality/extensionality. But it is obvious that in their duration and frequency they are of relevance also in the consideration of continuity/discontinuity, such that any property or indeed any group of properties consistently employed constitutes an added stratum of durationality.

Relationality

By relationality I mean to designate synchronic relationships among components of acts as well as the durational ones among acts in sequence. In both cases one is concerned with the consideration of either integration, by which one means that the properties of situation and of language are functionally or causally—in any event, meaningfully—related one to the other, or disintegration. It is characteristic of the continuous work that consequentiality characterizes the relationships among acts and larger patterns of acts, but such dependency does not characterize such relationships although, obviously, it must at the very least govern the relationships among the constituent elements comprising an act.

Experience

With respect to the medium of experience, one expects that it will tend to be more or less implicit and centripital in the intensive work and the opposite in the extensive one; that a constant state of evolving experience will characterize the continuous while a succession of estates of experience, doubtless unrelated, will characterize the discontinuous. Experience, one will recall, is that flush of pertinence that characterizes an affecting presence and makes it valuable, intimate, and believed.

Modelling

Modelling, which is not of course an affecting medium but is nonetheless a critical factor in considering the style of a people, will be either high or low, with the former leading to fully individuated characters and situations developed with marked credibility, and the latter leading to the characters' being portrayed as types, with their actions lacking something of both credibility and distinctiveness. Diachronically, in the case of high modelling, one sees characters develop and believes their change. This is less notably the case in low modelling. High synchronic modeling we would expect to characterize extensionality, and high diachronic modelling continuity. Conversely, low synchronic modelling would be equivalent to intensionality and low diachronic modelling to discontinuity.

It will be useful to present in schematic survey the characteristics of each of the media in intensionality and extensionality, in continuity and discontinuity.

There is, it must be noted, a difference between competence and lack of it, so that there is in effect excellence or failure in the practice of narrative, satisfaction or defect in the use of the media and their properties. Thus when best executed the intensional character is subtle, but when less well realized he is shallow and unbelievable. Similarly the extensional character at his best is complex and exciting, while at his worst he is disorganized, bombastic, hollow. The complexity of action or of language that characterizes the extensional is at best rich, and at worst rococo. The outward-tending, the reaching, in defect becomes mere disorganization; the intending, cramped; the subtle, shallow; the continuous, tiresome; and the discontinuous, chaotic.

As is sometimes true of models, they can reflect more entities than can in reality be readily found to exist. This is particularly the case with the question of continuity and discontinuity as it relates to narrative. This is to say that in point of actual fact, narrative existing in language and language being characterized by certain demands of consecutivity, absolute discontinuity would not be possible. Taken at the level of the smallest meaningful isolable unit—the act—it is inconceivable that either one of the only two possibilities of discontinuity would exist; namely, either that each act would be so explicitly defined and executed in such a way as to

213

| | SYNCHRONIC | |
	Intensionality	*Extensionality*
1. SITUATIONALITY *Sense detail*	There is an economy and close relevance to such sense detail as is included.	There is a richness to sense detail and it may or may not be tightly integrated into the structure of act.
Psychological detail	There is an economy and close relevance to such psychological detail as is included.	There is a richness to psychological detail and such detail may or may not be tightly integrated into the structure of act.
Motivation	Motivation is spare, pertinent, and closely integrated.	Motivation is elaborately conceived and intricately extended to the periphery of the act.
Action	Action is characterized by a strong focus, is definite and clear.	Action is complex, ranging, implicative.
Actor	The actor is well defined, executed with strong, clearly drawn lines.	The actor is richly drawn with a wealth of evocation, variety of motivation, complexity of personality (or simple personality completely, complexly shown).
2. RELATIONALITY	A narrow range of kinds of relationships among components of situation and other affecting media.	A wide range of kinds of relationships among components of situation and other affecting media.
3. LANGUAGE	Economical and rigorously pertinent use of images and other affecting properties of language so that the act is a tightly integrated synchronic event. Images tend to restrain the attention and focus the feeling.	Wide, indeed even lavish, use of images and other affecting properties of language so that act is a ranging affecting structure. Images are richly connotative and suggestive. Indefiniteness rules and implication and suggestion are vastly important.

DIACHRONIC

Continuity*	Discontinuity
Sense detail is closely controlled diachronically with attention to warp, and woof being either lavish (extensive) or restrained (intensive).	Sense detail shows little evidence of supporting any notion of through-development.
Psychological detail is closely controlled and the development of the psychological dimensions of the work (mood) are evolutionary.	Psychological detail is loosely controlled. There is no sense of careful, evolutionary development of successive psychological details.
Motivation is rigorously consequential and evolutionary.	Motivation is loosely consequential, or perhaps not consequential at all.
Action is carefully consequential and evolutionary.	Action is sequential and tends to interrupt forward movement.
The actor is developed in a carefully evolutionary fashion, such that all acts are logically derivable from previous conditions or referrable to future ones.	The actor is loosely evolutionary or not evolutionary at all. He is seen stroboscopically rather than realistically through causal time.
Temporal integration is tight and the principle of diachronic development is consequentiality. In the event of an episodic work, where sequentiality is apt to characterize the work, overall evidences of integrative relationality will occur.	There is a sense of disjuncture among the parts such that sequentiality characterizes the work. The discontinuous episodic is not clearly overridden by larger, integrative plans.
Carefully integrative patterns of use of images and other affecting properties of language.	A disregard for the temporal *patterning* of images and other affecting properties of language.

* Continuity by means of a dense frequency of discrete "atoms" poses different considerations. See text.

focus affective attention upon those acts themselves, at the expense of *before* and *after,* or that sequentiality would be handled in such a way that no act would follow from any other act. As we shall see when we come to consider *The Palm-Wine Drinkard*, this argument has special relevance to the episodic work, the existence of which would be made problematic under the mode of continuity. It is probably the case that there is an *intention* toward continuity and an *intention* toward discontinuity which are made manifest in the work. If this is true then it is in this area that we must search for continuity and for discontinuity. Once again, the discussion of Tutuola's work will make clear the evidences of such intentions in the case of a work which is episodic yet continuous, if not in terms of action, at least in other affecting media and their properties.

Amos Tutuola's *The Palm-Wine Drinkard* is one of those marvellous works of the human imagination which, rich with fancy, goes simply and directly to the heart of a perennial and profound human concern, that about the nature of the estate of being dead. It is therefore, although inevitably and inextricably involved with Tutuola's being Yoruba, equally inevitably and inextricably bound to the fact pure and simple of his being a man. Thus it is necessarily the case that the impact of much of what he writes is supracultural. It is, in a word, of the nature of that special and very basic level of pertinence which one calls Myth. I capitalize the term in order to distinuish it from that "myth" which the anthropologist sees culturally, a belief whose function is to "validate" action.

In *The Palm-Wine Drinkard* Tutuola relates the adventures of a first-person narrator whose palm-wine tapster has fallen from a tree while tapping palm-wine and been killed. The victim of a prodigious appetite for palm-wine and a generous host who is deserted by his friends once he can no longer supply them with the hospitality to which they have become accustomed from him, he sets off to find his palm-wine tapster.

> When I saw that there was no palm-wine for me again, and nobody could tap it for me, then I thought within myself that old people were saying that the whole people who had died in this world, did not go to heaven directly, but they were living in one place somewhere in this world. So that I said that I would find out where my palm-wine tapster who had died was. (p. 9)

This is not a "descent to the underworld" only because there is no underworld. The Town of the Deads is in the same world as the towns of the living. But in spirit, the mythic formula obtains, for the way to the town of the deads is fraught with harrowing escapes from monsters who would destroy the narrator and, eventually, the wife whom he acquires in one of his earliest experiences, that with the "incomplete gentleman." There is no river Styx for him to cross, although it must be noted that at the end of his odyssey the narrator encounters the last monsters in a mountain just across a river, but seven miles from his own village. The bush in which the Deads' Town is located (years away from his own village) is, there can be little doubt, raised to the power of Myth. But this radically generalizing action comes perhaps more easily to the Yoruba than to the urban European, and more readily to the Yoruba of Tutuola's generation (Tutuola was born in 1920), perhaps, than to the "enlightened" young of today. For the fact of the matter is that to the Yoruba the bush has traditionally been a place of mystery and often of fear. One encounters again and again in the fiction from the region accounts of experiences and of beliefs which would indicate a certain awe toward the bush. Because of the Mythization of the bush, therefore, one expects to encounter a functional equivalent of "crossing the Styx," and he is not disappointed. From the narrator's introduction—recounting his situation, the death of his tapster, and his determination to set forth in search—to the first adventures there is a perceptible boundary. The world of the introduction is a real world, save for the gargantuan appetites of the palm-wine drinkard, but the world of the first adventure is a world of the marvellous and the highly generalized—thus his first experience takes him on a labor whose objective is the capture of Death.

Not unlike some other accounts of the world of the dead, the deads of Tutuola's bush do not care for the living. In fact, the living are not allowed in the Deads' Town, though the drinkard and his wife succeed in visiting there. The deads behave differently from the living also—notably, they walk backwards, which we are to read as a primitive form of behavior, the evidence for which is to be found elsewhere in the story, notably in the section about the red people where we learn that at one time people had their eyes on their knees and walked backwards. In the long run the narrator learns that his trip was in vain. His tapster, once found, no longer wishes to return to the towns of the living. The tapster's transfiguration has been completed. He has visited some of the very towns the narrator himself has visited along the way, but having at last reached Deads' Town his transformation into a dead is both complete and irreversible.

The narrator himself is by no stretch of the imagination an ordinary

217

mortal. A person of enormous appetites, the palm-wine drinkard is not only somewhat gargantuan. When he begins his journey he is careful to take along with him both his own and his father's juju, or power-containing substances. But the merit of this juju is not only to ward off evil; it is also used to effect basic physical transformations of himself, his wife, and their possessions. The juju is more that of the magician than of the ordinary man protecting himself against witchcraft. Unlike the ordinary mortal, furthermore, he can "sell" his death and "lease" his fear. And the first characterization he gives of himself, once he has launched himself into the bush of adventure, is as "father of the gods." One does not necessarily believe that this is in fact who he is, nor indeed that he himself takes this self-description fully seriously, although at one point at least he does appear to do so. He is in a fair sense very much like the hero in Greek myths. He is as generic as they, and like them he can—as generic—engage in those highly generalized experiences which have within them the conditions essential to becoming Myth. We shall see something more of this subsequently when we have the occasion to discuss his lack of individuation.

So a hero he is, and though his task may lack something of the dignity of purpose of Prometheus', his ultimate objective is nonetheless of social worth and is to be viewed as heroic. For after having spent years in the search of his tapster, when he reaches Deads' Town and locates his tapster, he takes back with him not the tapster but a gift—a miraculous egg which will upon address fulfill all that is asked of it. He returns home to find that a famine has settled upon the earth, and whereas he had undertaken his journey in order that he might supply both himself and the men of his village with palm-wine, he uses the magical powers of the egg to become the universal provider, defeating the famine and alleviating the hunger of all who come to his compound.

It is obvious that *The Palm-Wine Drinkard,* because it is of a given type, is reminiscent of other works in world literature. Gerald Moore is particularly aware of these similarities, for he specifically cites—in his discussion of Tutuola in *Seven African Writers*—Bunyan and Dante, and likens the search of the palm-wine drinkard to Orpheus'. But what distinguishes Tutuola's work from that of Bunyan and Dante is perhaps more significant than the similarities they share. Notably, *The Palm-Wine Drinkard* lacks anything of the sense of explicit moral purpose to which *Pilgrim's Progress* and *The Divine Comedy* are dedicated. Especially in contrast with the latter work, Tutuola's masterpiece is not dedicated

218

to the purpose of summing up, as it were, a body of theological doctrine.

The two works with which *The Palm-Wine Drinkard* has most in common, though in very different ways, are the *Odyssey* and the *Canterbury Tales*. The *Drinkard* shares with the *Odyssey* many of its tale properties, notably the "descent" to the "underworld," wherein that special sense of the marvellous which characterizes the episodes of both Odysseus and the drinkard prevails. There are other points in common as well, chiefly a similarity of character which is to say that both Odysseus and the palm-wine drinkard live by the exercise of their cunning. But there is about the *Odyssey* a greater sense of the particular, and thus to some extent the mythic quality (which is always the more powerful the more nearly it approaches the general) of the *Odyssey* is less marked than that of *The Palm-Wine Drinkard*. Both these two works, and the *Canterbury Tales* as well, are similarly episodic, and they share in common the fact that each of them was written in a "popular" language, Chaucer in English rather than in the French of the Court, Dante in Italian rather than in Latin, and Tutuola in a marked English dialect rather than in Yoruba or in the standard "literary" English his contemporaries learned in their colleges and universities. Further, Tutuola's work has an added feature in common with Chaucer's—an immediacy, a forthrightness, a freshness, and a keen sense of delight, a delight particularly to be seen in the common determination to undertell the touching, the outrageous, the amusing.

Chinua Achebe notes that:

> The English language will be able to carry the weight of my African experience. But it will have to be a new English, still in full communion with its ancestral home but altered to suit its new African surroundings.[2]

This is clearly also how Tutuola has felt about and used the English language. Yet his diction, which is that of the proletariat rather than that of the university graduate, has undoubtedly caused some among his contemporaries to deny him the great esteem he deserves as a major literary artist. Such persons have perhaps been "embarrassed" by his "illiteracies." In this respect, his publishers were kinder and more honest than his African critics. It was the personal decision of Sir Geoffrey Faber[3] that Tutuola's English should not be "normalized," thus permitting a work of major significance to reach the public in all the striking and often breathtaking originality of its prose.

In the long run, however, comparisons of one work with others, particularly when those works are from different cultures, are of limited utility. In the final analysis, any work must stand naked in its own terms before those who come face to face with it in affecting interaction. The greater its universal features—as contrasted with those which are appreciable only by those who are co-cultural with the work—the greater the extent to which the work will win international acceptance. This has been the case with Tutuola's book.

This impressive fact notwithstanding, as well of course as its manifest and numerous other qualities, *The Palm-Wine Drinkard* has been rejected and maligned by those who should have been first to accept it—numerous of Tutuola's contemporaries, notably younger writers. Not only have they slighted the work on the mean basis of the normative considerations of grammar as indicated above, but they have also suggested that *The Palm-Wine Drinkard* is derivative. By such an observation, I suppose the intent has been somehow or other to demean the stature of the work. The sophisticated reader, however, jealously defends those works he values, and he is not to be put off by such observations. He knows there is much to be encountered in world literature that is borrowed. Embarrassment of his contemporaries or mean envy cannot hide the fact that Tutuola's work is rich with imagination (and if that imagination is the imagination of a people, to be encountered elsewhere in their works, it is then surely no less Tutuola's than anybody else's), incredibly inventive, superbly well told, touched with dignity and humor, with the poetic as well as the prosaic, with naiveté and with sophistication, with joy, with pathos, and with a strong appreciation of what is universal in the human condition.

At the other extreme of criticism, I have heard informed people criticize Tutuola because he has gone too far astray from the traditions of the oral tale as told by the Yoruba. Such people, typically Europeans and Americans, feel that Tutuola has not done the traditional tale well because he has not done it "properly." It appears to be the case that Tutuola is to be damned if he does and damned if he doesn't.

In any case, such evaluations, negative or positive, have as little to do with the grounds on which *The Palm-Wine Drinkard* is relevant to our present purposes as they do with the work itself. They constitute merely an interesting added dimension of context to the work's existence. What is of relevance here is solely the fact that the work was created by a Yoruba, and that it is in the narrative tradition of the Yoruba, a fact attested to by Ulli Beier, who points out that typical of the tradition is the use of "bizarre imagery," and the avoidance of moralizing and sentimentalizing. He also points out that in this last respect, in addition to drawing more heavily upon traditional folklore, Tutuola is more Yoruba than Fagunwa, from whom it is asserted Tutuola has somewhat derived.[4] Tutuola further provides the student with a unique advantage— authentic Yoruba narrative "behavior" which is in many significant respects traditional and yet written in English! This English of Tutuola's is as authentic a presentation of the language uses of the Yoruba in the achievement of narrative as is a presentation in Yoruba. I assume that one's method of telling a story is the same whether he does it in one language or in a very different one; he will assert metaphors at the same kinds of places, similarly shape incidents, similarly proportion them and invoke their relationships, and will even tailor the second language somewhat—if he is not a master of its own idiom—along the stylistic lines of that mother tongue he more perfectly knows, much as he will shape the sounds of a second language to conform to the phonemes of his mother tongue.

Even so, the work reflects acculturation. Thus its relationship to the traditional narrative is more nearly the relationship of Lamidi Fakeye, a contemporary carver who works in the tradition but with marked innovations, to the history of Yoruba art than it is that of young sculptors trained at the university to work in the idioms of Europe to that same history, for these, while doubtless influenced by the Yoruba tradition, are consciously and more greatly influenced by Europe. It is more nearly the relationship of a village drummer to the mainstream of Yoruba music than it is that of the music of the modern, symphonic composer Fela Sowande to that same tradition. Tutuola's relationship to the tradition of narrative is thus that of Fakeye to his carving and the traditional drummer to his music; the counterparts of the modern sculptor and Sowande are "university" writers, preeminently exampled by Wole Soyinka.

The mere fact that one searches for Yoruba features in Tutuola's work indicates that what I have said is taken for granted by scholars in the field, that is to say that he is of the tradition but acculturated. Beier's writing of "more Yoruba" and "less Yoruba" as between Tutuola and Fagunwa is a case in point. So is the essay of Bernth Lindfors, a work of admirable scholarly imagination which shows the common presence in contemporary Yoruba rhetoric of certain traditional devices, notably of a "string of hyperboles, the concern with number and amount, the climactic contrast."[5] He also lists as a feature of the traditional rhetoric the use of long strings of appositives and the enumeration of many items, which he calls "inventories."

In gross examination, the most immediately notable feature of *The Palm-Wine Drinkard* is its linear structure comprised of segments of action which are more or less independent of one another. These segments may be said to constitute separate stories, so lacking is any sense of contingency or geneticity in their interrelationships. With respect to one another, then, these segments are more accurately to be characterized as sequential rather than consequential. They are however contingently related to the basic condition of the story, which is the search by the drinkard for his palm-wine tapster. There is little doubt therefore that the work is to be called episodic.

The episodes of the story are of three kinds: those which involve fantastic monsters who attempt to victimize the protagonist—always to be defeated; those which are almost pastoral; and those which constitute the frame of the narrative. The first class of episodes tends toward the bizarre, the second toward the idyllic, and the third toward what we must accept as the "real" world. "The Complete Gentleman" sequence provides an example of the first class, a sequence in which a woman (later the drinkard's wife) is captivated by a handsome man whom she follows home only to learn that he is naught but a skull who has borrowed the various parts of his body and must return them. The sequence in the white tree with the Faithful Mother is one of the two developed idyllic interludes, and it provides the drinkard and his wife with an opportunity for happiness and security—respite from the awful experiences they have already endured and are yet to undergo. Episodes of the frame, and frequent allusions to the chief dramatic purpose of the story which the frame represents, taken together constitute the dramatic center of gravity for the work, while the two other kinds of episodes are constellar, dramatic forces which play about that center of gravity, endowing the total structure with a rhythm of the three forces.

The action of the story is thus constituted of discrete segments, and, as far as concerns the protagonist, these segments furthermore are almost wholly comprised of reactions of the drinkard to situations which have not been brought about as a result of anything he himself has done, save insofar as he made the initial decision to seek and subsequently to persist in his search for his palm-wine tapster. This is to say that as the episodes are not genetically related one to the other, neither are they genetically derived from the actions, the personality, or the free will of the protagonist. This leads to a narrative in which the protagonist persists outside of a dramatic framework described by the exercise of self and free will, with the result that, subjected to the inevitable encounter with bizarre and primarily evil forces which dominate the land in which he finds his adventures, he is subjected to events which are structurally of, radically limited kinds. One must note, however, that such limitation does not describe the substantive nature of the experiences he undergoes, for, by content, all that he endures is varied and richly inventive. The universe within which the palm-wine drinkard exists, then, is one characterized by acts which result not from his being but from his circumstance; by acts exerted upon him and to which he responds; by acts which are generically limited even though substantively varied. In a world where the protagonist cannot do as he will but as he must, the range of kinds of actions is limited and the cause of the protagonist's actions is external to himself.

Existence in a world of limited possibilities, most of which amount to a threat to the individual's well being, and where free will is irrelevant to all that happens to one, such existence entails a one-dimensionality of actor. Where reaction and not action is the rule, the scope of motivation is necessarily severely limited; and where what befalls one is universally physical, the development of character interiority is significantly restricted, if indeed it exists at all. The simultaneous operation of these two factors produces actors to match the world in which they find themselves —wooden beings subject to circumstance, victims rather than masters of their fate.

Perhaps it is not necessarily the case that characters who are primarily reactive lack something of believability, but in any case this is markedly true in *The Palm-Wine Drinkard*. Since there is no significant development of the interiority of characters, psychological detail is radically limited. Even where the narrator does acknowledge fear, that fear is asserted rather than created in prose. The actors are one-dimensional, stimulus-response creatures living in a story world whose apparatuses work neatly and inevitably, with precision, without ambiguity, in a world where clean action is all. It follows that the motivation which takes the actors from one action to the next is minimal, simple, and obvious, involving the preservation of one's self and the reduction of his needs. Further the actors exist and the story is enacted within a bizarre world which exists minimally in description and is not at all constituted in the work. Chiefly, this world may be said to exist only because we are presented with assertations to the effect that such and such a bizarre creature has come upon

223

the scene, or that an exotic condition of climate or of scene prevails. Even such assertations are rare, and it is thus readily to be concluded that scene, to the notably limited extent to which it is evoked, is not made integral to the story, and that it does not in any meaningful or believable sense exist. In the first instance it is intension by default, and in the second, as we shall see, contributory as a stratum to the continuity of the work.

As for language, it is marked by assertion rather than by connotation, and by description rather than by enactment. This latter characteristic would seem almost inevitable in view of the absence of any development of interiority and of sense and psychological detail. Imagistic devices are seldom used, and there is little evidence of any exploitation of the connotative edges of words, those which suggest color, texture. What is most notable is the exploitation of speed—though this is more properly to be considered a function of the pacing of actions rather than of language— a keen sense for the bizarre invention, and a propensity toward incredibly and therefore very funny precision, particularly in matters of quantity, size, and price. Thus the drinkard asserts:

> So my father gave me a palm-tree farm which was nine miles square and it contained 560,000 palm-trees, and this palm-wine tapster was tapping one hundred and fifty kegs of palm-wine every morning, but before 2 o'clock p.m., I would have drunk all of it; after that he would go and tap another 75 kegs in the evening, which I would be drinking till morning. (p. 7)

Further, he asserts, his wife:

> . . . used the canoe as "ferry" to carry passengers across the river, the fare for adults was 3d (three pence) and half fare for children. In the evening time, then I changed to a man as before and when we checked the money that my wife had collected for that day, it was £7: 5: 3d. (p. 39)

The total they make for the month is £56: 11: 9d. As for the physical description, the following:

> As we were going further, we did not travel more than one third of a mile on this riverbank, before we saw a big tree which was about one thousand and fifty feet in length and about two hundred feet in diameter. This tree was almost white as if it was painted every day with white paint with all its leaves and also branches. As we were about forty yards away from it, there we noticed that somebody

peeped out and was focusing us as if a photographer was focusing
somebody. (p. 65)
This striking image of the photographer "focusing" the drinkard and his
wife is one of the very few explicit imagistic devices in the entire narrative.

Yet this use of quantification to the point of spurious accuracy constitutes a kind of "metaphoric" (in the traditional, literary sense) device,
and although the more traditional classes of such devices are rarely to be
encountered, this one of spurious accuracy is rife and rich. There is an
effective difference of metaphor function that must be noted in passing,
however. Whereas images are traditionally used in Western literature to
suggest something of the nature of the unusual by creating some of its
parameters in metaphor and simile, here in contrast by means of spurious
accuracy, the bizarre is made discrete and familiar in this strange world
Tutuola has created for us. The image is therefore in fact a kind of anti-
image.

This use of the precise hyperbole is to be seen as an expression of the
drive toward concreteness, and it is, one suspects, a traditional Yoruba
narrative device. Certainly it is used equally by Tutuola and Fagunwa, as
Lindfors demonstrates with the following excerpt from *The Forest of a
Thousand Daemons:*

> My name is Akara-ogun, Compound-of-Spells, one of the formidable
> hunters of a bygone age. My own father was a hunter, he was also
> a great one for medicines and spells. He had a thousand powder
> gourdlets, eight hundred *ato,* and his amulets numbered six hundred.
> Two hundred and sixty incubi lived in that house and the birds of
> divination were without number. It was the spirits who guarded the
> house when he was away, and no one dared enter that house when
> my father was absent—it was unthinkable.[6]

The precise hyperbole is not only quantitative, however. Tutuola (and
Fagunwa as well) resorts to visual hyperbole as well, as indeed he must
if he is to communicate the bizarre creatures which inhabit his forests.
But it is something more than the mere fact of necessity that one notes in
Tutuola's writing—it is a positive delight in the astounding invention.
Here is the famous description of the red fish from *The Palm-Wine
Drinkard:*

> . . . its head was just like a tortoise's head, but it was as big as an
> elephant's head and it had over 30 horns and large eyes which sur-
> rounded the head. All these horns were spread out as an umbrella.
> It could not walk but was only gliding on the ground like a snake

and its body was just like a bat's body and covered with long red hair like strings. It could only fly to a short distance, and if it shouted a person who was four miles away would hear. All the eyes which surrounded its head were closing and opening at the same time as if a man was pressing a switch on and off. (pp. 79–80)

Such devices deliver us into a world of hard concreteness and sharp definition, one that is an intensive universe of discrete entities. But it is interesting to note that clarity of delineation and physical individuation do not have actional counterparts. The most bizarre monster yet acts *generically*, in much the same way that is expected of any monster. The monster is thus in no sense individuated in terms of his own, unique monster-ness. What is achieved by this drive toward precision and concreteness of the physical world is the evocation of the *category* of the specific rather than the specific itself. The affecting result of this process is that the unique is physically but not affectingly realized. On the contrary, it is the power of the general that is invoked. This amounts to a kind of paradox, and this paradox is a category of devices properly to be considered under the heading of the inhibition of range in the affecting medium of language in narrative.

The dramatic result of paradox is tension, and there is a system of such paradox-derived tensions in *The Palm-Wine Drinkard*. Take for example the situation near the end of the book where the drinkard is chased by the mountain-creatures. In order to escape, the drinkard:

... changed my wife into the wooden-doll as usual, then I put it into my pocket, and they saw her no more.

But when she had disappeared from their presence they told me to find her out at once and grew annoyed by that time, so I started to run away for my life because I could not face them to fight at all. As I was running away from them, I could not run more than 300 yards before the whole of them caught me and surrounded me there; of course, before they could do anything to me, I myself had changed into a flat pebble and was throwing myself along the way to my home town. (pp. 116–117)

The paradox involved in transforming one's wife and possessions into something one can carry and subsequently changing one's self into a pebble, then throwing one's self is that between the probable and the improbable, the possible and the impossible which typically occurs in the book. Further, there is the paradox which results when the discrete meets the universal, a situation which prevails when the drinkard encounters

"Dance," "Drum," and "Song," who aid him in his troubles with his monstrous son.

> When "Drum" started to beat himself it was just as if he was beaten by fifty men, when "Song" started to sing, it was just as if a hundred people were singing together . . . (p. 38)

Subsequently he encounters "Band" and "Spirit of Prey." Further, although these are somewhat different phenomena, in that they are not "Platonic" abstractions, yet they meet "images" of themselves and personifications of "Land" and "Heaven." The structure of these encounters running through the story creates a rhythmic counterpoint to the total structure which provides a dynamic factor of some importance.

Involved in these paradoxes is the affecting medium of relationship, for paradox implies contradiction and contradiction cannot exist without parts in interrelationship. Paradox is to be conceived of as a relationship in range, rather than in duration, and I have already said that its intent is to establish dynamics of tension. But because the terms of the paradoxes exist within the boundaries of a wildly improbable and circumstantial universe where the extraordinary is ordinary, their impact is by no means as great as it would be were they to appear in a more orderly, more "logical" context.

This is true also of the relationships which cement the work into a durational whole. Facts are not always related only in terms of simple cause-effect relationships. The Faithful Mother in the white tree is a sister of the Red King, but the Red King asserts that his whole family, indeed all his people, were turned red and sent to the place where they now reside. Now there is no mention of the Faithful Mother's being red, and so we assume she is not, for such an extraordinary fact would have been mentioned by Tutuola, who never fails to note the outlandish whenever it is possible to do so. On the other hand, neither are we given the circumstances under which she became other than red. Those numerous instances in which the drinkard is threatened with death also fall under this a-causal relationship, for he knows, as well as do his readers, that it is—as he often reminds himself—impossible for him to die since he has sold his death, and thus the threat of death is meaningless to him. The situation is not wholly reduced by the fact that he did not sell his fear, and thus is yet able to be afraid, for the fact of the matter is that he yet seems to entertain the prospect of death as a reasonable one. There are numerous instances in which actions are joined one to the other by means of relationships which defy the ordinary logic of the orderly procedure of human action.

Intension/Extension

We are here concerned with the question of range in *The Palm-Wine Drinkard*, such that if there may be said to be noticeable range in the situationality, language, relationality, and experience of the work we may say of it that it is extensive, whereas if the opposite is true we may say only that it is intensive.

With respect to the question of range as an inventory of classes of situations and of kinds of action-actor patterns, we have already noted that there are but three classes of actions which occur in the narrative, those which constitute the frame of the work, those which are idyllic, and those predominating ones which involve experiences with monsters. Even if we remove some of the generalization involved in this last and most numerous category, removing the consideration from so structural a level and glimpsing something of the particularities of experience, we see that there is little significant differentiation among the episodes with the monsters. The monster is always physically remarkable, always threatening to the welfare of the narrator, always outwitted by the narrator. The pattern of action-actor relationships is such that preponderantly the protagonist responds to actions initiated by agents other than himself.

The actors themselves also exhibit markedly limited variety. There are the good characters and the evil ones, and there is no significant moral shading, with the result that none of them is morally problematic. Their motivations are of limited variety as well, involving primarily action from the monsters and reaction from the narrator and his wife. The use of details of sense and psychology in scene and character creation are so minimally used that there is little point even to mentioning them here.

The situation is not markedly different for language. Only one kind of "imagistic" device is typically used, that of the precise hyperbole which we have described as an anti-image. As for diachronic relationships, it may be said that these tend to display greater variety than is characteristic of the other media, for in durational terms not only does cause beget adequate and predictable effect in many instances, but in others it does not. Examples of the first sort are commonplace, and even those of the second are numerous. But perhaps these latter ones require an example or two since they are far and away less common in narrative. The fact that the narrator and his wife produce a monster for a child, one who grows to

228

maturity within days and who outstrips his parents, relegating them to the role of servants, is such an a-causally related eventuation. So also are the relationships among the various episodes a-causal. These relationships contrast with even the most remarkable of the other kinds of events in the narrative, for as bizarre as they might be, they yet are rooted in causality, either in the power of the narrator's juju (such as the magical transformations) or in the nature of the peculiar laws of the spiritual world of the bush (the strange habits of the deads).

The synchronic dimension of relationality lacks careful definition and integration. There is thus no necessary relationship between the kinds of monstrosity of character, of which there is great variety if not great range, and the kinds of actions those monsters commit. Neither is particularity of place related to the kind of action which occurs, nor even the general place (i.e., the bush of monsters and the Town of the Deads), for the prodigious, the strange, and the magical happen as readily in the "real" world of the protagonist's village as they do in the bush of monsters and the Town of the Deads. In short, there is no close exploitation of relational integration such as one would expect of the intensional work, but on the other hand, neither is there the complexity or richness of relationality one would expect to find in the extensive work.

Finally, as for the medium of experience, which we have defined in terms of its relevance to man and his human condition, one can assert only that it is limited, for there is little of universality in the affairs of the drinkard. Raised to the level of Myth, however, the search takes on rich significance for every man.

Range is also to be understood in terms of the "spread" of given instances of the above items, as opposed to their taxonomy. In this connection, one can say only that range is inhibited in nearly every case,[7] the sole exceptions being in two areas: the first of these is in terms of the richness of invention applied to the devising of the physical and behavioral characteristics of the monsters and the deads on the one hand, and the prolific use of the images of discreteness on the other. There is thus a certain amount of extensiveness—of spread—to the medium of language, though as we have suggested, since it is in the direction of concreteness its net effect is intensive. The second area is to be found in the use of language, which since it tends to create a world of the particulate and is used toward the ends of invention rather than of imagination—of artifice rather than of constituting experience—has its focus on the discrete, the specific, the quantified and the evaluated. There is in the work a drive toward precision and clarity, despite the substantive fantasy of the work. The inhibition of imagination, connotation and evocation is an exercise in the direction of the reduction of ambiguity, and is thus an exercise in intension. There is, in short, range in invention if not in imagination—as we here define the term.

Otherwise the draft of the media is shallow. For situation, actions reach but feebly and without marked penetration into the depths of possibility of subtlety, variety, richness of experience and of the exercise of the human fancy. Motivation is neither profound nor revealing and the actors, in large measure because of these factors, are one-dimensional, even though lively, and there is hardly any development at all of the physical world within which actions occur, let alone the careful elaboration of its properties. There is present in the work a radical inhibition of the complexity of causality, with the result that there cannot be said to be any significant range to relationality either. Language, as we have said, denotes rather than connotes.

The philosophical framework within which the work exists is one characterized by the proscription of the exercise of free will. The narrator persists in a world in which he has no choice over what happens to him. But since he endures by his own free will at least, even though in a world where freedom of will is abrogated, he submits to a moral order that is one of imposed and unpredictable outrage. In this world in which free will does not exist, only limited evil can happen—the protagonist cannot die, for example. It is a world in which planned, logical, and genetic action is severely limited if not impossible. The revocation of free will must be seen as the sufficient cause of the action-reaction pattern described earlier as well as of the absence of the meaningful development of motivation. The inhibition of the possibility of doing as one will restricts the volitional world, shrinking the world of will almost to the point of nonexistence. The fact that actions happen to the protagonist does not alter the situation, both by reason of the limited variety of those actions and by reason of the fact that no matter how varied they might conceivably be such variety would not change this fact about the moral universe of the work.

The philosophical nature of *The Palm-Wine Drinkard*, the restriction of range in situation and its properties of scene, actor, action, motivation, in language, and in relationality—all bespeak the influence of a strong drive toward intension in the execution of narrative. All elements which would tend to make acts extensive are avoided—the connotative values of words, the use of imagination as opposed to invention, full-dimensioned characters rather than types, and a full spectrum of human motivations and actions.

Continuity/Discontinuity

The absence of geneticity of relationality characterizes the durational dimension of *The Palm-Wine Drinkard*, which is thus episodic, and, in effect, discontinuous. If this is true, then narrative in this respect negates the mode of continuity we have hypothesized for it, as indeed it negates the argument of the essay, for we have maintained the existence of an affecting system of similetic equivalents as a condition of a homogeneous culture. We have assumed late, traditional Yoruba culture to have such homogeneity, at least as far as concerns the affecting presence in it.

But the relevant question now is whether it is the discontinuity between episodes which is affectingly important, or whether it is that episodicism itself. The former is suggested to be false by the test of system (which is the case in the other forms), while the latter would appear to be affirmed by the same test, for in the other forms we have seen continuity asserted not in the way Europeans and Americans should have chosen—which is to say by means of long lines of through-development—but rather atomistically, for in the temporal works of the Yoruba, continuity is to be seen as a function of the density of multiple, discrete parts. Continuity as a function of a high frequency of discrete integers can be achieved in narrative only by means of the episodic, and in order to come into being the episodic requires a certain amount of disjuncture with respect to the relationships among its components and their immediate contexts.

Looked at somewhat differently, the situation amounts to this: we cannot regard the discontinuity of episodicism as an important feature in its own terms, since discontinuity defines the conditions under which episodicism may be said to exist. Were we to stress the fact of discontinuity as of critical import, we should have to deny to those peoples, who in their affecting works assert the mode of continuity, the possibility of creating an episodic work. We should therefore have to run the risk of denying the possibility of much of oral literature, for it is obvious that the conditions of oral tale telling are such as to be favorable to the generation of the episodic. *The Palm-Wine Drinkard*, then, is to be seen as achieving continuity through density, in much the same way, which is to say as a similetic equivalent to the way in which the discrete beats of drumming

231

occur with such dense frequency as to create a temporal "solid," or continuity.

This, I think, is our most important evidence in support of the continuity of Tutuola's work, and it thus defends the integrity and ultimately the reality of the system we have described. There is other evidence, however. There are in the work certain constants which clearly indicate a drive toward continuity. At least five of these constants can be readily identified, and doubtless the researches of others would reveal even more.

1. The constancy of the improbable. The total, durational fabric of the work is to be characterized by a markedly high frequency of appearance of the remarkable, the wondrous, the unlikely—the improbable, in short.

2. The constancy of the permanence of the **narrator.** One means by this not only the constancy of point of view as a technical device of executing the narrative, but also—and indeed primarily—the constancy of the dramatic value of knowing that the **protagonist,** having sold his death, is bound to endure.

3. The constancy of the generalized character of the event. We have adequately discussed this point elsewhere in connection with the absence of individuation..

4. The constancy of the contrast between the real world of the reader and the fanciful one of the narrative. This is perhaps best regarded as the equivalent in scene of the improbability of event discussed under the first entry above.

5. The constancy of the frame. It is above all the unity of protagonist and of purpose which demonstrates the narrative's drive toward continuity.

But continuity through density is achieved not only by means of the episodic characteristics of the work. There is a noticeable drive toward the proliferation of entities that gives further support to the view that with respect to duration the esthetic of the Yoruba is expressive of the atomistic approach to continuity. Doubtless this is conditioned by the predominance of percussive instruments in music, which (save for the pressure drum) cannot sustain sound, and by the basically oral nature of the narrative, including *The Palm-Wine Drinkard* of which it may justifiably be maintained that the fact that it is written is purely accidental to its nature.

How else does one explain the frequency of the precise hyperbole? Does one maintain that it is only a nonfunctional, decorative element found as a characteristic of the execution of the language of Yoruba narrative, or does one assume on the contrary that there is some reason for having opted for this out of all possible kinds of images—indeed out of all kinds of hyperbole? Reason would seem to me to argue in support of the latter alternative, and when one says that one drinks seventy-five barrels of palm-wine of an evening rather than "some," or "a great quantity," or even "barrels," one is stressing the atomistic aspect of the situation—he is searching for the proliferation of entities, composing the situation of its bits and pieces and calling attention to them..

It is doubtful, given the nature of the content of the narrative, whether one can maintain that the invention of the story, essential as it is to create the bizarre with which the story is concerned, reflects in any direct way the imperative toward atomistic density. Yet one cannot help but note that there seems to be a kind of special interest in the particulateness of the monsters' enormities, so inventively are they made, so lovingly are they noted. In order to demonstrate this, I merely invite the reader's attentions to the description of the Red Fish quoted earlier above.

An excellent instance of the interest in the particulate is to be seen in the following:

> My wife had said of the woman we met: "She was not a human-being and she was not a spirit, but what was she?" She was the Red-smaller-tree who was at the front of the bigger Red-tree, and the bigger Red-tree was the Red-king of the Red-people of Red-town and the Red-bush and also the Red-leaves on the bigger Red-tree were the Red-people of the Red-town in the Red-bush. (p. 83, punctuated thus.)

It is difficult to doubt that in this passage, which is perhaps the most remarkable one (for the terms of our discussion) in the entire work, Tutuola takes delight in being as specific as he can, in maximizing every opportunity to give to his prose a density of discrete reference which indeed is contributory to *constituting* the mode of continuity in the work.

I am not the first to mention the "drumming" feature of the contemporary Yoruba popular prose style. Ulli Beier says of Fagunwa, "He is a master of rhetoric, who can make repetitions and variations swing in a mounting rhythm, like Yoruba drumming."⁵ One notes this same characteristic in Tutuola—in the passage quoted immediately above, in the pace of his inventions, in the rhythm of his actions, and in his regulation of pace with the diminuendo effect brought about by the inclusion of idyllic interludes. But the work of Tutuola is like drumming in more respects than these, for the narrative exists in terms of its properties of situation and language, its system of tensions, its relationality, the contrasts between its world and the world of the reader, between the general and the specific, the probable and the improbable. These various voices, like the voices of different drums, assert their own drives toward continuity and one has an interwoven structure therefore, all contributing their strata of particulate reality to the general density by which the continuity of the narrative is constituted.

All that *The Palm-Wine Drinkard* esthetically *is* is to be accounted for by that network of synapses and interstices (which feeling ultimately fills in) comprised of the nerves of media and properties I have identified. The affecting reality of the work is this, and nothing more. Who wrote it, under what circumstances, his role in society, the identity and social placement of his readers, their opinions of the work as to its quality, originality, and impact—all such considerations, while of undoubted import in other considerations, are irrelevant here.

As one would expect, *The Palm-Wine Drinkard* actualizes the Yoruba esthetic as it has been described in this essay, owing its affecting existence to the discipline of those same principles of intensive continuity as characterize the other forms of the affecting presence. To be sure, intensive continuity has determined the nature of the narrative's media in ways proper to narrative.

Those conditions of the affecting media which express or execute intension, as well as those which express or execute continuity, are esthemes. The contributions these esthemes make toward the systemic whole are such that, even more ˈsurely than was the case after we concluded our examinations of sculpture, dance, and music, we may speak of intension and continuity as para-esthemes of the part and of intensive-continuity as the para-estheme of the whole. The estheme of the whole in *The Palm-Wine Drinkard* is obviously that confluence of the expression of intension and continuity such that the work may be demonstrated to exhibit intensive continuity.

There can be no doubt that Amos Tutuola is closer to the traditional esthetic of the Yoruba than are those of his contemporaries who have turned to the novel. This is a relative estate at best, to be sure, for the traditional culture has been heavily acculturated. One would expect therefore, upon further study, to perceive a continuum of "Yorubaness," extending from Tutuola at the deeply Yoruba end to Wole Soyinka at the more Europeanized, modernized end, with T. M. Aluko standing somewhere in between.

234

Raised to the level of the culture area, at least as far as concerns those writers publishing in English, one would expect to explain in terms of the suasion of the traditional esthetic many of the characteristic "flaws" or "shortcomings" Europeans often appear to see in the West African practice of narrative. Thus episodicism is to be seen as the affecting desire to achieve continuity by means of a density of discrete elements rather than by the attenuation of long lines of dramatic—actional, psychological—development. "Shallowness" of draft, lowness of modelling in the delineation of characters and of scene development, is to be seen as the exercise of the imperative to achieve intensivity—that on the one hand, and on the other hand as the drive toward the generalized presentation of character, the concern with the type, the role.

All West African, English-speaking writers show these characteristics to one degree or another, and that critic who fails to take into account the operation of the imperatives of an esthetic *system* at the unconscious, cultural level practices the art of criticism irresponsibly. One can only wonder what innovations might have been wrought in the perpetration of narrative if the writers of West Africa had pursued and developed their craft in accordance with the dictates of their traditional esthetic.

FOOTNOTES

[1] Amos Tutuola, *The Palm-Wine Drinkard* (London: Faber and Faber, paper, 1962).

[2] Chinua Achebe, "English and the African Writer," *Transition* 18 (1965), p. 30.

[3] Told to me through personal communication.

[4] Ulli Beier, "Fagunwa: A Yoruba Novelist," *Black Orpheus* 17 (1965), pp. 52, 54.

[5] Bernth Lindfors, "Characteristics of Yoruba and Igbo Prose Styles in English," (Paper given at seminar on Contemporary African Literatures held at the annual meeting of the Modern Language Association of America, New York, December 27, 1968), p. 5.

[6] Daniel O. Fagunwa, *The Forest of a Thousand Daemons: A Hunter's Saga,* trans. Wole Soyinka (London: Nelson, 1968), p. 9.

[7] See the outline of the features of range of these various respects in the preceding table.

[8] Beier, "Fagunwa," p. 53.

Amos Tutuola: Literature and Folklore, or the Problem of Synthesis

Sunday O. Anozie

The publication in 1952 by Faber and Faber in London of Amos Tutuola's first narrative, *The Palm-Wine Drinkard and his Dead Palm-Wine Tapster in the Deads' Town,*[1] was a great event in West African English literature. This publication not only brought to this Yoruba author from Nigeria a precocious fame, which has stirred up controversy among critics and English writers,[2] including the celebrated poet Dylan Thomas, but it has also drawn the attention of the English-speaking literary world to what, it appears, might be the determinative tendency of the future of the West African novel, namely, traditional folklore.

If this literature has not become ineluctably involved in the exploration of mythology and popular folklore, it is for the reason that the West African novelists were all influenced by Christianity through the teachings of the missionaries. And since they used first of all an art form which can be styled as Christian, these novelists tried to express more concrete values, those which were related more to the actual social reality, values which traditional folklore and myths embody but

---

1. Translated into French by Raymond Queneau as *L'ivrogne dans la brousse,* Paris, 1953.

2. Among the numerous commentaries on Tutuola, the following are emphasized: Elspeth Huxley, *Four Guineas* (London, 1954), p. 175; Geoffrey Parrinder, Foreword to Tutuola's *My Life in the Bush of Ghosts* (London, 1954); and Gerald Moore, *Seven African Writers* (London, 1962), chap. iv.

Reprinted from *Cahiers d'études africaines*, 10 (1970), 335-51. Translated into English by Judith H. McDowell. The same essay can be found in Anozie's *Sociologie du roman africaine: Réalisme, structure et détermination dans le roman moderne ouest-africain* (Paris, 1970), pp. 65-88.

little.[3] Tutuola's largely folkloristic inspiration, on the other hand, can be explained by his double vision, quite opposite from that of his colleagues.

For certain critics, Tutuola is a marvelous storyteller, gifted with an original and gripping creative genius; for others, his fame is not without pretension, if one considers the syntactical extremes of this writer who knows so poorly the English language in which he pretends to write. For still others, the cult of the "primitive," the "surrealistic" matter of Tutuola's stories can only be the sign of "Neo-Africanism."[4]

Thus, throughout the diverse impressions and opinions called forth in Africa as well as in Europe by Amos Tutuola's marvelous tales, differing tendencies are revealed. There is, first, the literary and intellectual snobbishness of novelists and critics in Africa who do not hesitate to underestimate Tutuola's talent and who are not anxious to recognize him as a fellow writer. On the other hand, in Europe especially, one ascertains in the enthusiasm of English-speaking readers a certain current of paternalistic conservatism which seeks to magnify everything bizarre and exotic, whether in African art or African literature.

If one wants to speak of Amos Tutuola as a West African novelist, if it is justifiable to devote an entire article to him, it is because *The Palm-Wine Drinkard* holds in African literature a historical importance analogous to that of *Don Quixote* in European literature. In the characters of both Tutuola and Cervantes, one discerns a certain consciousness of the individual's internal conflict; one perceives a hero in chivalrous quest of the ideal, an individual whose dilemma, or mediatory desire,[5] consists in coming to grips with a certain elusive

---

3. Cf. George Balandier, *Sociologie actuelle de l'Afrique noire* (Paris, 1963), p. 518. Though referring to the formation of the messianic ideology of the Bakongo, Balandier's statement is equally valid for African novelists: "Traditional folklore and myths associated with ancient rituals offered few usable themes or none at all; they encouraged submissiveness and conformity more than rebellion and actions suited to shape the course of history."

4. Cf. Janheinz Jahn, *Muntu: the New African Culture* (New York, 1961), p. 195. According to Jahn, "Whether the work of an author, whatever his colour, belongs to Western or to African culture, depends on whether we find in it those criteria of African culture . . . ." Those criteria are called *ntu*, *nommo*, and *muntu*.

5. Cf. René Girard, *Mensonge romantique et vérité romanesque* (Paris, 1961), pp. 11-13. The "mediator," according to Girard, is the model, the desire. For Don Quixote, the chivalrous life is the imitation of Amadis, in the sense that the Christian life is the imitation of Jesus Christ. For the palm-wine drinkard, this model changes into the desire to find his dead palm-wine tapster in the Deads' Town.

finality and in reconciling his spiritual and psychological ambivalence.

Tutuola's Folkloristic World, or the Extension of the Social Utopia

We shall try here to understand this baroque world of folklore and popular mythology in its totality. We shall try to see precisely how Tutuola's work is a mythical recreation of the African social reality. Our aim, within the limits imposed by the unconscious obscurity of the stories themselves, will be to appreciate Tutuola's creative intention as an attempt to reconstruct, by means of a series of folkloristic anec-dotes, a central though embryonic character as a vehicle for his individualistic vision of the real African world.

With Tutuola, one ascertains that myth assumes a cosmic grandeur embracing both the grotesque and the true, traditional morality and conventions. Tutuola's works are not the figments of a morbid imagination, nor are they simple representations of terror and combats with gods which take place in a confined and marvelous place. The traditional tale, for Tutuola, is above all a means for analyzing the daily reality. Hence, on the one hand, the interaction, on the level of style, between Tutuola's creative consciousness and the mythological material, and, on the other hand, the thematic rapport between the elements of daily life and the folkloristic events do not take place in logical inconsequence but in the perspective of synthesis: Tutuola recreates a world of social utopia.

With Tutuola, to look for a work full of esthetic delights, a work like that of Proust or Kafka, is a useless task. Because of his limited formal education, Tutuola remains relatively free from the influence of European writers.[6] Belonging to the Yoruba tribe of Western Nigeria, a tribe renowned for the richness of its folklore, Tutuola naturally finds in folklore a fertile source for his creative demands. However, the imagination which gets hold of this traditional world is not an inventive or an original imagination but one which seeks to give the illusion of coherence to disconnected facts. This is all the more true because the world of folklore and mythology—Tutuola's world also—is a disturbed world, prelogical and sometimes crepuscular, in which, moreover, events take place by themselves without any logical, intellectual

---

6. Tutuola has read the Bible, of course, and the religious literature of the Anglican missionaries, but he has read neither *The Divine Comedy* of Dante nor *The Pilgrim's Progress* of Bunyan, authors who are sometimes said to have imparted to him the allegorical spirit.

connection. Nevertheless, in traditional African society, these are events which, in the primitive context of the collective consciousness, provide an ethical perspective and constitute an efficacious means of education.

This didactic purpose, foremost in all popular folklore, is incontestably present in Tutuola's work. Thus, the author of *The Palm-Wine Drinkard* is not an African writer of science-fiction, but a storyteller and a traditional moralizer, in whom one also discovers an almost childish joy before the marvelous world. The habitual procedure of this storyteller is, first, to try to capture for us the illusion or the quality of the world of folklore, then, above all with his explosive, humorous style, to make us participate fully in the successive events through which he allows the moral and allegorical lessons to filter.

Tutuola's folkloristic world rests upon a system of antitheses and ambiguities. In it, one discovers order and disorder, happiness and unhappiness, continuity and change, good and evil, crime and punishment. His hero is a weak man suddenly made omnipotent through traditional magic power.

Will Tutuola's character be classed with similar creations, the "Invisible Man" of H. G. Wells, or the "Robot-Man" made by Dr. Frankenstein, the fictions of a technological culture? With them all, one observes a certain subversion of established values and a denial of the conventional. In the case of Tutuola, the subversion is mostly directed toward the cosmic hierarchy, as the hero, who claims the title "Father of gods who could do anything in this world," amuses himself immensely by terrifying the real gods by carrying out an astonishing variety of supernatural tasks. This, therefore, is an individual in the state of infancy, who is tending toward a nostalgic divinity or toward a certain mastery of two worlds: that of the living and that of the dead.

For Tutuola, the town of the living and the Deads' Town are not perceptibly separated in any way. Although each one strictly keeps its identity in its ways and customs, Tutuola nevertheless ascertains a complementariness, a continuity between the two. It is in this attempt to extend the values of one town into those of the other that Tutuola's utopian meaning seems to come forth. Put in another way, it is on the utopian plane, which is reality, of course, in folklore, that Tutuola wants to bring about a synthesis of tradition and modernity in Africa. This preoccupation alone justifies the consideration of Tutuola as a modern writer.

To specify his hero's principal aspiration, this thirst to extend himself into the invisible, Tutuola seems to insist that we first consider the Drinkard wholly as a man impressed by injustice, divine and human, a man obsessed by fear of failure in his world. From this fear a certain utopia emerges, which may be styled as pessimistic, recalling Tutuola's didactic intention: to turn man away from his false pride, from the complacent self-satisfaction which characterizes his daily life, in short, to make the Drinkard give up his hedonism, that pleasure of which he boasts at the beginning of the narrative:

> I was a palm-wine drinkard since I was a boy of ten years of age. I had no other work more than to drink palm-wine in my life. . . . I was drinking palm-wine from morning till night and from night till morning. By that time I could not drink ordinary water at all except palm-wine.[7]

Yet, the obsession with failure can bring forth from a man what could be called an optimistic utopian vision, to the extent that his awareness of being a victim of injustice makes him resolve to seek his spiritual equilibrium for himself and to assure himself of the continuation of his happiness. The heroism[8] of Tutuola's Drinkard consists in the fact that he considers the gods hostile forces, against whom man must do battle to obtain satisfaction. By thus making the supernatural powers assume the responsibility for all his misfortunes, symbolized by the death of his tapster, the Drinkard gives himself a single goal: to put an end to injustice by recovering his dead tapster and, to accomplish that, subduing and taking possession of the Deads' Town. Whether or not there is in this an unconscious allusion to the European experience in precolonial Africa (the appearance of the Drinkard in that strange world of the dead presents a kind of analogy with Achebe's vision of the appearance of the first white man in precolonial Ibo society), Tutuola establishes a system of contrasts in his masterpiece. He poses the scientific imagination against the imagination fastened upon traditional folklore, and, opposite the time machine or the interplanetary spaceship, he places traditional magic, the external means by which the hero undergoes the desired metamorphoses.

Thus, in *The Palm-Wine Drinkard*, Tutuola creates an extensive other-world, where abortive dreams, endured blows, and human ambitions are found.

The foremost intention of the hero remains, nevertheless, this ambiguous enterprise, undertaken without reflection and having the recovery of his dead tapster as its object. This desire for the Other, whose death symbolizes for the hero the loss of an ideal, daily happiness (for the Other is the poetic construction of values, otherwise perishable), is an archetype of popular mythology, as in the classical

---

7. *The Palm-Wine Drinkard* (New York: Grove Press, 1953), p. 7.

8. Cf. Vladimir Propp, *The Morphology of the Folktale* (Bloomington, 1958), p. 46. According to Propp, the folklore hero is the one who suffers directly from the initial action of the villain or the one who alleviates the misfortunes of others by means of a magic power he possesses.

story of Orpheus and Eurydice.[9] Impressed by the arbitrary decree of the gods because the departure from the ordinary has undermined his personal well-being, for as a result he has lost all his best friends, the Drinkard immediately hits upon a primitive idea of purgatory which makes no distinction between Christian orthodoxy and traditional mythology:

> When I saw that there was no palm-wine for me again, and nobody could tap it for me, then I thought within myself that old people were saying that the whole people who had died in this world, did not go to heaven directly, but they were living in one place somewhere in this world. So that I said that I would find out where my palm-wine tapster who had died was.[10]

This resolve of a troubled hero, out of his mind, to search for that "one place somewhere in this world," this nostalgic thought of acquiring or rediscovering something, of absolute freedom, constitutes the essential thematic substructure of Tutuola's masterpiece. But an ambiguity is set up from the beginning: the fact that the hero himself is not yet dead. The rational mind thinks that this necessary transformation would be the only means by which the Drinkard could enter the Deads' Town. It is precisely at this point of discrepancy between the logic of conventional rationalism and traditional thought that the mediating role of "juju," or the magic amulet, becomes evident. Armed and strengthened by this traditional magic power, the Drinkard proceeds with complete confidence toward the discovery and the conquest of the Deads' Town. One might say, by way of analogy, that in this second half of the twentieth century, in which each day the race to the moon becomes accelerated and more and more displays the attributes of conquest, the technological civilization of the West is in the same manner setting out on an enterprise, the outcome of which is still uncertain.

The effective result of all we have said up to this point is that on the unconscious level of myth, Tutuola carries out the complete transposition and the fusion of the two authentic poles of his world: the Deads' Town and the land of the living, between which the main character moves with the facility of an astronaut. On the stylistic level, this process manifests itself in the form of the interpenetration of the

---

9. Jean Paul Sartre does well to give his celebrated introduction to a collection of poets of negritude the title "Black Orpheus" (in L. S. Senghor, *Nouvelle anthologie de la poésie nègre et malgache*, Paris, 1948). Because of his nostalgia for the romantic and the messianic, Tutuola belongs to this school of Black writers.

10. *The Palm-Wine Drinkard*, p. 9.

symbols which come from European technocracy and the images which have African cosmo-mythic significance. From this comes a series of apparent contradictions and inconsistencies. With Tutuola, however, these are a kind of meta-language,[11] which is disclosed in the peculiar narrative form of his works and even in the syntactical structure of his phrases. It is significant, extraordinary rhetoric, which allows us to perceive the allusions Tutuola is constantly making to industrial products in a world of folklore not necessarily as simple indications of a primitive, undisciplined sensibility but rather as mythic statements of plot or inner conflict—in short, as the flashing of a mind in contact with a foreign culture, in the grip of another mode of thought, another value system, that of the technological West. It is, therefore, the purpose of this laborious connecting of the external, technological reality to a traditional, creative consciousness (a direct result of the contact of Europe and Africa and the social changes it has occasioned) to bring about the effect of the images and objects Tutuola often uses, sometimes ironically, as helpful clues to the meaning of the work.

Some examples will suffice to confirm that observation. First, there is the portrait of the complete gentleman,[12] which is a direct reference to the *nouveaux riches*, the African elite said to be Westernized and to have bourgeois pretensions, since the role of this handsome character is to seduce a young girl. Next, there are the security measures taken by the hero and his wife before entering the white tree, the abode of the Faithful Mother:

> Now by that time and before we entered inside the white tree, we had 'sold our death' to somebody at the door for the sum of £70: 18: 6d and 'lent our fear' to somebody at the door as well on interest of £3: 10: 0d per month, so we did not care about death and we did not fear again.[13]

Logically, these measures can only reflect an awareness on Tutuola's part of the means of exchange in the modern economy and of the idea of life insurance. To intensify even more these allusions to social changes coming into the traditional mental and physical order of African society, Tutuola uses other industrial products as images: gold jewelry, household gadgets, and even military accoutrements such as

---

11. Considered as a language within a language, Tutuola's style of writing, contrary to what some of his critics pretend, should not be difficult to understand. The syntactical structure of his phrases is itself the absolute condition of the mythic existence of his subject.

12. *The Palm-Wine Drinkard*, p. 18.

13. *The Palm-Wine Drinkard*, p. 67.

bombs. One might add that he divides the land beyond the grave into miles and measures its time by the clock.

One does not expect to find such diverse phenomena of Western technological culture side by side with primitive African magic in the same folkloristic world. This coexistence has socio-psychological importance. For example, it shows us, first, how much Tutuola is aware of the problems of acculturation and colonial alienation, physical as well as psychic, in Africa. It is brought, then, into the central plot only because it serves to reinforce and better clarify the Drinkard's conflict. The main character, who may be considered as "inner-directed," experiences the desire to probe into his own psychological equilibrium, to overcome his inner agitation, and to reconcile the contradictions of his world. In this, Tutuola's Drinkard once again resembles other characters: Samba Diallo, Clarence, and Okolo, the heroes of Cheikh Hamidou Kane's *L'aventure ambiguë*, Camara Laye's *Le regard du roi*, and Gabriel Okara's *The Voice*, respectively. These heroes have one common characteristic: the ambiguity of their experience, stemming from the anguished collision of the European technological ethic and the African cosmo-mythic values. Also, their single goal is to rediscover a coherence in their lives and to fuse the values of the living and the dead, that is to say, of modernity and tradition. In the mythic situation itself, Tutuola clearly shows how man's powerful will collides ineluctably with the antagonistic will of the supernatural powers. This didactic humanism, which Tutuola shares with Kane, Laye, and Okara, gives his hero a tragic dimension superior to that of Danson, the hero of David Ananou's novel, *Le fils du fétiche*. Spoiled by propaganda and polemic, this author's method is to manipulate his main character through extremely complex situations in the animistic bush of Dahomey, so that, as he says, he can "point out certain pagan anomalies and deplore . . . the grotesqueness of fetishism in order to show the glories of the Christian faith."[14]

It is now fitting that we analyze more deeply the structure of the plot and the conflict of the hero in *The Palm-Wine Drinkard* and show how Tutuola, a humanistic and utopian writer, has built or reconstructed an anomalous universe from sixteen episodes, the contents of which are invested with a coherent organization according to a genuine mythic process.

---

14. David Ananou, *Le fils du fétiche* (Paris, 1955), p. 193. Cf. also the introduction to this work.

Structure of a Utopian Conquest

By isolating the beginning and the end of Tutuola's masterpiece and also by grouping together the rest of the anecdotes under three principal instants, we arrive first at a simple breakdown of the structure of the tale, thereby also revealing its heterogeneous and anecdotal character. The narrative unity is insured by the authentic and central presence of the hero. (See fig. i.)

There is a parallelism in structure and function between the three anecdotes which make up the group A, and it is upon those mainly that our analysis will bear. The other groups consist of more or less gratuitous repetition of the same type of marvel. The function of the three anecdotes is to validify the identity of the hero by proving, in particular, .his pretensions to omnipotence. Into these anecdotes Tutuola introduces a number of variations on a theme, common to all folklore, of the rogue expert in malicious cunning, while at the same time he preserves the taste for pleasantries and the moral instruction common among traditional storytellers. We have employed the symbols β, γ, θ, δ to denote the four different levels on which the principal conflict is articulated, from the arrival of the hero at the home of the agent of information (the king-god) to the moment of his departure. All, however, is inscribed within the global context of one grand quest for the Deads' Town. (See fig. ii.)

The incidents can be summed up as follows:

Anecdote A. 1: Moderate Test. The hero is requested by the god to fetch an object which he has confided to a smith; triumphant, the hero returns with a bell.

Anecdote A. 2: Intermediate Test. The hero is requested by the god to fetch Death in a net from his house. By a successive intervention of magic and superb trickery, the hero succeeds in returning with Death in a net to the home of the incredulous god.

Anecdote A. 3: Supreme Test. The hero is asked by the god to find out and bring home his daughter who has allegedly been kidnapped by a strange, unknown creature. The hero succeeds in identifying the "complete gentleman" who turns out to be only a Skull. His chivalrous success is then crowned with a recompense: marriage between the saviour and the saved. Result of the marriage: the birth of a prodigy who menaces the life of his parents, until he finally disappears in company of the musical trio: "Drum," "Song," and "Dance." (See fig. iii.)

Considered as a social or moral structure elaborated on the level of the collective unconscious, Utopia is a form of myth.[15] Thus, the three anecdotes whose contents have just been summarized above, constitute tests whose function is dual:

First, they reveal a structural homogeneity in the enactment of the dramatic action. Second, they show that Tutuola's thematic vision is inscribed within an incomplete utopian or mythical construction. This central quest-theme logically implies the formal schema of an intrigue type: departure → voyage → protective intervention → peril → delivery → return → manifestation of gratitude. The final objective remains the same: to satisfy the capricious demands of the gods in order to win from them a reward by way of an information relative to the Deads' Town, where the Drinkard hopes to encounter his tapster.

The gods remain forever suspicious and difficult to please, even scornful of all man's attempts to deal with them. In this respect, one can cite the hero's confrontation with Death. More than anything else in Tutuola's work, this test of strength is the best evidence of his humanism. In it he conveys man's tragic greatness and indomitable spirit and his sometimes arrogant determination to overcome all obstacles in order to attain his goal. Shall one conclude, then, given the final triumph of the hero over his formidable adversary, that Tutuola has truly found in the realm of folklore and popular mythology, or in the collective unconscious, a logical foreshadowing of "the death of God," a concept upon which the atheistic existentialists, among them Nietzsche, have placed great moral significance? Be that as it may, caught between the necessity to exert his human will and the cosmic obstacle which the divine will puts in his way, sometimes with no reason, man can realize only a partial success. One finds this idea also in the works of Chinua Achebe and other Ibo novelists of Eastern Nigeria. The setting of their works, however, is much more realistic, and, with Tutuola, the conflict is not just between the human and the divine will but also between the individual and the collective consciousness.

If one focuses briefly on Anecdote A. 3, one sees how Tutuola has introduced the latter theme into his work. At this point, the author emphasizes his modern views and his awareness of the real social problem, that is, the disintegration of traditional family bonds, the

---

15. It is to be noted that C. G. Jung raised the problem of myth and the phenomenon of archetypes as a part of the activity of the collective unconscious (cf. *Psychologie de l'inconscient*, Zurich, 1916; and *L'inconscient dans la vie psychique normale et anormale*, Paris, 1952). Karl Mannheim has also elaborated upon the connection between ideology and utopia on the unconscious and on the conscious level (cf. *Ideology and Utopia: an Introduction to the Sociology of Knowledge*, London, 1936).

result of social change. The kidnapping victim is a young woman who has rebelled against the despotism of her father because of a marriage into which he wanted to force her.

She is, therefore, an "other-directed" character. Betrayed by her parents, made vain by her beauty, the young woman foolishly falls in love with a "complete gentleman," a stranger whom she has met purely by chance in the market. Here again one gets a clear idea of the virtuosity, the mystical energy with which Tutuola has described the result of that casual meeting. In short, after having drawn a flattering, indeed exaggerated, picture of his "complete gentleman," the author of *The Palm-Wine Drinkard* next proceeds step by step to the unravelling of his mystery, which is truly a *reductio ad absurdum*. Consisting of a progressive unveiling of the gentleman's true self, this mythic process reveals the enormity of the cynicism and scorn Tutuola himself feels toward the "westernized gentlemen" of Lagos. These are the so-called advanced men, the *nouveaux riches*, seducers and betrayers of young women who rebel against their families in the bush. In this matter, Tutuola is like other novelists and social critics, notably Abdoulayi Sadji and Cyprian Ekwensi, who have used a similar theme in *Maimouna* and *Jagua Nana*, respectively. It is through such episodes that Tutuola clearly reveals his socially and morally didactic purpose. For this writer, oriented toward the traditionally absolute, toward magical or folkloristic reality, the main point is in unveiling a myth, in diminishing the bourgeois pretensions of his complete gentleman most logically to the point of absurdity. The next most important thing is to show the would-be modern young woman the foolishness of her choice and the stupidity of her rebellion against traditional family values by making her undergo the most traumatic experience possible. Perhaps this is a way of requiring a ritual expiation from her.

It would seem possible also to consider the birth of Zurrjir, the prodigy, as punishment and expiation. He is the result of the sacrilegious marriage of the hero and a devil-woman. One is reminded that Abdoulayi Sadji also used a similar device in *Tounka*. Throughout the plot of this novel, one observes a psychological element: the criticism of cross-breeding in Senegal. Since then, Sadji has given greater socio--psychological dimensions to this theme in his novel, *Nini, mulâtresse du Sénégal*. What is more disconcerting and more revealing in the mythic use Tutuola has made of this event is the way in which the unhappy parents finally get rid of their prodigy. So, the meeting with Drum, Song, and Dance is a messianic meeting. They may be considered as anthropomorphic characters of traditional reality, or as three aspects of the collective African soul, for the prodigy immediately ran off with them. What Tutuola is trying to do thus takes on a new allegorical dimension, the sublimation of individual conflict and unhappiness in the therapeutic ritual which reflects the collective consciousness.

Chinua Achebe's novels display a similar process of ritual exorcism, which is especially seen through the role of the principal guardian of the clan's authority, above all during the traditional festivals in which the whole community participates.

The Abortive Denouement

A number of events take place before the Drinkard finally meets his tapster in the Deads' Town. This is after he has encroached with the liberty of an astronaut or the impunity of a nineteenth century European explorer in Africa upon the democratically delimited frontiers of the under-world beings. Each intrusion into the territorial frontier constitutes on the part of the hero a transgression more or less serious according to the actual psychological disposition of the interested inhabitants. Thus at B. I (see fig. i) the hero and his wife are exposed to disapproval and ridicule. This even provokes in Tutuola a striking anatomy of the psychology of "Laughter."[16] One sees in particular how Tutuola's prose explodes into a veritable incantatory ritualism in order to capture in dramatic suspense the prolonged and native affectivity of this phenomenon. Once mythically recreated, this unhappy atmosphere is later contrasted with the idyllic reception reserved for the hero in the Wraith-Island (B. II). The procedure is repetitive, for the monstrous avarice of the Spirit of Prey (B. III) is also contrasted with the Faithful Mother, proprietress of the White-Tree (B. IV). By such a system of contrasts and alternation of characters, Tutuola transmits a moralizing vision of the society implicit in all popular folklore. Besides, one can see in Tutuola some influences of the Bible: first that of the Genesis in the Old Testament based upon inspired prophecies and the myths of prenatal man; then those of the Apocalypse of John and the New Testament founded upon conflicts with dragons or the myth of man in becoming. One of the experiences lived by the hero in the course of his return voyage (C. III) is a variation on the biblical theme of Jonah trapped in the stomach of the whale.

The actual confrontation between the Drinkard and his tapster, or between the hero and the finality of his search, is an abortive denouement. This does not necessarily imply a failure in the mythical organization of the work itself. Not having any esthetic pretensions at

---

16. J. Jahn, p. 103, considers Tutuola's use of "Laughter" as *Kuntu*, a "modal force."

all, Tutuola's intention is to leave the events and episodes within the fairy land without seeking to impose on them any artistic unity. The generic interest of the work itself lies, therefore, in the fact that the hero is conducted through an incoherent series of rites of passage into what can be regarded as a final initiation or self-knowledge. With Camara Laye, a more conscious artist than Tutuola and one who employs a similar ritualistic structure of initiation in his novel, *Le regard du roi*, the effect is entirely different. Here the sequence of events as well as the nature of the experience of the hero are adapted to a veritable ritualistic and artistic mode of initiation. By contrast, the author of *The Palm-Wine Drinkard* entertains us to a repetitive pattern of marvels. This is evident especially in group C, where the anecdotic functions are duplicated with the effect, sometimes, of crescendo and even boredom. The logical deduction is that Tutuola has not succeeded in completely dominating the substance of folklore, in penetrating in any satisfactory way its monolithic forms in order to construct a novel in the classic sense of the term. Instead of a total transposition of the folkloristic into the real world, Tutuola betrays a modern individualistic vision within which both traditional values and technological data are confounded. His hero is not a human personage but a "sample" of man. He is presented to us as a mythical synthesis of two forms of individual, which we have examined in another study:[17] the tradition-directed and the inner-directed.

Having arrived at the end of his journey, the hero is astonished to ascertain the reality of his individual failure, which is conveyed through the immense strangeness of the Deads' Town, through the novelty of its values and its ways, and through the extent of his tapster's adaptation to them.

> He told us that both white and black deads were living in the Deads' Town, not a single alive was there at all. Because everything that they were doing there was incorrect to alives and everything that all alives were doing was incorrect to deads too.[18]

The Drinkard, however, is compensated for his so apparent devotion:

> . . . when he came, I told him that we should leave here tomorrow morning, then he gave me an 'EGG'. He told me to keep it as safely as gold and said that if I reached my town, I should keep it inside my box and said that the use of the egg was to give me anything that I wanted in this

---

17. *Sociologie du roman africain* (Paris, 1970).
18. *The Palm-Wine Drinkard*, p. 100.

world and if I wanted to use it, I must put it in a big bowl of water, then I would mention the name of anything I wanted.[19]

Thus, the magic egg becomes a war trophy for the hero. It is, moreover, the only nostalgic reminder of a journey to the extremity of darkness, but, as a compensation or as a gift from a god to a mortal, how fragile it is! Perhaps Tutuola's metaphysical realism makes itself known gradually, as one observes in folklore or in popular mythology, not as simple games of gratuitous interaction between gods, men, and beasts, but as questions of great moral and philosophic bearing. One can ask oneself, for example, why in the last anecdote of the narrative Tutuola chose to bring in the magic power of the egg precisely at the moment when a cosmic drama is beginning about a disagreement between Heaven and Land over as insignificant a matter as the sharing of a mouse. Since this disagreement provokes great misfortune for human beings, is not Tutuola's intention to save innocent victims from a capricious interplanetary conflict and to reinforce even more the opposition of moral categories such as crime and punishment, gratitude and ingratitude? In the end, Tutuola's work shows how reality eludes total comprehension. It also shows that traditional magic cannot constitute an effective instrument of research and absolute knowledge.

It cannot therefore be asserted that at the time when he wrote *The Palm-Wine Drinkard* Tutuola had totally abdicated every consciousness of the social reality and the transformations taking place in his African traditional environment. His creative orientation toward folklore and mythology stands as evidence of his personal nostalgia, which an essentially dramatic mind feels with respect to traditional realism, and of the desire to identify himself with an experience lived and integrated within the totality of collective life, and to seek the primitive source of group ethics which is their folklore. The result of such a quest is the ultimate illumination of a fundamental paradox, the schism between the real and the illusory, the possible and the impossible. These ethical aberrations have a sociopsychological nature evident even in the structure of the images and language of Tutuola whose origin can be accounted for by the fact of culture-contact in Africa as well as by the rapid transition from tradition to modernity. A major difference between Tutuola and Achebe is that the author of *Things Fall Apart* has not only transformed this phenomenal paradox, this absence of cohesion in traditional structure into a formal principle for his novels, but also has situated the historical and human peripeties of the dramatic conflicts within one concrete traditional society, that of the Ibos of Nigeria, utilizing for this flesh and blood characters.

---

19. *The Palm-Wine Drinkard*, p. 101.

BEGINNING	MIDDLE			END
	A HERO ALONE	B HERO MARRIED	C RETURN OF COUPLE	
Engagement of Tapster → Death of Tapster → Desertion by Friend → Ingratitude Triumphant → Hero's Resolution and Departure	I. Bell II. Death III. Skull	I. Termites' House II. Wraith-Island III. Spirit of Prey IV. The Unreturnable-Heaven's Town V. The Faithful Mother in the White Tree VI. The Red-People in the Red-Town VII. The Wise King in the Wrong Town with the Prince Killer VIII. I and My Palm-Wine Tapster in the Deads' Town	I. Dead-Babies on the Road to the Deads' Town II. Terrible Creatures in Bag III. Both Wife and Husband in the Hungry-Creature's Stomach IV. The Mixed Town V. The Mountain-Creatures on the Unknown Mountain	Heaven/Land Conflict → Famine → 1st Intervention of Magical Egg → Friends' Return → Loss of Egg → 2nd Flight of Friends → 2nd Intervention of Magical Egg → Ingratitude Punished → Sacrifice & Pacification of Heaven → Rain

Fig. i. **Simple Breakdown of the Structure of the Tale**

251

Fig. ii. Basic Structure of the Episodes

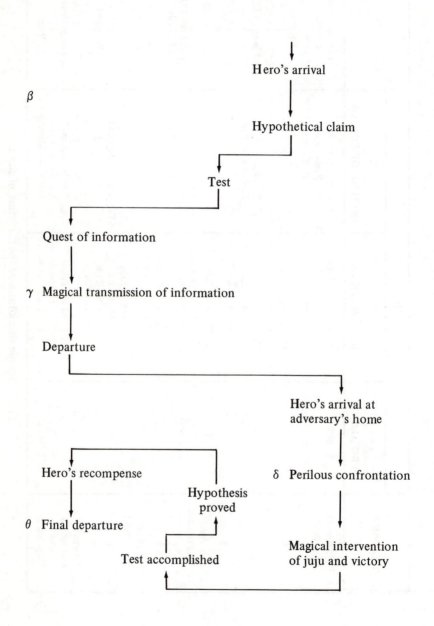

Fig. iii. Progression and Denouement θ

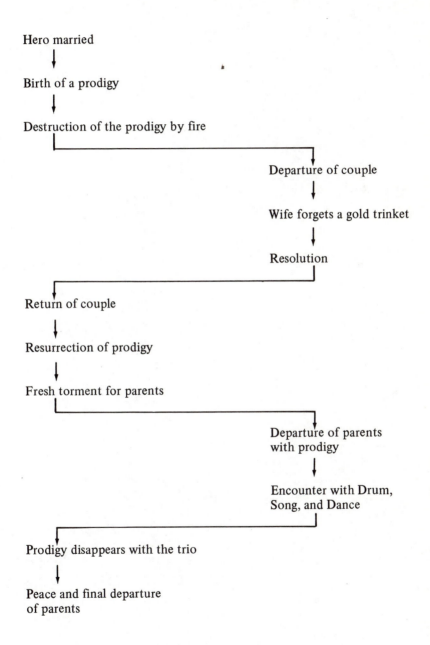

Hero married

Birth of a prodigy

Destruction of the prodigy by fire

Departure of couple

Wife forgets a gold trinket

Resolution

Return of couple

Resurrection of prodigy

Fresh torment for parents

Departure of parents
with prodigy

Encounter with Drum,
Song, and Dance

Prodigy disappears with the trio

Peace and final departure
of parents

The Farm and the Wilderness in Tutuola's
The Palm-Wine Drinkard

PAUL EDWARDS

Amos Tutuola's novel is more commonly admired for its free-running fancy than for anything that could be called its structure, and apart from its archetypal form of the quest, there might appear to be little evidence of patterning. Omolara Leslie's[1] article stresses this view: '. . . the novel is picaresque hence episodic.' Indeed, what seems to be a clear instance of the absence of form is the introduction of the tale of the quarrel between earth and heaven into the novel's closing pages. But I suggest that it might be less arbitrary than it appears, and that the episode is given its peculiar prominence as the culmination of a central and repeated image.

Writing of the quest motif in the tale, Omolara Leslie remarks: 'Tutuola has come to the pattern naturally and not through an intellectual choice conceived as "structure". Tutuola is certainly not aware of such monsters as "monomyths" and "archetypes".' This may or may not be true – we are aware of more things than we attach labels to, and Omolara Leslie acknowledges this fact in a footnote which draws attention to Northrop Frye's categories in 'The Archetypes of Literature'. I propose to begin my case by referring to Northrop Frye's *Anatomy of Criticism*,[2] particularly to his description of opposed apocalyptic and demonic worlds, imaged characteristically as farm or garden on the one hand, wilderness on the other.

Frye writes that 'the apocalyptic world, the heaven of religion, presents, in the first place, the categories of reality in the forms of human desire, as indicated by the forms they assume under the work of human civilization. The form imposed by human work and desire on the *vegetable* world, for instance, is that of the garden, the farm, the grove, or the park.'[3] He notes that the biblical image of the divine

Reprinted from *The Journal of Commonwealth Literature*, 9 (1974), 57-65.

equivalent to the vegetable world of farm or garden is 'the One Tree (of Life)'. Opposed to apocalyptic symbolism is 'the presentation of the world that desire totally rejects: the world of the nightmare and the scapegoat, of bondage and pain and confusion; the world as it is before the human imagination begins to work on it and before any image of human desire, such as the city or the garden, has been established'.⁴ Frye points out that 'one of the central themes of demonic imagery is parody',⁴ and that the apocalyptic vegetable world of farm or garden is parodied in demonic imagery by 'a sinister forest like the ones we meet in *Comus* or the opening of the *Inferno,* or a heath which from Shakespeare to Hardy has been associated with tragic destiny, or a wilderness like that of Browning's *Childe Roland* or Eliot's *Waste Land'.⁵* It can also be 'a sinister enchanted garden' like that of Circe, and parodies the tree of life with a tree of death of which 'scaffolds, gallows, stocks, pillories, whips, and birch rods are or could be modulations'.⁵ It is also a world of dragons and other monstrous beasts, of human violence and labyrinthine wanderings.

It is clear that these opposed worlds resemble those of the Drinkard. At the start of the tale we learn that he is a kind of farmer, but living complacently in a world of false fertility. One of a family of eight brothers, he tells us that 'all the rest were hard workers, but I myself was an expert palm-wine drinkard'.⁶ The use of the word 'expert' here appears an ironic acknowledgement of the drinkard's complacent state. His father gives him a palm-tree farm, and engages the 'expert palm-wine tapster', and the Drinkard himself emerges as an exploiter of nature's fertility, unaware that this abundance is threatened in an organic world. Dearth suddenly enters this false Paradise when first his generous father, and then his skilled tapster die, the two men on whom he has been dependent; nature too now demands her fee, the farm goes to waste; and the Drinkard's vulnerability is defined in social terms as his fair-weather friends desert him. So he enters the wilderness in which he is to stray, searching for Deads' Town, and his journey is to be characterized by a rhythmic movement between, on the one hand, states of terror and distress, and, on the other periods in temporary Edens associated with farming, trees, and another recurrent image of harmony, music and dance.

The Drinkard's powers of endurance and his ability to deal with suffering begin to emerge in his adventures in Death's house and the underworld of the skulls where he wins his wife. Burdened with the half-bodied baby (the demon child, seemingly a parody of natural fertility, born from its mother's thumb), the drinkard and his wife begin their long pilgrimage. The baby both parodies and parallels the Drinkard's own parasitism in the opening part of the novel; its vast appetite ('he could eat the whole food of this world without satisfaction' – p. 37) recalls the Drinkard's gigantic capacity for palm-wine in Chapter One. The Drinkard feels the burden of his own helplessness: 'Ah, how could we escape from this half-bodied baby?' It is at this point that he first hears the music of the trio, Drum, Song, and Dance, who are to play a crucial role in the tale. With his wife he follows them, 'dancing for a good five days without eating' (p. 38), reluctantly ('We did not want to follow them up to that place, but we could not control ourselves as we were dancing along with them' – p. 89). This period of fasting and penitential dancing delivers them from the burden of the monstrous child, however, and natural harmony has overcome the unnatural.

Other terrors and pains are endured; white creatures surround them crying, 'cold! cold! cold!' (p. 42); they travel through a field with no trees or palm-trees, 'only long wild grasses grew there, all resembled corn plants, the edges of its leaves were as sharp as razor blades and hairy' (p. 43); they come to a decaying palace, 'almost covered with refuse, it resembled an old ruined house, it was very rough', which belongs to a king who 'himself was refuse, because he was almost covered with both dried and undried leaves and we could not see his feet and face etc.' (p. 45) The king has them stabbed with a sharp stick. Characteristic of these episodes of the journey is the sense of dereliction, waste, and pain in the vegetable world, and it is at this point that the travellers reach their first temporary Eden, Wraith-Island. These paradise-people of the island 'were very kind and they loved themselves, their work was only to plant their food, after that they had no other work more than to play music and dance. They were the most beautiful creatures in the world of the curious creatures and also the most wonderful dancers and musicians' (p. 47). So the two key images of harmony and accommodation, the farm and the dance, come together for the first of several times in the tale. The Drinkard plants his first farm but after a while a terrible creature begins to eat his crops. It turns out, however, that it is the Drinkard, not the creature, who has disturbed the delicate harmony of the island, for the monster is really the spirit-owner of the land, and wishes for no more than his proper share. The Drinkard makes his gift (or sacrifice) and the creature, now a benevolent spirit, returns the honour with a gift of magical fast-growing seeds. The Drinkard grows these wonderful crops 'and when dried, I cut them and kept their seeds as a reference as we were travelling about in the bush' (p. 48). These seeds are to reappear at a later point in the tale, another harmonious moment imaged in the farm and the great dance of nature.

But Wraith-Island is not their destination, and after eighteen months of contented farming and dancing they feel the impulse to move on through the wilderness. After describing the beneficent send-off that he and his wife experience, the Drinkard comments: 'If it was in their power, they would have led us to our destination, but they were forbidden to touch another creature's land or bush.' (p. 51)

Whether good or evil, the creatures of the bush are unable to move from their own places, but the Drinkard is established as the one who can, indeed must, keep moving. To farm is delightful, but the Drinkard has entered upon the journey of the imagination and must pursue it to its end. His seven hardworking brothers of the opening page will never go through his terrors or experience the sharpness of his joys, nor will they need to for their state is one of contented existence, and the story is not concerned with it. But the Drinkard is the imaginative man, the teller of his own tale (like the Ancient Mariner or Conrad's Marlow), the mental traveller, and his stage is one of continuing excited or terrified consciousness. He is the poet, the madman, the drunk.[7]

So he and his wife move on into the worlds of the 'cruel, greedy and merciless creatures' (p. 60) and of monstrous appetites: 'To my surprise, he had eaten off the dead body of the buffalo within four minutes' (p. 55) – yet another parody-echo of the Drinkard's own initial appetite. They build but only 'a small temporary house' in the threatening bush, fenced with sticks 'so that it might keep us from the animals etc.' (p. 64) They live by killing 'bush animals', and picking 'edible fruits'. This is the life of the wilderness, the life of mere survival and constant threat, and Wraith-Island is behind them, an 'Unreturnable-Heaven's Town'. They are committed to their journey:

We thought that to go back to the town of my wife's father was dangerous, because of various punishments, and we could not trace out the right way on which we travelled from that place again. To go back was harder and to go further was hardest, so at last we made up our mind and started to go forward. (p. 64)

So they move towards the next stage of peace and harmony after their period in the wilderness. At first it appears yet another terror as the great white tree seems to be 'focusing us as if a photographer was focusing somebody'. But the tree is a Tree of Life,[8] the home of 'Faithful-Mother' and a place of abundance, kindly care, and inevitably, music and dance:

This beautiful hall was full of all kinds of food and drinks, over twenty stages were in that hall with uncountable orchestras, musicians, dancers and tappers. The orchestras were always busy. The children of seven to eight years etc. of age were always dancing, tapping on the stage with melodious songs and they were also singing with warm tones with non-stop dance till morning. (p. 68)

But this is no permanent Eden either, and the Drinkard is due to be cast out again into the wilderness of the world. The generosity of the Faithful-Mother and the absence of threat and activity lead the Drinkard to the edge once more of complacent parasitism. 'Within a week that we were living with this mother,' he tells us, 'we had forgotten all our past torments.' (p. 69) When the time comes for them to move on, they try to avoid their commitment to the journey:

But after we had completed the period of one year and two weeks with Faithful-Mother, one night she called my wife and me and told us that it was time for us to leave there and continue our journey as usual. When she said this we begged her not to let us leave there ever, then she replied that she had no right to delay anybody more than a year and some days, she said again that if it had been in her power, she would grant our request. (pp.70–71)

As with the people of Wraith-Island, the Mother 'must not go beyond the boundary' and can do no more than provide them with gifts and show them the way. They emerge from the tree and 'both of us (my wife and I) said suddenly "We are in the bush again." '

They move on towards their next adventure, amongst the people of Red-Town, where there is a curious twist of appearance. This time it is the Drinkard himself who seems like a monster, and when he becomes the destroyer of the grotesque red-fish and red-bird, far from feeling relief the people of the town see him as an even greater demon and threat:

But when the Red-king saw the two red creatures already dead, he said – 'Here is another fearful and harmful creature who could ruin my town in future.' (He called me a fearful and harmful creature.) (p. 81)

His astonished tone indicates his sudden realization of yet another aspect of himself, that he is simultaneously victim and killer, and when the whole of the Red-people vanish in the form of two disappearing red trees ('and all the leaves on these trees were singing as human beings' – p. 82) taking his wife along with them, he pursues them and seeks friendship. At this moment, the 'three fellows', Drum, Song, and Dance, re-appear, and are called, curiously, at one point, 'the tree fellows' (p. 83). It may simply be a misprint, but bearing in mind that 'three' and 'tree' are pronounced almost identically in West African English speech, and that the Tree of Life and the two red trees have been associated with harmonious music, it seems possibly a deliberate pun. At any rate, the great harmonious dance of nature now takes place as a preliminary to the planting of the magical seeds brought from Wraith-Island:

But when the day that they appointed for this special occasion was reached, these fellows came and when 'Drum' started to beat himself, all the people who had been dead for hundreds of years, rose up and came to witness 'Drum' when beating; and when 'Song' began to sing all domestic animals of that new town, bush animals with snakes etc; came out to see 'Song' personally, but when 'Dance' (that lady) started to dance the whole bush creatures, spirits, mountain creatures and also all the river creatures came to the town to see who was dancing. When these three fellows started at the same time, the whole people of the new town, the whole people that rose up from the grave, animals, snakes, spirits and other nameless creatures, were dancing together with these three fellows and it was that day that I saw that snakes were dancing more then human-beings or other creatures. When the whole people of that town and bush creatures started dancing together none of them could stop for two days. But at last 'Drum' was beating himself till he reached heaven before he knew that he was out of the world and since that day he could not come to the world again. Then 'Song' sang until he entered into a large river unexpectedly and we could not see him any more and 'Dance' was dancing till she became a mountain and did not appear to anybody since that day, so all the deads rose up from the grave returned to the grave and since that day they could not rise up again, then all the rest of the creatures went back to the bush etc. but since that day they could not come to the town and dance with anybody or with human-beings.

So when these three fellows (Drum, Song, and Dance) disappeared, the people of the new town went back to their houses. Since that day nobody could see the three fellows personally, but we are only hearing their names about in the world and nobody could do in these days what they did. After I had spent a year with my wife in this new town, I became a rich man. Then I hired many labourers to clear bush for me and it was cleared up to three miles square by these farm-labourers, then I planted the seeds and grains which were given me in the 'Wraith-Island' by a certain animal (as he was called) the owner of the land on which I planted my crops, before he gave me the seeds and grains which germinated the same day as I planted them. As the seeds and grains grew up and yielded fruits the same day, so it made me richer than the rest of the people in that town. (pp. 84–5)

This passage describes the high-point in the Drinkard's journey, his vision of a golden age which vanishes almost at the moment of perception, as the three fellows leave the world to its inevitable broken harmonies and the cycle of life and death implicit in the harvesting. The dance gives way to a world of disharmony as the Drinkard exploits the labour of the Invisible-Pawn, and is in turn exploited and cheated by him, for his other name is Give and Take, an ironic re-interpretation of the normal meaning of the expression, mutual tolerance. He is back in the waste land again: '. . . they could not plant other crops throughout that year again and had nothing for themselves and their children to eat at all and all of my own crops were taken away too . . .' (pp. 89–90)

The people of the town, his former friends, now threaten to kill the Drinkard, and his only way to survival is to call on Invisible-Pawn to help him. Invisible-Pawn marches in from the bush, 'then the whole of them started to fight these people and killed the whole of them and left my wife and me there alone' (p. 91). What began as universal dance ends in a fallen world of treachery and violence; the rest of the journey, apart from the conversation with the dead tapster and his gift of the magical productive egg (another seed), is through suffering and enmity, with echoes of the world that came before the apocalyptic vision of the harmonious dance. There are more demonic babies (p. 102) followed by more monstrous eating, when even the Drinkard and his wife are consumed (p. 108) and crazily reborn through the shattered belly of the monster. They now reach 'mixed town', where the Drinkard is asked to give judgement in two court cases. But the cases are dilemma tales, with no solution possible. 'So', he says, 'I shall be very much grateful if anyone who reads this story-book can judge one or both cases', and explains that the cases are 'still pending and waiting for me' (p. 115). Only in the ideal or visionary world can the contraries be reconciled, as in the great dance: but in the fallen world of the journey there appear to be no harmonious solutions, only continuing dilemmas and confrontations. Even the dance now takes on a sinister quality as they meet 'the mountain creatures on the unknown mountain' (p. 115), a parody of the tree-home of Faithful-Mother. At first all seems pleasant enough, but the Drinkard's wife is invited to join the dance, and finds herself trapped. She wants to stop after a while but the creatures grow angry and will not let her go. The Drinkard uses his magic and they escape with their lives, but it is their last adventure in the wilderness. It seems that his father is still alive ('I met my parents safely too'), even though he died in the opening section of the tale. But it would be unwise to demand rational happenings in a dream-tale such as this. The impression here is of a return to the world of the Drinkard before the disasters of his father's death, the loss of the tapster, the wasting of the farm and the departure of the friends. His father is still alive, his friends are around him as before, and he settles down to drink two-hundred kegs of palm-wine, having hidden away the egg which will now do for him all that the tapster had done before. The tale has come full circle, 'and so all our trials, difficulties and many years' travel brought only an egg or resulted in an egg' (p. 118). It looks as if the original tale ended here, for the next paragraph closes: 'That was how the story of the palm-wine drinkard and his dead tapster went.' But Tutuola had not said all he wished to say, and the tale ends with a curious account of how Famine was caused by a quarrel between Land and Heaven. During the famine, the Drinkard feeds the whole world with his magic egg. But people demand more and more of the egg, eat and drink too much, start fighting, and smash the egg. The Drinkard repairs it with glue, but now it will produce nothing but whips, to whip mankind out of the tale. The moral point is obvious enough, but the tale is still not concluded, for the famine remains. A sacrifice is made to 'Heaven in heaven', the rain falls for three months and 'there was no famine again'.

What has happened is a return to natural harmony on earth, which might parallel the vision of harmony in the great dance, also associated with the second of the Drinkard's farms. The tale ends with the reconciliation of Heaven and Earth by Water, the three elements, it will be remembered, into which Drum, Song, and Dance vanished. There does seem to be a shaping imagination at work here of a more complex kind than is usually associated with this tale. The Drinkard has grown, through experience and vision, from a layabout to a man of spiritual powers. Through his vision and knowledge, he is able to serve the land and the men who work it, men like his seven diligent brothers. He has passed through various sufferings without which he could never have experienced the harmonious farm-and-dance life of Wraith-

Island, the tree-dance of Faithful-Mother, or the universal dance of Drum, Song, and Dance. In each case, the harmony of song and dance is associated with vegetable life, either in the image of the farm, or that of the tree. And he brings back with him from Deads' Town another image of creation, the egg. Fallen mankind destroys the egg, but the Drinkard's knowledge remains, and it is he who knows how the gods are to be propitiated, and his people ultimately saved.

That something like the pattern described exists in the tale is, I think, unquestionable. That it is the only pattern, or that I have interpreted it fully or correctly is another matter entirely. I have insufficient knowledge to take into account the Yoruba consciousness which Omolara Leslie very properly refers to as a fundamental feature of the work and if I had that knowledge it might have led me to very different conclusions. What is striking, all the same, is the similarity of so many elements of this work to those of European and Oriental myth, and the discovery which we need to make over and over again, it seems, that in spite of surface differences, men continue to bring up remarkably similar things from the mental underworld.

University of Edinburgh

NOTES

1 Omolara Leslie, '*The Palm-Wine Drinkard*: A Reassessment of Amos Tutuola', *JCL*, 9 (1970), pp. 48–56.
2 Northrop Frye, *Anatomy of Criticism*, Princeton, 1957.
3 ibid., p. 141.
4 ibid., p. 147.
5 ibid., p. 149.
6 Amos Tutuola, *The Palm-Wine Drinkard*, Faber, 1953, paperback edn., p. 7; subsequent references to the book are given in parenthesis in the body of the article.
7 A connection between the three is widely recognized. In north-west European tradition, for example, Odin is the generous mead-giver in his banqueting hall Valhalla, but also the god of poetry, which is called Odin's mead. His name is cognate with the Anglo-Saxon *wod*, mad (*Wodan id est furor* notes Adam of Bremen) and with the Welsh *gwawd*, which means both poetry and mockery or abuse. In *A Midsummer Night's Dream* Shakespeare links the lunatic with the poet, but adds the lover instead of the drunk.
8 For another close association of tree and dance as images of harmony, see Yeats's 'Among School Children'.

Tutuola, the Riddler

Richard Priebe

Criticism, if it is worth anything, should ultimately propose models that help to explain, clarify, or simply give the reader a handle on whatever is going on in a given creative work. A disproportionate amount of the criticism on Tutuola has been directed at assessing his literary value, at the question of whether Tutuola is "extraordinarily good, extraordinarily bad, or extraordinarily lucky."[1] The fact, however, that Tutuola is generally more highly regarded in the West than in Africa is quite significant—not because, as has been asserted on one side, Africans have willfully refused to recognize a native son who is a literary genius, nor, as has been asserted on the other side, because Europeans have been naive and patronizing in their praise of a man who has simply written down stories that many young Yoruba children could tell, but because they do show us how relative culture-based perceptions, or more specifically, esthetics, are. Knowing that the story of the "beautiful complete gentleman" is commonplace in West Africa does not necessarily lessen one's enjoyment in reading Tutuola's interpretation of it any more than knowing that phrases such as "he would not have to listen before hearing" or "bad-bye function"[2] are non-standard English, or possibly transliterated Yoruba, ruins the freshness and vitality of these figures of speech. At the same time, for one who already finds Tutuola commonplace or tedious, learning that his tales conform to some monomythic pattern will do little to change that opinion.

1. Bernth Lindfors, "Amos Tutuola: Debts and Assets," *Cahiers d'études africaines*, 10 (1970), 333.

2. *The Palm-Wine Drinkard* (New York: Grove Press, 1953), p. 27, and *My Life in the Bush of Ghosts* (New York: Grove Press, 1954), p. 156. Page references in parentheses will refer to these editions.

This essay was read at the Annual Meeting of the African Studies Association held in Chicago in October 1974.

The difficulties we face in dealing critically with Tutuola are legion. His works are as difficult to pin down as the monsters he writes about. In talking about the form of these stories, we have no label we can easily use. For convenience it is commonly referred to as the novel, but arguments have also been advanced that the form is that of the extended folktale, the prose epic, or the romance. The structure no less than the language of these works is often confusing, the characters as well as the settings are more often than not fantastic, and the situations we and the characters are presented with are always problematical. While there is a great deal of disagreement over the assessment he should be accorded, it is clear that the words, images and even the sense of what Tutuola is saying more often than not violate our prevailing notions of propriety, Western or African.

This sense of propriety being violated points to a rather significant aspect of Tutuola's work that has not yet been fully explored, namely the rhetorical stance of the author and the relationship between the authorial voice in these works and the audience. The rhetoric, of course, has been touched on by the critics who have recognized that Tutuola is more like a fireside raconteur than a conscious literary artist, but the implications have not been pursued. His rhetoric is that of a riddler; he generates confusion, transgresses propriety, and inverts our normal perceptions of the real, physical world, leaving us with the sheer joy we derive out of participating in that confusion as well as the astonishment we get on emerging from fictional chaos and finding the world re-ordered.

In his book, *The Philosophy of Literary Form*, Kenneth Burke puts forth the idea that complex literary works can be seen as "proverbs writ large." [3] The proverb, he argues, is a very primary unit through which we can see art as equipment for living. Proverbs name and encompass ranges of strategies or attitudes for handling recurrent situations. A good strategy must, of course, be functional and realistic—in other words, it must size things up rather accurately. Above all, the proverb must have vitality:

> The point of issue is not to find categories that "place
> the proverbs once and for all. What I want is categories that
> suggest their active nature. Here is not "realism for its own
> sake." Here is realism for promise, admonition, solace, fore-
> telling, instruction, charting, all for the direct bearing that
> such acts have upon matters of welfare. [4]

Yet not all complex literary works are written in a realistic mode, nor do they, like the proverb, necessarily function in any realistic manner.

---

3. (New York: Vintage Books, 1957), p. 256.

4. Ibid., p. 255.

It might help us to extend Burke's idea and think not only of "proverbs writ large" but also of "riddles writ large." Proverbs are often structured around a metaphor, but if the proverb is to function when used in a social context, the analogue to the real situation must be readily apprehended by those to whom the proverb is directed. In contrast, whatever is being described in a riddle must not be very apparent. All the clues may be there, but the description must lead the audience away from any easy answer. The riddle thus tends to be problematic rather than normative, confusing rather than clear. It creates artificial conflict and opens speculation, whereas the proverb smooths over conflict and closes further thought. Even when a proverb is metaphorical in its form, it must function as a simile, showing clearly that one thing is like another. The riddle, however, must always function metaphorically, drawing together apparently incongruous elements, a point first noted by Aristotle in his *Poetics*: "For the essence of a riddle is to express true fact under impossible combinations. Now this cannot be done by any arrangement of ordinary words, but by the use of metaphor it can." [5]

This is also the very nature of what Tutuola is doing in each of his works. *The Palm-Wine Drinkard, My Life in the Bush of Ghosts*, and all the other books are, in effect, riddles writ large. Tutuola spins us into a world where the impossible is always possible. There is always just enough of the world and language we recognize for us to follow what he is doing, but he continually startles us by rearranging the pieces in ways we never imagined. As a riddler he cannot be second-guessed, for he is always creating his own grammar.

Tutuola's works, like myth, explore the riddles of existence. In *The Palm-Wine Drinkard* he deals with the very primary question of death. In *My Life in the Bush of Ghosts* the riddle we confront is hatred. A young boy, not old enough to know what is "good" or "bad," learns what hatred does as he is driven into a bush of terrors. Simbi, in *Simbi and the Satyr of the Dark Jungle*, leaves her wealthy family to discover and "experience the difficulties of the 'Poverty' and of the 'Punishment'," in short, to fathom the meaning of suffering. The young lady in *The Brave African Huntress*, like the Drinkard, is one who has "sold death." Here, however, the end is to explore the nature of bravery. The "entertainments" narrated by the Yoruba chief in *Feather Woman of the Jungle* explore the mystery of wealth. Finally, in *Ajaiyi and His Inherited Poverty*, we have another look into the

---

5. Trans. S. H. Butcher, ed. Milton C. Nahn (New York: Library of Liberal Arts, 1956), p. 29. For a further discussion of this, see Robert A. Georges and Alan Dundes, "Toward a Structural Definition of the Riddle," *Journal of American Folklore*, 76 (1963), 111-18.

mystery of suffering, though this time from the perspective of one born into it. For later reference we might note that in all these works the characters must confront death. Simbi, for example, starts off her adventure heading down "the Path of Death."

Looking at *The Palm-Wine Drinkard*, let us now specifically apply the things we have been saying about the riddle. The story starts off as if there is going to be a plot centering around the Drinkard's search for his dead tapster, but as soon as we get past the first few episodes we realize that situation becomes more important than narrative development. The capture of death and the remarkable escape from the "Skull's family house" have almost no significance in terms of bringing the Drinkard closer to his tapster, though these and other episodes have a great deal of rhetorical impact as dramatically and cleverly resolved conundrums. Our attention is drawn away from any ultimate or final resolution and focused on the manner in which the Drinkard extricates himself from each of the successive agonistic moves. As in a riddling session, we derive pleasure from this pattern of tension and relief, since "what in everyday life proves disruptive, in play form is able to create fun and pleasure [this is simply a restatement of a bylaw of esthetics that threatening motives, when re-enacted in artificial form, create a sense of pleasurable control and completeness which is absent in everyday life]."[6]

Noting again that we are looking at *The Palm-Wine Drinkard* from a rhetorical and not a formal perspective, we must recognize that such a pattern is not limited to riddling sessions. Nevertheless, this pattern, coupled with the overriding presence of death, the ultimate riddle, the ultimate source of confusion and disorder, does distinguish it. Between his departure in search of his dead tapster and his return to his village the Drinkard has some nineteen or twenty adventures.[7] In all but two he faces the threat of death, and as we shall see later, the two exceptions add to our argument. Death, *the* riddle without an answer, must not simply be confronted and overpowered. The Drinkard is able to do this at the outset, but it does not get him to his tapster. He must first come to understand and resolve the enigma that death represents; then and only then can he "sell his death" and "lend his fear." This involves an understanding of death not in the biological sense as an absence of life, but in a mythic sense where death is seen as a necessary complement to life, and as an event that infuses life with value. Just as the

6. Roger D. Abrahams, "The Literary Study of the Riddle," *Texas Studies in Literature and Language*, 14, 1 (1972), 191.

7. This figure is somewhat arbitrary, as one might see a few of these adventures as constituting more than one distinct adventure.

resolution of a riddle is predicated on shifting modes of perception (in many cases simply shifting the way we perceive a certain word is being used), myth is able to resolve the life-death contradiction by playing off an alternative reality against our sensory reality. In other words, unless one sees into another order of things, namely a mythic order, death remains in its realistic frame as an annihilator of order and inducer of chaos.

To the extent that one of the basic functions of myth is to explain the primary contradictions of existence, mythic narrative tends to have the rhetorical structure of a riddle. Before going on to examine the Drinkard's coming to terms with death, it would be instructive to see the way this rhetoric works in an actual traditional myth.

In northern Ghana the Lo Dagaa have a secret society, Bagre, with which two very long narratives are associated. The first of these, "The White Bagre," appears to be a fairly straightforward narrative in which the Bagre ritual and explanation of the ritual are set forth. In contrast, the second piece, "The Black Bagre," appears from its opening lines to be problematical:

> In the beginning was god,
> the god of the initiates
> and their gods,
> the god who comes,
> the god with the mark between the eyes,
> the god with the white and black stripes,
> the god with the white arse,
> the thieving god,
> the lying god,
> the troubling god.[8]

Five thousand lines later we are given an explanation of who these gods are, no simple feat in a piece of oral literature of this length. We find, for example, that "the lying god" is a trickster who attempted to deceive man into thinking he could banish death if he learned to perform the Bagre. In a very immediate way, this trick has taught man, as the neophyte is continually taught, a very skeptical approach to one's sensory apprehension of reality:

> I had this sense [of banishing death]
> but it changed
> into a treacherous sense.
> I had this sense
> but it changed
> into an untruthful sense.

---

8. Jack Goody, *The Myth of the Bagre* (London: Oxford Univ. Press, 1972), p. 224.

> Too much sense
> is the thing
> that ruins a man's head.
> Too much foolishness
> is also what ruins a man's head,
> though not as readily.[9]

In an ultimate way, "the lying god" is no liar, for although man cannot efface the physical reality of death, his "foolishness" will enable him to transcend that reality, to overcome his sensory perception of death as absolute extinction. If man has too much "sense," he will only perceive myth as a deceptive attempt to make something out of nothing. Operating here is a meaningful play between sense and nonsense. Through a process of symbolic inversion the lie becomes truth and foolishness becomes wisdom that results in the restructuring of the neophyte's world view.

In a similar manner the Drinkard feels confident at the outset of his journey that, armed simply with his own wit, he can recover his dead tapster and thus, in effect, plumb the secrets of death. He soon meets Death, but his victory, as we pointed out earlier, does not prove to be much of a help to him. He must plunge deeper into a world where natural laws do not operate, and, in fact, he finally winds up in a town where natural order is entirely inverted. Here, in the "Unreturnable-Heaven's Town," he and the wife that joined him shortly after his adventure began, must undergo a most incredible series of agonizing tortures. First they have their heads shaved, rather scraped with broken bottles. Then they have pepper rubbed into their bare scalps and their heads burnt with fiery rags. As if this is not enough, their heads are scraped again, and the two are buried up to their heads out in an open field. They are flogged and then tortured by the presence of food they cannot touch. Finally, an eagle is left to peck at their heads. But this is only the first day's treatment—they undergo a similar series on the second day.

With this, the Drinkard's initiation into the world of myth is halfway complete. He is dead, as it were, to the world of physical reality. Now he must learn to cope with riddles.

The first episode not dealing with any direct confrontation with death significantly comes at this point, literally halfway through the story. The Drinkard and his wife recuperate in the hospital of the Faithful-Mother, and at the end of this rest continue on their way, having now "sold their death." The wife, generally quiet up to now, takes a more active role, serving as a mentor who instructs her husband

---

9. Ibid., pp. 290-91.

through the use of riddles. As the two leave the Faithful-Mother, they immediately meet another female figure who leads them into a frightening "Red-Town." On approaching this town the wife predicts that their adventures there will only be "fear for the heart but not dangerous to the heart" (p. 73). The wife, of course, already sees the implications of their having "lent fear" and "sold death."

At other crucial points the wife predicts and teaches through her riddles. When they are close to death among the Red-people she tells her husband "This would be a brief loss of woman, but a shorter separation of man from lover," (p. 78) a prediction that comes true when she is transformed for a short period into a tree along with the Red-people and their town. Later, she warns that "The Invisible-Pawn" will be a "Wonderful hard worker, but he would be a wonderful robber in future" (p. 86). Again, the Drinkard only realizes the significance of her words after he finds that the pawn takes far more than he gives.

The "mixed town" episode, which occurs just prior to the Drinkard's last adventure before returning to his village, appears to be a total digression from the series of adventures the Drinkard has recounted. Certainly from any formal critical perspective, the episode does not seem to fit into the over-all pattern of a particular genre. If we look at the rhetorical unity of the work, however, its position is clear. While in a real sense the Drinkard has been engaged in a search for his dead tapster, he has in a metaphysical sense been engaged in developing a certain attitude toward, and understanding of death.

While telling of the "mixed town" the Drinkard relates two dilemma tales involving death and calls on the reader to render a judgement in each of the cases. In the first, a debtor and a bill collector have a fight and kill each other while performing their respective jobs, owing money and collecting money. A third man, doing his duty as a neutral onlooker, kills himself to see how the conflict is resolved in heaven. We are asked to decide who is responsible in this conflict where everyone was doing what he should have been doing. In the second narrative, a man who had three wives dies. They all perform special tasks in bringing him back to life. One, however, must be given to a wizard for his work in reviving the dead man. Again we are asked to make a judgement.

In its problematical structure the dilemma tale is in many respects very much like a riddle. As William Bascom has pointed out, however, it differs in that it involves choices and not answers.[10] In his own process of coming to terms with death, the Drinkard himself has been involved

---

10. "African Dilemma Tales: An Introduction," in *African Folklore*, ed. Richard M. Dorson (New York: Anchor Books, 1972), p. 155.

with a series of choices, the most important being his very decision to undertake the journey. The choice necessarily comes before the discovery of an answer. In effect, what the Drinkard is telling us is that he can give us no answer to the riddle of death; we must find it ourselves through first making the proper choices in our lives. The Drinkard has at this point completely made the transition from neophyte to teacher and can return to the real physical world.

On telling us that he came back to his village to find a great famine, the Drinkard interrupts his narrative to explain through myth the causes of famine. The myth relates how two friends, Heaven and Land, fought over the possession of a mouse they had killed. Because of their greed they could not resolve the conflict and went back to their homes. Heaven then punished Land by withholding rain and thus bringing famine into the world. Having himself in a sense unlocked the mysteries of life, the Drinkard has returned with a boon that will provide an answer to the problem the people face. His answer, in the form of a magical egg that will produce food on command, proves too fragile an item for the people to handle. They break the egg and in their greed bring punishment upon themselves. Having been properly punished, the people are then in a position to learn from the Drinkard the proper sacrifice and course of action necessary to stop the famine and restore life to the land.

Another Nigerian writer, Chinua Achebe, uses a close variant of this same myth in his novel, *Things Fall Apart*.[11] However, considering Achebe's work as a whole, and his particular use of this myth in symbolically supporting the structure of the novel,[12] we can see that he is engaged in the process of writing proverbs, not merely in the literal sense that he uses them, but in the metaphorical sense that his novels provide a clear moral orientation. Tutuola, on the other hand, engages us in the process of resolving riddles. In *The Palm-Wine Drinkard* the . riddle is death, a riddle whose answer we find to be eclipsed only by our own insufficiency. The Drinkard addresses us directly as we follow him make his choice and move from his own insufficiency to fulfillment, from chaos to order, and through death into life. In a parallel, but foreshortened process, we see an entire community go through the same experience at the end of the book.

Tutuola's language, whether or not it is the accidental or unconscious transliteration of Yoruba expressions, or use of Nigerian vernacular English, lends itself very effectively to these "riddles writ large."

11. (New York: Fawcett, 1969), pp. 52-53.

12. For a discussion of Achebe's symbolic use of this tale see Donald Weinstock and Cathy Ramadan, "Symbolic Structure in *Things Fall Apart*," *Critique: Studies in Modern Fiction*, 2 (1969), 22-41.

Tutuola's Drinkard journeys into the mysteries of death and returns to tell his tale of this other reality. The very fact that there are no direct correspondences between that world and our physical reality necessitates the bending of our perceptions, not merely by what is said, but by the manner in which it is said. The unimaginable horror of the inverted utopia that the Drinkard goes through is thus far better expressed by the term "Unreturnable-Heaven's Town," than by any conventional expression he might have employed. As Michael Linn has pointed out in a paper on Tutuola's language, the very word "Drinkard" is a felicitous choice as it conveys a sense of present and on-going time as opposed to the standard term "drunkard."[13] The past has no reality in the Drinkard's experience, for he has stepped into mythic time, coterminous with past, present and future.

Had Tutuola bent his language any more, he would have been totally unintelligible, but almost always it operates on the level of metaphor. To the extent that it does this, it approximates the riddle in its effect. This is not exactly what Aristotle would call the perfection of style, but then we need not accept his value judgement. It is, however, worth returning to Aristotle's *Poetics* here, as his comment on diction does clarify what we have been saying about Tutuola:

> The perfection of style is to be clear without being mean. The clearest style is that which uses only current or proper words; at the same time it is mean . . . That diction, on the other hand, is lofty and raised above the commonplace which employs unusual words. By unusual, I mean strange (or rare) words, metaphorical, lengthened— anything, in short, that differs from the normal idiom. Yet a style wholly composed of such words is either a riddle or a jargon; a riddle if it consists of metaphors; a jargon if it consists of strange (or rare) words.[14]

Tutuola employs large numbers of strange words, but mainly in contexts where the metaphorical effects of these words can be seen or felt. Almost always there is enough balance between the familiar and the strange that we can follow him, confident that we are being led by a genius. He riddles and we peer into chaos; he resolves conundrums and we see order restored. Nothing, however, is made perfectly clear, and in the end we are left with enough questions to respect the mystery and beauty, no less than the humor, this riddler conveys.

---

13. "Degrees of Grammaticalness in Amos Tutuola's *The Palm-Wine Drinkard*" presented at the Annual Meeting of the African Studies Association, Chicago, October, 1974.

14. p. 29.

BERNTH LINDFORS

Amos Tutuola : Debts and Assets

Amos Tutuola began writing out of boredom. In 1948 he had taken a job as a messenger in the Government Labour Department in Lagos, an "unsatisfactory job,"[1] he said, which left him with a lot of free time on his hands. The job must have been something of a comedown for him, for he had had six years of schooling, some professional training as a blacksmith, and experience working as a coppersmith for the RAF during the war. But post-war demobilization had thrown him out of work, and after an unsuccessful attempt to start his own workshop and a year of unemployment, he was ready to trade in his apron for a messenger's uniform. The trouble with his new job was that often there was nothing at all for him to do. So to keep himself busy during office hours, he started to write down on scrap paper the stories he heard on Sundays from an old man on a palm plantation. He has spoken of composing his first story, *The Wild Hunter in the Bush of Ghosts*, because "in a day I cannot

---

[1]. Amos TUTUOLA, *The Palm-Wine Drinkard and his Dead Palm-Wine Tapster in the Dead's Town* (New York, 1953), p. 130. All quotations are taken from this Grove Press edition which contains Tutuola's autobiographical sketch, "My Life and Activities", pp. 126-130. Other important sources of biographical information are: Anon., "Portrait: A Life in the Bush of Ghosts", *West Africa*, May 1, 1954, pp. 389-390; Harold R. COLLINS, "Amos Tutuola: Folk Novelist Among the Ghosts", MS. of a book to be published in Twayne's "World Author Series" (The biographical account in chapter one of this MS. is based largely on the *West Africa* portrait but also includes unpublished information Collins received from Tutuola's publishers. I wish here to express my thanks to Professor Collins for making the MS. of his book available to me); Eric LARRABEE, " Palm-Wine Drinkard Searches for a Tapster", *Reporter*, May 12, 1953, pp. 37-39; and "Amos Tutuola: A Problem in Translation", *Chicago Review*, X (Spring 1956), pp. 40-44; Nancy ACKERLY, "WLB Biography: Amos Tutuola", *Wilson Library Bulletin*, XXXVIII (September 1963), p. 81.

Reprinted from *Cahiers d'études africaines*, 10 (1970), 306-334.

sit down doing nothing. I was just playing at it. My intention was not to send it to anywhere."[1]

Then one day in 1950 he read an advertisement in a local paper listing the publications of the United Society for Christian Literature, and he conceived the idea of sending this organization his latest story, *The Palm-Wine Drinkard and his Dead Palm-Wine Tapster in the Deads' Town*, which he had written in two days.[2] He spent three months enlarging the story, then drafted a final copy in ink and sent it off. The United Society for Christian Literature replied that they did not publish novels, but they would try to help Tutuola find a publisher. Faber and Faber received the manuscript from the society's Lutterworth Press on February 20, 1951,[3] and published *The Palm-Wine Drinkard* on May 2, 1952. Grove Press brought out an American edition the following year, and by 1955 the book was available in French, Italian, German and Serbo-Croatian translations.[4] Thus the bored messenger became the first Nigerian author to win international recognition and acclaim.

A writer almost by accident, Tutuola must have been greatly encouraged by Faber and Faber's acceptance of *The Palm-Wine Drinkard*. Eighty days after it appeared in print they received his second manuscript, *My Life in the Bush of Ghosts*, which they published on February 5, 1954.[5] Like *The Palm-Wine Drinkard* it had been 'composed' in two days and 'revised' and expanded over a period of three months.[6] Since then Tutuola has written four other major works of fiction—*Simbi and the Satyr of the Dark Jungle* (1955),

---

1. *West Africa*, May 1, 1954, p. 389. He may have written at other times of the day as well. In *The Literature and Thought of Modern Africa* (London, 1966), p. 74, Claude WAUTHIER quotes him as saying he began writing because "I had nothing else to do in the evenings."
2. *West Africa*, May 1, 1954, p. 389. In another account Tutuola is said to have written the book "roughly with lead pencil three hours each day for five days": *Listener*, November 13, 1952, p. 819. In a 1964 interview Tutuola said, "*The Palm-Wine Drinkard* took me about [. . .] three days": *Africa Report*, IX (July 1964), p. 11.
3. Information in a letter to the author from Sarah Lloyd of Faber and Faber, May 1, 1968.
4. Today it is also available in Danish and Swedish translations. For details, cf. Janheinz JAHN, *A Bibliography of Neo-African Literature from Africa, America and the Caribbean* (London, 1965), pp. 62-63.
5. Information in a letter to the author from Sarah Lloyd of Faber and Faber, May 1, 1968.
6. *West Africa*, May 1, 1954, p. 389. However, in 1964 Tutuola said "*My Life in the Bush of Ghosts* took me about two or three weeks": *Africa Report*, IX (July 1964), p. 11.

The Brave African Huntress (1958), *Feather Woman of the Jungle* (1962), *Ajaiyi and his Inherited Poverty* (1967)—and has published several short stories in literary journals.[1]

All six of Tutuola's longer works follow a similar narrative pattern. A hero (or heroine) with supernatural powers or access to supernatural assistance sets out on a journey in quest of something important and suffers incredible hardships before successfully accomplishing his mission. Invariably he ventures into unearthly realms, performs arduous tasks, fights with fearsome monsters, endures cruel tortures, and narrowly escapes death. Sometimes he is accompanied by a relative or by loyal companions; sometimes he wanders alone. But he always survives his ordeals, attains his objective, and usually emerges from his nightmarish experiences a wiser, wealthier man. His story is told in an unorthodox but curiously expressive idiom which is nearly as unpredictable as the bizarre adventures he undergoes in outlandish fantasy worlds.

The critics who have ventured to comment on Tutuola's peculiarities have almost without exception tried to relate his works to more familiar forms of oral or literary expression. This is an understandable ploy, one which puts the critic at ease while exploring a bewildering new territory, but is has led to unfortunate terminological confusion. Gerald Moore, for example, argues that Tutuola's "affinities are

---

1. Hereafter the titles of Tutuola's books will be abbreviated as follows: *The Palm-Wine Drinkard* (London, 1952) – *PWD; My Life in the Bush of Ghosts* (London, 1954) – *MLBG; Simbi and the Satyr of the Dark Jungle* (London, 1955) – *SSDJ; The Brave African Huntress* (London, 1958) – *BAH; Feather Woman of the Jungle* (London, 1962) – *FWJ; Ajaiyi and his Inherited Poverty* (London, 1967) – *AHIP*. All quotations will be taken from these editions, except *PWD* (cf. n. 1, p. 306).

Tutuola often reworks his stories to fit them into his books. "Ajayi and the Witchdoctor", *Atlantic*, CCIII (April 1959), pp. 78-80, which is reprinted in *Black Orpheus*, 19 (1966), pp. 10-14, can be found in *AHIP*, pp. 219-235. "Don't Pay Bad for Bad", *Présence Africaine*, English ed., II, 30 (1960), pp. 78-81, which is reprinted in Frances ADEMOLA, ed., *Reflections: Nigerian Prose and Verse* (Lagos, 1962), pp. 33-36, also reappears in *AHIP*, pp. 76-84. This story is based on a traditional Yoruba tale, one version of which can be found in E. Bolaji IDOWU, *Olódùmarè: God in Yoruba Belief* (London, 1962), pp. 160-161. "The Duckling Brothers and their Disobedient Sister", *Présence Africaine*, English ed., VIII, 36 (1961), pp. 73-78, takes a rather different form in *FWJ*, pp. 12-35. "The Elephant Woman", *Chicago Review*, X (Spring 1956), pp. 36-39, which was published earlier and in a different form in *MLBG*, pp. 112-135, is based on a familiar folktale, "The Hunter and the Hind", Yoruba versions of which are listed in n. 4, p. 329. Another story, "Ajantala, the Noxious Guest", is anthologized in Langston HUGUES, ed., *An African Treasury* (London, 1961), pp. 121-127. The character Ajantala reappears in *BAH*, pp. 121-132.

really with Bunyan, Dante and Blake rather than with the Western novel [. . .]. He is something much rarer and more interesting than another novelist; he is a visionary, and his books are prose epics."[1] Ann Tibble, objecting to such ambitious comparisons and "wide-of-the-mark praise," reduces Tutuola's books to a "blend of psychological fantasy, myth and fable" but concedes they are "fine fairy tales as well as contriving to be something more."[2] Harold Collins, on the other hand, likes to speak of him as a "folk novelist" who writes "ghost novels," but he uses Northrop Frye's terms to carefully define Tutuola's genre as the "naive quest romance" which verges on myth.[3] Martin Tucker considers Tutuola "more a mythologist than a novelist" and suggests he relies on a "personal mythology."[4] However, Ben Obumselu, a Nigerian critic, asserts that "Tutuola stands within the Yoruba tradition" and not only makes extensive use of the material of Yoruba folklore but also models the formal organization of that material "on the folktale about the hunter who ventures into the bad bush or the wrestler who takes his mortal challenge to the denizens of the spirit world."[5] In a similar vein John Ramsaran, a West Indian who teaches in Nigeria, notes that Tutuola's writings "preserve at least two essential qualities of the native folktale: its dramatic spirit and its identity as lived experience integrated into the whole of life as seen and felt by the writer."[6] Another Nigerian, Emmanuel Obiechina, conceives of Tutuola's

1. *Seven African Writers* (London, 1962), p. 42.   Earlier versions of Moore's essay on Tutuola can be found in *Black Orpheus*, 1 (September 1957), pp. 27-35, and *Odu*, 4 (n.d.), pp. 44-47.   Margaret LAURENCE, in her chapter on Tutuola in *Long Drums and Cannons: Nigerian Dramatists and Novelists, 1952-67* (London, 1968), pp. 126-147, relies heavily on Moore.

2. *African-English Literature: A Survey and Anthology* (London, 1965), pp. 96 and 101.

3. MS., pp. 55-56.   This definition, based on Northrop FRYE's analysis of the "romance mode of fiction", in *Anatomy of Criticism* (Princeton, 1957), can also be found in H. R. COLLINS, "Founding a New National Literature: The Ghost Novels of Amos Tutuola", *Critique*, IV (Fall-Winter 1960-61), p. 22.

4. *Africa in Modern Literature: A Survey of Contemporary Writing in English* (New York, 1967), pp. 69 and 72.

5. Ben OBUMSELU, "The Background of. Modern African Literature", *Ibadan*, 22 (June 1966), p. 57.   The Yoruba are not the only tribe with such a tale.   Jack BERRY, in his *Spoken Art in Africa* (London, 1961), p. 9, mentions an Ashanti cycle of tales about a "hunter, who (sometimes with the help of the long-haired little men) defeats not only the dangerous animals he encounters, but Sasabonsam the forest monster in the silk cotton tree and other supernatural spirits."

6. J. A. RAMSARAN, "African Twilight: Folktale and Myth in Nigerian Literature", *Ibadan*, 15 (March 1963), p. 17.

writing "in the context of a transition between the oral tradition and the literary tradition."[1]   Thus, in seeking some common ground on which to come to grips with Tutuola, critics have applied variety of familiar labels to his works.

The trouble with such labels is not that they differ but that they are too often applied so loosely or with so little backing that they fail to stick.   The critic is content to merely suggest a likely parallel or link or source without bothering to present evidence to show that the suggestion has some validity.   Assumptions take the place of research.   For example, although everyone seems to agree that Tutuola has his roots in oral tradition, they differ markedly in their estimates of how deeply into cultures other than his own these roots extend.   The comparative mythologists who draw parallels between Tutuola's works and Indo-European narratives have arrived at some interesting conclusions, but a modest research effort shows that critics who sift the evidence available on Tutuola's native soil are on the safest and most rewarding ground.

Among the few remarks Tutuola has made on his own writing is the statement that he heard the story of *The Palm-Wine Drinkard* from a very old man on a Yoruba palm plantation.   Tutuola's amusing account of this incident is worth quoting in full.   After roasting a big yam, the old man had offered Tutuola palm-wine.

"He started to serve the wine with bamboo tumbler.   This bamboo tumbler was as deep as a glass tumbler, but it could contain the palm-wine which could reach half a bottle.   Having taken about four, my body was not at rest at all, it was intoxicating me as if I was dreaming.   But when he noticed how I was doing, he told me to let us go and sit down on the bank of a big river which is near the farm for fresh breeze which was blowing here and there with strong power.   Immediately we reached there and sat under the shade of some palm trees which collected or spread as a tent I fall aslept.   After an hour, he woke me up, and I came to normal condition at that time.

When he believed that I could enjoy what he wanted to tell me, then he told me the story of the Palm-Wine Drinkard."[2]

On several other occasions Tutuola has admitted that he has always enjoyed hearing and telling folktales.   Geoffrey Parrinder

---

1. E. N. OBIECHINA, "Transition from Oral to Literary Tradition", *Présence Africaine*, 63 (1967), p. 147; "Amos Tutuola and the Oral Tradition", *Présence Africaine*, 65 (1968), pp. 85-106.   I pursue this idea as well in my "Amos Tutuola's The Palm-Wine Drinkard and Oral Tradition", *Critique*, XI (1968-69), pp. 42-50.

2. *Listener*, November 13, 1952, p. 819.

reports that "Tutuola has told me how he and his boyhood playmates would listen to such yarns on their farms in the evening."[1] In an interview Tutuola said, "When I was attending school [. . .] I was always telling folklore stories [. . .], short stories to the other children in the school. So from the beginning I always liked to listen to the old people in my village when they were telling short stories in the night."[2]

Tutuola has also stated that he began writing because "it seemed necessary to write down the tales of my country since they will soon all be forgotten."[3] In a recent letter he explained, "I wrote the *Palm-Wine Drinkard* for the people of the other countries to read the Yoruba folk-lores [. . .]. My purpose of writing is to make other people to understand more about Yoruba people and in fact they have already understood us more than ever before."[4] Even if one were to doubt the veracity of these statements, Eric Larrabee, who may have been the first one to interview him, confirms that "Tutuola does not think of himself as the creator of his stories. Stories exist objectively; he merely sets them down. When I asked him if he planned to write more, the question had no meaning to him. 'But there are many stories', he said."[5] Furthermore, a Nigerian correspondent for *West Africa* reported in 1954 that Tutuola felt "written out" after his first two books and intended "to return to Abeokuta for a short time to rest and draw fresh inspiration from listening to old people re-telling Yoruba legends."[6] The evidence that Tutuola has been influenced primarily by Yoruba oral tradition thus appears to be conclusive.

Even without such evidence, the reader familiar with oral literature from Africa or elsewhere will immediately recognize points of similarity between Tutuola's writing and oral narrative art. The content, structure and style of his works bear the earmarks of oral tradition. An analysis of *The Palm-Wine Drinkard* will serve as an illustration.

---

1. Foreword to *MLBG*, p. 10.
2. *Africa Report*, IX (July 1964), p. 11.
3. WAUTHIER, p. 74.
4. Information in a letter to the author from Amos Tutuola, May 16, 1968.
5. *Chicago Review*, X (Spring 1956), p. 42. In another article (1953, p. 39), LARRABEE says: "When I asked him what his future writing plans were, he said that possibly there were more stories down on the farm and that if I liked he might be able to get some."
6. *West Africa*, May 1, 1954, p. 390.

It is perhaps best to begin with a plot summary. One can do no better than to quote Dylan Thomas who in a book review entitled "Blithe Spirits" summarized *The Palm-Wine Drinkard* as a

"brief, thronged, grisly and bewitching story, or series of stories [. . .] about the journey of an expert and devoted palm-wine drinkard through a nightmare of indescribable adventures, all simply and carefully described, in the spirit-bristling bush. From the age of ten he drank 225 kegs a day, and wished to do nothing else; he knew what was good for him, it was just what the witch-doctor ordered. But when his tapster fell from a tree and died, and as, naturally, he himself 'did not satisfy with water as with palm-wine', he set out to search for the tapster in Deads' Town.

This was the devil—or, rather, the many devils—of a way off, and among those creatures, dubiously alive, whom he encountered, were an image with two long breasts with deep eyes; a female cream image; a quarter-of-a-mile total stranger with no head, feet or hands, but one large eye on his topmost; an unsoothing something with flood-light eyes, big as a hippopotamus but walking upright; animals cold as ice and hairy as sandpaper, who breathed very hot steam and sounded like church bells; and a 'beautiful complete gentleman' who, as he went through the forest, returned the hired parts of his body to their owners, at the same time paying rentage, and soon became a full-bodied gentleman reduced to skull.

Luckily, the drinkard found a fine wife on his travels, and she bore him a child from her thumb; but the child turned out to be abnormal, a pyromaniac, a smasher to death of domestic animals, and a bigger drinkard than its father, who was forced to burn it to ashes. And out of the ashes appeared a half-bodied child, talking with a 'lower voice like a telephone' [. . .]. There is, later, one harmonious interlude in the Father-Mother's house, or magical, techni-colour night-club, in a tree that takes photographs; and one beautiful moment of rejoicing, when Drum, Song, and Dance, three tree fellows, perform upon themselves, and the dead arise, and the animals, snakes, and spirits of the bush dance together. But mostly it's hard and haunted going until the drinkard and his wife reach Deads' Town, meet the tapster, and, clutching his gift of a miraculous, all-providing Egg, are hounded out of the town by dead babies." [1]

As can be inferred from this incomplete summary, *The Palm-Wine Drinkard* is pure fantasy, a voyage of the imagination into a never-never land of magic, marvels and monsters. But the beings and doings in this fantasy world are not entirely unfamiliar. The journey to the land of the dead, the abnormal conception, the monstrous child, the enormous drinking capacity, the all-providing magical object, the tree-spirits, the personifications, the fabulous monsters—these are standard materials of oral tradition, the stuff folktales are made of all over the world.

1. London *Observer*, July 6, 1952, p. 7.

281

The palm-wine drinkard himself appears at first to be an unpromising hero. He has, after all, done nothing but drink palm-wine
all his life. But once he starts on his journey to Deads' Town his
extraordinary cleverness and unusual powers of endurance enable
him to circumvent or survive numerous misadventures. He carries
with him a substantial supply of juju so he can transform himself
at will whenever he gets into a tight corner. However, even though
he is part-trickster, part-magician, part-superman, he cannot overcome every adversary or extricate himself from every difficult situation;
supernatural helpers have to come to his assistance from time to time.
Eventually he finds his tapster in Deads' Town but cannot persuade
him to re-enter the world of the 'alives'. The palm-wine drinkard
and his wife leave Deads' Town and, several adventures later, arrive
home only to discover that their people are starving. Heaven and
Land have had a bitter quarrel and Heaven has refused to send rain
to Land. The ensuing drought and famine have killed millions.
The palm-wine drinkard springs into action and in a short time
manages to feed the remaining multitudes, settle the cosmic dispute,
end the drought and famine, and restore the world to normal functioning order. The unpromising hero who had set out on his quest with
limited powers and purely selfish ambitions becomes in the end a
miracle worker, the savior and benefactor of all mankind. He
changes, in other words, from a typical folktale hero into a typical
epic hero. Such a change does not take him outside the stream of
oral tradition.

Further evidence that *The Palm-Wine Drinkard* is largely derived
from oral tradition can be found in the inner structure of the story.
Some critics have overlooked this evidence because they have focused
only on the overall narrative pattern. Gerald Moore, for example,
praising Tutuola's "grasp of basic literary forms," describes the palm-
wine drinkard's deliberate quest for his dead palm-wine tapster, a
quest in the course of which the drinkard experiences many trials,
labors and revelations, as a "variant [. . .] of the cycle of the heroic
monomyth, Departure-Initiation-Return."[1] This is a perceptive
comment on the overall narrative pattern, but a close examination
of the inner structure, of the way in which individual episodes are
constructed, set in sequence and woven together suggests that Tutuola
should be credited with a grasp of the basic forms of spoken art rather

---

1. MOORE, p. 44. Here Moore cites Joseph CAMPBELL, *The Hero with a
Thousand Faces* (New York, 1949), a study of the monomyth.

than with a "grasp of basic literary forms." Indeed, the fact that the story consists entirely of a series of short, separable episodes immediately arouses a suspicion that it is little more than a collection of traditional tales strung together on the lifeline of a common hero. This suspicion is strengthened when we find many of these episodes rounded off with closing formulas (e.g., "This was how I got a wife," "That was how we got away from the long white creatures," "That was how we were saved from the Unknown creatures of the 'Unreturn-able-Heaven's town'," "This was the end of the story of the bag which I carried from the bush to the 'wrong town'."[1] Several episodes even have etiological endings (e.g., "So that since the day that I had brought Death out from his house, he has no permanent place to dwell or stay, and we are hearing his name about in the world," p. 16). Etiological tales and closing formulas are quite common in West African oral tradition.

The Palm-Wine Drinkard's neat cyclical narrative pattern rests on a very loosely coordinated inner structure. The hero is involved in one adventure after another but these adventures are not well integrated. Like boxcars on a freight train, they are independent units joined with a minimum of apparatus and set in a seemingly random and interchangeable order. There is no foreshadowing of events, no dramatic irony, no evidence of any kind that the sequence of events was carefully thought out. Tutuola appears to be improvising as he goes along and employing the techniques and materials of oral narrative art in his improvisations.

To search for an orderly system or well-developed artistic pattern in the succession of disjointed episodes in *The Palm-Wine Drinkard* is to search for symmetry in chaos, for deliberate design in chance. Some critics have risen to the challenge with bold imagination. Gerald Moore has found it

"of the utmost significance that the first of all the trials imposed upon the Palm-Wine Drinkard in his journey is the binding and bringing of Death [. . .]. It stands as a clear enough indication that the Drinkard's adventure is not merely a journey into the eternal African Bush, but equally a journey into the racial imagination, into the sub-conscious, into that Spirit World that everywhere co-exists and even overlaps with the world of waking 'reality'."[2]

---

1. *PWD*, pp. 31, 43, 63, 95. Henceforth page numbers will be noted in the text.

2. MOORE, pp. 44-46.

Unfortunately, this interesting creative interpretation is built on a factual error. The first of the trials imposed upon the palm-wine drinkard in his journey is not the binding and bringing of Death but rather the fetching of an unnamed object from an unnamed blacksmith in an unnamed town. An old man has promised to tell the drinkard where his tapster is if the drinkard can accomplish this impossible task. The drinkard succeeds in fetching the object, and the old man, instead of rewarding him, sets him a still more impossible task—the binding and bringing of Death. When the drinkard accomplishes this dreadful task, the old man and all the rest of the people in the town flee in terror.

The plot of this adventure resembles that found in many folktales. A hero must perform impossible tasks in order to gain important information. Each successive task is more difficult to perform. When the hero succeeds in performing the most difficult task, usually one in which he must risk his life, the task-setter, amazed and terrified, flees and never bothers the hero again. In such tales the function of the impossible tasks is to provide opportunities for an extraordinary hero to display his extraordinary abilities. But neither the tasks nor the hero's special skills in coping with them need figure in the tale again. Each successful performance of an impossible task can stand as a complete and independent tale within the main tale, an event which need not be closely related to previous or subsequent events.

And such is the case in the episode of the binding and bringing of Death. Nothing in this episode carries over into other episodes. The drinkard's triumph over Death is not permanent; he soon faces threats on his life again. What is most significant about this first contest with Death is not its place in the overall narrative pattern but its place in one segment of the inner structure; not, in other words, the fact that it launches the reader on a journey into the eternal African Bush, the racial imagination, the subconscious or the African Spirit World, but the fact that it has the form, place and function of an enclosed motif in an extended folktale. This episode affords structural evidence of Tutuola's debt to oral tradition.

The style of *The Palm-Wine Drinkard* is essentially an oral style. The story is told by the drinkard himself, and right from the beginning we sense that he is speaking, not writing, of his experiences. Here are his first words:

"I was a palm-wine drinkard since I was a boy of ten years of age. I had no other work more than to drink palm-wine in my life. In those days we did not know other money, except COWRIES, so that everything was very cheap, and my father was the richest man in our town.

My father got eight children and I was the eldest among them, all of the rest were hard workers, but I myself was an expert palm-wine drinkard. I was drinking palm-wine from morning till night and from night till morning. By that time I could not drink ordinary water at all except palm-wine.

But when my father noticed that I could not do any work more than to drink, he engaged an expert palm-wine tapster for me; he had no other work more than to tap palm-wine every day.

So my father gave me a palm-tree farm which was nine miles square and it contained 560,000 palm-trees, and this palm-wine tapster was tapping one hundred and fifty kegs of palm-wine every morning, but before 2 o'clock p.m., I would have drunk all of it; after that he would go and tap another 75 kegs in the evening which I would be drinking till morning. So my friends were uncountable by that time and they were drinking palm-wine with me from morning to a late hour in the night" (p. 7).

The entire story is told in this naive tall-tale style, an idiom which preserves the flavor and rhythm of speech. Mabel Jolaoso, a Yoruba reviewer of Tutuola's books, notes that the "loose structure of his sentences, his roundabout expressions, and his vivid similes, essentially African, remind one very forcibly of the rambling old grandmother telling her tale of spirits in the ghostly light of the moon."[1] Tutuola did not have to work to create this style; it was perfectly natural to him. A *West Africa* interviewer reported in 1954 that his "spoken and written English are identical and he writes exactly what presents itself to his mind."[2] Another Yoruba critic confirmed this, adding only that Tutuola's writing "consists largely in translating Yoruba ideas into English."[3] According to anthropologist Paul Bohannan, many felt that *The Palm-Wine Drinkard* was "the same sort of thing that any Lagos Yoruba could talk."[4] It was merely oral art written down.

The influence of Tutuola's native language on his prose style can be seen in the passage quoted above. Unorthodox constructions such as "I had no other work more than to drink," "I could not do any work more than to drink," "he had no other work more than to tap," and "we did not know other money, except COWRIES" are taken

---

1. *Odu*, 1 (January 1955), p. 43.
2. *West Africa*, May 1, 1954, p. 389.
3. Babasola JOHNSON, "The Books of Amos Tutuola", *West Africa*, April 10, 1954, p. 322.
4. "Translation—A Problem in Anthropology", *Listener*, May 13, 1954, p. 815.

directly from Yoruba *(mọ owó mǐràn, àfi ẹya owó)*. The phrase "by that time" *(n'igbà yẹn)* is also used in typical Yoruba fashion.[1] It may have been stylistic eccentricities like these that led Mabel Jolaoso to remark that "the very imperfections of Tutuola's English have made him the perfect African storyteller."[2] In syntax as well as imagery and narrative content he sounded exactly like a Yoruba raconteur.

In sum, it is evident that *The Palm-Wine Drinkard* has been greatly influenced by oral tradition.   The hero appears to be a composite of the heroes found most frequently in West African oral narratives —the trickster, the magician, the superman, the unpromising hero, the culture hero—and he tells his story in an oral style.   The story itself is little more than a cleverly woven string of loosely connected episodes many of which appear to have been borrowed or derived from folktales.   The content, structure, and style of *The Palm-Wine Drinkard* reveal that Tutuola is not a novelist but a writer of concatenated folktales.[3]

It is not difficult to prove that many of the folktales Tutuola uses exist in Yoruba oral tradition.   Any sizable collection of Yoruba tales will yield a number of parallels, and some of Tutuola's most striking episodes can be found in more than one collection.   For example, the celebrated passage in *The Palm-Wine Drinkard* in which a "beautiful complete gentleman" lures a lady deep into the forest and then dismembers himself, returning the hired parts of his body to their owners and paying rentage until he is reduced to a humming skull, appears in at least four different versions in Yoruba folktale collections.[4]   There are just as many texts of the incident

---

1. I wish to thank Edward Fresco, doctoral candidate in Linguistics at UCLA, for helping me to locate the Yoruba elements in this passage.

2. *Odu*, I (January 1955), p. 43.

3. COLLINS (MS., p. 36) observes that "Tutuola's novels have the episodic structure of the more extended Yoruba folk tales; they are simply extended a little longer."   It would be more accurate to say that they are extended a lot longer and that Tutuola extends them by concatenating different tales rather than by expanding a single tale.

4. *PWD*, pp. 17-29; A. B. ELLIS, *The Yoruba-Speaking Peoples of the Slave Coast of West Africa* (London, 1894), pp. 267-269; M. I. OGUMEFU, *Yoruba Legends* (London, 1929), pp. 18-20 and 38-40; Abayomi FUJA, *Fourteen Hundred Cowries* (London, 1962), pp. 44-49; Kolawole BALOGUN, *The Crowning of the Elephant and Other Stories* (Oshogbo, n.d.), pp. 25-29.   Professor William Bascom of the University of California at Berkeley has informed me of three additional published texts: Margaret I. BAUMANN, *Ajapa and the Tortoise* (London, 1929), pp. 96-103; and *Sons of Sticks* (London, 1933), pp. 41-43; Pierre BOUCHE, *Sept ans en Afrique Occidentale: la Côte des Esclaves et le Dahomey* (Paris, 1885), pp. 151-152.

of the all-providing magical object which produces first an abundance of food and later an abundance of whips.[1] Many other tales and motifs in this book—the quarrel between heaven and earth,[2] the carrying of a sacrifice to heaven,[3] the tiny creature that makes newly-cleared fields sprout weeds,[4] the *enfant terrible*,[5] the magical transformations[6]—can be documented as traditional among the Yoruba. For those that cannot be so documented we have the word of Adeboye Babalola, a prominent Yoruba scholar, that

"the Yoruba are lovers of the marvellous, the awe-inspiring, the weird, the eerie. It is a small minority of [Yoruba] folk-tales that concern human beings only. The great majority of the tales feature human beings, animals behaving like humans, and often also superhuman beings: demons, ogres, deities."[7]

Further confirmation of Tutuola's debt to Yoruba oral tradition comes from his Yoruba critics who insist that his stories are well-known.[8]

They are known not only in Yorubaland but throughout West Africa. The distinguished anthropologist Melville Herskovits remarks in the introduction to a collection of Fon tales from Dahomey that "it will be instructive for one who reads the narratives in this volume to go to Tutuola's books with the motifs and orientations of the tales given here in mind. He will find them all."[9] Though this is certainly an overstatement, it serves to emphasize the fact that folktales known to the Yoruba are known to other West African peoples as well. Tutuola's tale of the self-dismembering "complete gentleman," for instance, has been found among the Fon of Dahomey,[10] the Ibo,[11]

1. *PWD*, pp. 120-124; OGUMEFU, pp. 80-84; FUJA, pp. 125-128; Phebean ITAYEMI and P. GURREY, *Folk Tales and Fables* (London, 1953), pp. 81-85; J. A. LOMAX, "Stories of an African Prince", *Journal of American Folklore*, XXVI (1913), pp. 10-12.
2. *PWD*, pp. 118-119; IDOWU, pp. 50-51.
3. *PWD*, pp. 124-125; IDOWU, pp. 50-51; FUJA, pp. 34-36.
4. *PWD*, pp. 48-50; FUJA, pp. 88-91; ELLIS, pp. 254-255.
5. *PWD*, pp. 31-37; ITAYEMI and GURREY, pp. 46-50. Cf. also. Ajantala in Tutuola's story, "Ajantala, the Noxious Guest", in HUGHES, pp. 121-127.
6. There are 23 magical transformations in *PWD*. One of the most striking is the hero's transformation into a pebble (*PWD*, p. 117) which is thrown across a river, thereby enabling the hero to escape from his pursuers. This motif can be found in ITAYEMI and GURREY, p. 43.
7. A. BABALOLA, "Yoruba Folktales", *West African Review* (July 1962), p. 49.
8. JOHNSON, p. 322.
9. Melville J. HERSKOVITS and Frances S. HERSKOVITS, *Dahomean Narrative: A Cross-Cultural Analysis* (Evanston, 1958), p. 13.
10. *Ibid.*, pp. 243-245.
11. Cyprian EKWENSI, *Ikolo the Wrestler and Other Ibo Tales* (London, n.d.), pp. 65-68; reprinted in EKWENSI's *The Great Elephant-Bird* (London, 1965),

and Ibibio[1] of Nigeria, and the Krio of Sierra Leone.[2] According to Jack Berry, the tale of the magical food-and-whips producer is very widely distributed in West Africa, as are tales of ogres and other supernatural beings.[3] Alice Werner, in her study of African mythology, reports that stories of people who have penetrated into the world of ghosts and returned "are not uncommon"[4] and that shape-shifting transformations are not only present in many folktales but also "are believed in as actual occurrences at the present day."[5] Thus *The Palm-Wine Drinkard*, a lineal descendant of Yoruba oral tradition, hails from a large family of West African oral narratives.

What has been said about *The Palm-Wine Drinkard* also applies to Tutuola's other books, for his method and content have not changed much over the years. The quest pattern basic to his fiction has already been described: a hero or heroine sets out on a journey in search of something important and passes through a number of concatenated folktale adventures before, and sometimes after, finding what he seeks. Though Tutuola varies this pattern from book to book, he never abandons it entirely. He never chooses a totally different pattern. One suspects that his roots in oral tradition run so deep that he knows of no other way to compose book-length fiction.

Nevertheless, minor changes in Tutuola's writing are worth noting, for they reveal that though Tutuola has not moved any great distance from where he was in 1950 when he wrote *The Palm-Wine Drinkard*, he has not been standing still all these years. His most radical departure from the quest pattern came in his second book, *My Life in the Bush of Ghosts* (1954), which opens with its narrator-hero, a boy of seven, being maltreated and abandoned by his stepmothers,

---

pp. 57-60. Two variants can be found in his *The Boa Suitor* (London, 1966), pp. 1-5 and 11-13. Cf. also his reviews of *PWD*, in *West African Review* (July 1952), p. 713, and *African Affairs*, LI (July 1952), pp. 257-258.

1. Alta JABLOW, *Yes and No: The Intimate Folklore of Africa* (New York, 1961), pp. 184-188; another version, perhaps not Ibibio, appears in Elphinstone DAYRELL, *Folk Stories from Southern Nigeria, West Africa* (London, 1910), pp. 38-41. I am grateful to Harold COLLINS (MS., p. 73) for these references.

2. Eldred JONES, "Amos Tutuola—The Palm-Wine Drinkard: Fourteen Years On", *Bulletin of the Association for African Literature in English*, 4 (March 1966), pp. 24-30.

3. BERRY, p. 9.

4. Alice WERNER, "African Mythology", in John Arnott MacCULLOCH, ed., *The Mythology of All Races* (New York, 1964), p. 118.

5. *Ibid.*, p. 121. A correspondent for *West Africa*, May 1, 1954, p. 389, reports that "Tutuola confesses that he more than halfbelieves the tales he writes."

separated from his older brother, and left to wander in the bush during a tribal war. Frightened by the sounds of gunfire and unable to distinguish between bad and good, he enters the Bush of Ghosts and spends the next twenty-four years wandering in an African spirit world replete with towns, kings, civic ceremonies, festivals, law courts, even a Methodist church. He has experiences both harrowing and happy and at one point considers taking up permanent residence in the "10th town of ghosts" with his dead cousin. But he can't bring himself to do it because he keeps longing to return to his earthly home. Eventually a "Television-handed ghostess" helps him to escape, and he is reunited with his mother and brother and begins to lead a more normal life.

As can be seen from this brief summary, the hero's journey is not really a quest. Harold Collins describes it as a "West African Odyssey," [1] and Gerald Moore sees it as "a kind of extended Initiation or 'rite of passage' [. . .] or Purgatory [in which the] initiation of the boy-hero is not sought, but is imposed upon him as the price of his development into full understanding." [2] Both of these interpretations are apt, but they presuppose a degree of premeditation, of careful organization and methodical development, which cannot be found in the story. [3] Again the plot consists of a string of loosely-connected episodes set down in random order. There is a distinct beginning and a distinct end but the middle is a muddle. When Geoffrey Parrinder asked Tutuola "the reason for the apparently haphazard order of the towns of the ghosts" in this book, Tutuola replied: "That is the order in which I came to them." [4] Here is confirmation of the improvisatory nature of Tutuola's art. He moves from one tale to another not by calculation but by chance. And when he gets to the end of the chain, when all conflicts are resolved and his hero returns to a state of equilibrium, as most folktale heroes do, Tutuola rounds off the narrative with a moral: "This is what hatred did." The moral reminds the reader that the hero's sufferings and misfortunes

---

1. H. R. COLLINS, "The Novel in Nigeria", in Priscilla TYLER, ed., *Writers on the Other Side of the Horizon: A Guide to Developing Literatures of the World* (Champaign, 1964), pp. 51-52; MS., p. 21. V. S. PRITCHETT also terms this book an Odyssey in a review in *New Statesman and Nation*, March 6, 1954, p. 291.

2. MOORE, pp. 49-51.

3. MOORE, p. 50, admits that Tutuola does not sustain the idea of the extended Initiation or 'rite of passage' and fails to relate the hero's "disorganized adventures" to it.

4. Foreword to *MLBG*, p. 11.

can be blamed on his stepmothers who rejected him twenty-four years before.   Tutuola thus ends his story in typical folktale fashion by using it to teach a lesson about human behavior.

In his third book, *Simbi and the Satyr of the Dark Jungle* (1955), Tutuola returns to the quest pattern.   Beautiful Simbi, an only child who has never known poverty and punishment, desires to set out on a journey "to know and experience their difficulties."   Her mother and others warn her not to, but she feels she must.   One hundred and twenty pages later she is fed up with poverty and punishment: She has been kidnapped, sold into slavery, beaten, starved, almost beheaded, set afloat on a river in a sealed coffin, carried off by an eagle, imprisoned in a tree trunk, half-swallowed by a boa constrictor, attacked by a satyr, shrunk and put in a bottle, bombarded by a stone-carrying phoenix, and petrified to a rock.   Fortunately, she is a talented girl who can sing well enough to wake the dead and she gets plenty of assistance from girl-friends, gods and a friendly gnome, so that in the end she manages to return home to her mother.   Then, "Having rested for some days, she was going from house to house she was warning all the children that it was a great mistake to a girl who did not obey her parents" (p. 136).   Simbi, too, has a lesson to teach.

Although it resembles Tutuola's other books in matter and manner, *Simbi and the Satyr of the Dark Jungle* marks a new stage in Tutuola's development as a writer, for it displays definite signs of formal literary influence.   It is the first of his books to be divided into numbered chapters, each encompassing a major adventure, and the only one to be written in the third person.   Gerald Moore has pointed out that it contains far more dialogue and more frequent adverbial 'stage directions' than the earlier books.[1]   Furthermore, there are creatures such as goblins, imps, a gnome, myrmidon, phoenix, nymph, and satyr whose names, at least, derive from European mythology.[2] And there is one passage which closely resembles an episode in a Yoruba novel by D. O. Fagunwa, whose influence on Tutuola will be discussed later.   It is clear that Tutuola must have been doing some reading between July 22, 1952, and November 26, 1954, the dates *My Life in the Bush of Ghosts* and *Simbi and the Satyr of the Dark Jungle* were submitted for publication.[3]   When Eric Larrabee

1. MOORE, p. 54.
2. *SSDJ*, pp. 74, 47, 61, 25, 74, 90, 73 ff.
3. Information in letters to the author from Sarah Lloyd and Rosemary Goad of Faber and Faber, May 1 and 14, 1968.

interviewed him in 1953, Tutuola owned no books and did not think of himself as an author,[1] but after his second book was published, another interviewer found that he had "decided to attend evening classes to 'improve' himself, so that he [might] develop into what he describes as 'a real writer'."[2] Reading was no doubt a part of Tutuola's program for self-improvement. When Larrabee offered to send him books, Tutuola requested *A Survey of Economic Education* published by the Brookings Institution, Aldous Huxley's *The Devils of Loudun*, and "some other books which contain stories like that of the P.W.D. [*The Palm-Wine Drinkard*] which are written by either West Africans, White men or Negroes, etc."[3] Larrabee recalls that of the other books sent, "the two he seemed most to enjoy were Joyce Cary's *Mr. Johnson* and Edith Hamilton's *Mythology*, which he said contained stories similar to those he had heard as a child."[4] It is not surprising then to find traces of literary influence in *Simbi and the Satyr of the Dark Jungle*. Between 1952 and 1954 Tutuola was becoming conscious of himself as an author, was reading more widely, and was trying hard to 'improve' his writing. He could still tell only one kind of story, but should the nearby palm plantation or the campfires of Abeokuta ever fail to provide him with sufficient material, he could now turn to a number of other sources for fresh inspiration.

Tutuola did succeed in improving the structure of his narratives considerably. His last three books do not differ markedly from his first three in content or narrative pattern, but they tend, like *Simbi and the Satyr of the Dark Jungle*, to be organized into rather more neatly demarcated chapters. In *The Brave African Huntress* (1958) and *Ajaiyi and his Inherited Poverty* (1967), he adopted the practice of citing one or more proverbs at the head of a chapter and then using the action in that chapter to illustrate the proverbs. In *Feather Woman of the Jungle* (1962), his most stylized work, he created an Arabian Nights structure by having a 76 year old chief entertain villagers every night for ten nights with accounts of his past adventures. Both of these narrative techniques must have entered literature from oral tradition. If Tutuola picked them up from his reading, as appears likely,[5] he is to be commended for selecting those that suited his

---

1. Larrabée, 1953, p. 38.
2. *West Africa*, May 1, 1954, p. 389.
3. Larrabee, 1956, pp. 40-41.
4. *Ibid.*
5. In a letter to the author dated May 16, 1968, Tutuola says that he read *The Arabian Nights* in 1948.

291

material perfectly.   Using such techniques he could remain a raconteur and at the same time could link and unify his concatenated tales more effectively.

The tales were still woven into the familiar quest pattern.   Adebisi, the heroine in *The Brave African Huntress*, ventures into the dangerous Jungle of the Pigmies to rescue her four brothers.   The chief in *Feather Woman of the Jungle* sets out on a series of hazardous journeys in quest of treasure and adventure.   Ajaiyi in *Ajaiyi and his Inherited Poverty* simply wants to get out of debt and is willing to go to the Creator, the God of Iron, the Devil, and assorted witches, witchdoctors and wizards to ask for help.   Each of these adventurers, after a succession of ups and downs, achieves his objective.

As for the tales themselves, Tutuola appears to have continued to rely more heavily on traditional Yoruba material than on non-Yoruba material.   In *The Brave African Huntress* there are references to "elves, genii, goblins, demons, imps, gnomes" and a "cyclops-like creature,"[1] but the actual monsters encountered and the adventures undergone are not unlike those in Tutuola's earlier books.   The episode in which Adebisi the huntress cuts the hair of the king of Ibembe Town and discovers he has horns has been cited by critics as a possible example of European or Indian influence because it resembles the story of King Midas and the Ass's Ears,[2] but Tutuola, in a letter to Harold Collins, has stated: "The king who has horns is in the traditional story of my town."[3]   In published Yoruba folktale collections it is not difficult to find parallels to other tales and motifs such as Adebisi's palace adventure in Bachelors' Town[4] in *The Brave African Huntress;* the three dogs that rescue their master from woodchoppers,[5] the journey to the underwater kingdom,[6] and the town where people eat only water[7] in *Feather Woman of the Jungle;* and the dead rats that come alive,[8] the person who hides in the pupil

1. *BAH*, pp. 9 and 25.
2. OBUMSELU, p. 57; RAMSARAN, p. 18.   This tale is number 782 in Antti AARNE and Stith THOMPSON, *The Types of the Folktale: A Classification and Bibliography* (Helsinki, 1964).   Literary redactions appear in OVID's *Metamorphoses* (Bk. XI) and CHAUCER's *Wife of Bath's Tale* (III, 951 ff.).
3. 1960-61, p. 28.
4. *BAH*, pp. 112-119; Barbara K. WALKER and Warren S. WALKER, *Nigerian Folk Tales* (New Brunswick, New Jersey, 1961), pp. 19-21.
5. *FWJ*, pp. 53-66; WALKER and WALKER, pp. 17-19; FUJA, pp. 155-161.
6. *FWJ*, pp. 72-83; LOMAX, pp. 10-12.
7. *FWJ*, pp. 69-72; LOMAX, *ibid*.
8. *AHIP*, pp. 137-166; ITAYEMI and GURREY, p. 40.

of a blacksmith's eye,[1] and the quarrel between lenders [2] in *Ajaiyi and his Inherited Poverty*.   Moreover, these later books are packed with Yoruba deities, towns, customs, superstitions, and proverbs. Tutuola, despite his reading and increased sophistication, apparently chose to remain a teller of Yoruba tales.

A few critics, seeking to demonstrate how Tutuola improves upon the material he borrows, have contrasted passages in his books with analogous folktales. [3]   This type of argument, no matter how well documented, is not very persuasive because the critic cannot prove that the particular folktale text chosen for comparison is the version of the tale that Tutuola knew.   Perhaps Tutuola had heard a different version, perhaps even a better version than he himself was able to tell.   Eldred Jones makes the mistake of assuming that the Yoruba traditional tale on which Tutuola based his account of the self-dismembering "complete gentleman" in *The Palm-Wine Drinkard* is very similar to the Krio version of this tale.[4]   Jones therefore credits Tutuola with the invention of several striking details which, though absent from the Krio version, are quite common in published Yoruba texts of the tale.   Even a critic familiar with all the published Yoruba versions would not be able to draw a firm line between borrowed and invented details in Tutuola's redaction   Without knowing exactly what Tutuola borrowed, it is impossible to know how much he contributed to the stories he tells.

Critics who search for literary influences on Tutuola's writing are on safer ground insofar as texts are concerned, but very few serious comparative studies have been attempted.   Despite several excellent leads for research, Tutuola's reading has been virtually ignored. Tutuola claims that he read only textbooks while in school,[5] but some of these must have been literary works.   It is known, for example, that Aesop's fables were read in Nigerian schools in the 1930's[6] and that John Bunyan's *The Pilgrim's Progress* was available in Nigeria in a simplified English version as early as 1937.[7]   It is also known that at least twenty-six school books classified as 'General

1. *AHIP*, pp. 163-164; ITAYEMI and GURREY, p. 44.
2. *AHIP*, pp. 76-83; IDOWU, pp. 160-161.
3. JONES, pp. 24-29; COLLINS, MS., pp. 70-100.
4. JONES, pp. 24-27.
5. Information in the above-mentioned letter to the author from Tutuola, May 16, 1968.
6. OBUMSELU, p. 57.
7. *Books for Africa*, VII (April 1937), p. 21.

Literature' were published in Yoruba between 1927 and 1937,[1] and that many others have been published since.[2] Moreover, in recent years Tutuola has acknowledged that there are many stories like his written in Yoruba[3] and has admitted in a letter that he read *The Pilgrim's Progress* and *The Arabian Nights* in 1948,[4] just two years before *The Palm-Wine Drinkard* was written. As noted earlier, he also told Eric Larrabee[5] that he enjoyed reading Joyce Cary's *Mister Johnson* and Edith Hamilton's *Mythology*, which presumably is the book responsible for the enrichment of his mythological vocabulary. But the effects of such reading on Tutuola's writing have not yet been adequately studied.

The influence of Bunyan on Tutuola appears to be one of the most promising avenues for future research. Like *The Pilgrim's Progress*, each of Tutuola's narratives takes the form of a quest. Persevering heroes journey through supernatural realms and encounter many marvels and monsters before finding what they seek. Sometimes their adventures are almost identical to those Christian experiences on his way to the Celestial City. For example, the episode in which Death shows the palm-wine drinkard the bones of his former victims appears to be modeled on Christian's meeting with the giant of Doubting Castle.[6] A number of the towns the drinkard and other Tutuolan heroes visit bear a distinct resemblance to Vanity Fair. And Tutuola's monsters often seem to belong to the same sub-species as Bunyan's Appolyon who was "clothed with-scales, like a fish, [. . .] had wings like a dragon, feet like a bear, and out of his belly came fire and smoke, and his mouth was as the mouth of a lion."[7] However, unlike *The Pilgrim's Progress*, Tutuola's narratives are not religious allegories. They have been influenced far more by Yoruba oral tradition than by the Bible. Bunyan may have taught Tutuola how to put an extended quest tale together but he did not convert him to Christianity. In substance and spirit Tutuola remained a thoroughly African storyteller.

1. "A Survey of Literature in African Languages", *Books for Africa*, IX (January 1939), pp. 9-10.
2. Cf. JAHN, pp. 11-66.
3. *Africa Report*, IX (July 1964), p. 11.
4. Information in the above-mentioned letter to the author from Tutuola, May 16, 1968.
5. 1956, p. 41.
6. *PWD*, p. 13. John BUNYAN, *The Pilgrim's Progress*, Alexander M. Witherspoon, ed. (New York, 1957), p. 113.
7. BUNYAN, p. 55.

Another author whose influence on Tutuola has not gone entirely unnoticed is Chief Daniel Olorunfemi Fagunwa, a Yoruba writer who before his death in 1963 produced five 'novels',[1] a collection of stories, two travel books, and a series of graded readers for schools.[2] Fagunwa was an extremely popular author in Yorubaland. His first novel, *Ogboju Ode Ninu Igbo Irunmale (The Brave Hunter in the Forest of the Four Hundred Spirits)*, published in 1938, immediately established his reputation and became a standard textbook in Yoruba schools.[3] His second novel did not appear until ten years later, but it was quickly followed by his third in 1949.[4] These new works were so enthusiastically received that Fagunwa's publishers brought out a new edition of *Ogboju Ode Ninu Igbo Irunmale* in 1950, the year Tutuola wrote *The Palm-Wine Drinkard*. Since then Fagunwa's novels have seldom been out of print (one had been reissued sixteen times by 1963), and the total printing of his six major works is estimated to run into the hundreds of thousands.[5]

At mid-century Fagunwa was Nigeria's most prominent and prolific man of letters. Between 1948 and 1951 he published at least nine books.[6] Tutuola, who had read Fagunwa's first novel at school,[7] must have been aware of this extraordinary outburst of literary activity. Indeed, it is conceivable that he got both the idea of writing stories and the idea of submitting them for publication from seeing Fagunwa's works in print. The title of Tutuola's first

1. With perhaps one exception *(Irèké Oníbùdó)*, Fagunwa's books are no more novels than Tutuola's. L. Murby, an editor for Fagunwa's publisher, calls them indigenous epics or allegories which "bear definite resemblances to the *Odyssey* and *Beowulf* and the early medieval romances on the one hand, and on the other hand to that great cornerstone of the English novel, Bunyan's *The Pilgrim's Progress*." Cf. "Editor's Foreword", in *Ogboju Ode Ninu Igbo Irunmale* by D. O. FAGUNWA (London, 1950). Wole SOYINKA has recently published an English translation of this novel, entitling it *The Forest of a Thousand Daemons: A Hunter's Saga* (London, 1968).

2. A. OLUBUMMO, "D. O. Fagunwa: A Yoruba Novelist", *Odu*, 9 (September 1963), p. 26.

3. *Ibid.*, pp. 26-27. JAHN's bibliography and J. A. RAMSARAN's *New Approaches to African Literature: A Guide to Negro-African Writing and Related Studies* (Ibadan, 1965) do not list the 1938 edition of this work.

4. *Ibid.*, p. 26. However, the first publication date listed in the Nelson editions of these two works—*Igbo Olodumare* and *Irèké Oníbùdó*—is 1949.

5. Ulli BEIER, "Fagunwa, a Yoruba Novelist", *Black Orpheus*, 17 (June 1965), p. 51.

6. Besides the three fictional works he published two travel books—*Irinajo Apa Kini* and *Irinajo Apa Keji*—and four "Taiwo and Kehinde" school readers during this period. See *Books for Africa*, XXI (April 1952), p. 34.

7. Information in the above-mentioned letter to the author from Tutuola, May 16, 1968.

short story, *The Wild Hunter in the Bush of Ghosts*,[1] which was not written for publication, is suspiciously close to the title of Fagunwa's first novel, *Ogboju Ode Ninu Igbo Irunmale*. And there is abundant evidence in critical articles[2] and English translations of excerpts from Fagunwa's fiction[3] that Fagunwa's influence on Tutuola extends well beyond titles.

A. Olubummo, a Yoruba critic, describes the general pattern of Fagunwa's first four' books in the following manner:

"One fine day, a brave hunter finds his way into a thick jungle in search of big game. He encounters the most fearful monsters, fights with a giant snake with a human head and wrestles with a ghost with one eye in front and one eye at the back of his head. Armed with his gun, the charms of his fore-fathers and an unshakable belief in an omnipotent God, he comes out success-fully in all these encounters. On returning home, he is appointed by the chief of his town to lead a group of men to a far-off land in search of wisdom. They miss their way into the outskirts of hell and wander through curious places like the city of dirt where nobody has ever thought of the idea of having a bath and the city where all the inhabitants eat, drink, laugh or weep simulta-neously. After more trouble and hair breadth escapes, they reach their goal and return home richer and wiser."[4]

This sounds very much like a description of Tutuola's books. In addition to the quest, the monsters, and the curious places, one finds some of the same motifs: e.g., the city of dirt,[5] the hunter in search of game,[6] the outskirts of hell.[7] Moreover, Ulli Beier compares Fagunwa's plot structure to "a rambling, somewhat disorganized fairy tale. It is a succession of adventures, loosely strung together."[8] This could serve as an excellent characterization of Tutuola's plots.

1. *West Africa*, May 1, 1954, p. 389. There are two references to a "Bush of the Ghosts" story in *PWD*, pp. 40, and 53.
2. BEIER, pp. 51-56; OLUBUMMO, pp. 26-30; Anon., "Teller of Yoruba Tales", *West Africa*, October 2, 1954, p. 917.
3. "The Bold Hunter in the Forest of Zombis", trans. A. Akikiwo, *Odu*, 9 (September 1963), pp. 35-37; "The Beginning of Olowo Aiye", trans. Bakare Gbadamosi and Ulli Beier, *Odu*, 9 (September 1963), pp. 31-34; "The Forest of the Lord", trans. E. C. Rowlands, in Wilfred WHITELEY, ed., *A Selection of African Prose (2. Written Prose)*, (London, 1964), pp. 69-84; "Igbako", trans. Wole Soyinka, *Black Orpheus*, 15 (August 1964), pp. 5-7; "Kalo", trans. Wole Soyinka, *Black Orpheus*, 19 (March 1966), pp. 17-21.
4. OLUBUMMO, p. 26.
5. *PWD*, pp. 44-45.
6. *BAH*.
7. "Deads' Town", *PWD*, pp. 90-102; the visit to the Devil, *AHIP*, pp. 171-193.
8. BEIER, p. 52.

But there are several significant differences between Fagunwa and Tutuola. Ulli Beier notes that although there are elements of traditional Yoruba folktales in Fagunwa's books, he "does not draw as heavily on Yoruba folklore, as Tutuola. Most of the stories are invented, many of them are also taken from European tradition."[1] Tutuola, writing in a foreign language and largely for a foreign audience, remains more closely tied to Yoruba oral tradition.

Beier goes on to state that "Tutuola differs from Fagunwa in two major points: Tutuola does not moralize and he is never sentimental. Fagunwa is much more a Christian writer [. . .], [one who] loses no opportunity to moralize and improve his reader. He can also be sentimental and even sloppy."[2] Although Beier overlooks Tutuola's tendency to append folktale morals to many of his heroes' adventures, he is quite right about the absence of missionary zeal and sentimentality in his writing. Olubummo confirms that "Fagunwa's code of morality and philosophy of life are decidedly Christian. In this connection, it is interesting to compare him with a writer like [. . .] Amos Tutuola whose ideas of right and wrong on the whole seem to spring from more indigenous sources."[3]

Aside from these differences, they are in the same class. Beier claims that "as an observer of the Yoruba mind at work Fagunwa is still unsurpassed," but that "Tutuola rivals him as a story teller."[4] Perhaps one reason both are excellent story tellers is that both learned to tell good stories by hearing good stories told. Perhaps another reason is that what Tutuola did not learn from oral tradition he learned from Fagunwa.

Certainly they share a lot of common ground. Tutuola has been praised for the way he uses "the paraphernalia of modern life to give sharpness and immediacy to his imagery."[5] The classic example is his description of the terrible "red fish" in *The Palm-Wine Drinkard:*

"Its head was just like a tortoise's head, but it was as big as an elephant's head and it had over 30 horns and large eyes which surrounded the head.

---

1. *Ibid.*, p. 54. However, OBUMSELU (p. 57) says that "they both make extensive use of the material of folklore", and *West Africa*, October 2, 1954, p. 917, says that the tales Fagunwa heard in his youth "formed in his mind the basis of the fascinating adventure stories for which he is now so well known throughout Yoruba country, and Nigerian children in primary and secondary schools are learning the folk-lore of their country through this medium."
2. BEIER, p. 54.
3. OLUBUMMO, p. 29.
4. BEIER, p. 56.
5. MOORE, p. 43.

All these horns were spread out as an umbrella. It could not walk but was only gliding on the ground like a snake and its body was just like a bat's body and covered with long red hair like strings. It could only fly to a short distance, and if it shouted a person who was four miles away would hear. All the eyes which surrounded its head were closing and opening at the same time as if a man was pressing a switch on and off" (pp. 79-80).

Arresting images such as the umbrella-like horns and the electrically operated eyes seem quite original, but Fagunwa had used images of this sort in his first novel. Here is part of Fagunwa's description of Agbako, an evil spirit:

"His head was long and large, the sixteen eyes being arranged around the base of his head, and there was no living man who could stare into those eyes without trembling, they rolled endlessly round like the face of a clock. His head was matted with hair, black as the hearth and very long, often swishing his hips as he swung his legs." [1]

Fagunwa's manner of describing monsters appears to have made a profound impression on Tutuola, leading him to strive for similar hallucinatory effects.

Sometimes Tutuola will base an entire scene on something he has read in Fagunwa. In *Simbi and the Satyr of the Dark Jungle*, for example, Simbi's first encounter with the Satyr closely resembles Olowo-Aiye's meeting with *Esu Kekere Ode* ("Little Devil of the Ways") in *Igbo Olodumare*, Fagunwa's second novel. The monsters themselves are very much alike. Here is Fagunwa's *Esu Kekere Ode:*

"He wore no coat and he wore no trousers; he had no hat on his head and tied no cloth round his loins, for it was with leaves that the wretch covered his nakedness. He had only one eye and that was wide and round like a great moon. He had no nose at all because his eye was so much bigger than the ordinary bounds of an eye. His mouth was as wide as a man's palm and his teeth were like those of a lion, and these teeth were red as when a lion has just finished eating a meal of raw meat. The sprite's body was covered with hair like a garment and resembled that of a European dog. A long tuft of hair grew on the top of his head. From his shoulder there hung a scourge and from his neck a great bag which filled one with fear. This bag was smeared all over with blood and on this blood was stuck the down of birds, while various medicines were attached to its sides." [2]

---

1. *Black Orpheus*, 15 (August 1964), p. 6.
2. WHITELEY, pp. 73-74.

Here is Tutuola's Satyr:

"He did not wear neither coat nor trousers but he wore only an apron which was soaked with blood. Plenty of the soft feathers were stuck onto this apron. More than one thousand heads of birds were stuck to all over it. He was about ten feet tall and very strong, bold and vigorous. His head was full of dirty long hairs and the hairs were full up with refuses and dried leaves. The mouth was so large and wide that it almost covered the nose. The eyes were so fearful that a person could not be able to look at them for two times, especially the powerful illumination they were bringing out always. He wore plenty of juju-beads round his neck" (pp. 73-74).

Some of the descriptive details are different but a great many are the same. Moreover, the action that follows is almost identical. Fagunwa's monster first interrogates the presumptuous earthling that has trespassed on his domain and then boasts of past conquests:

"Who are you? What are you? What do you amount to? What do you rank as? What are you looking for? What do you want? What are you looking at? What do you see? What are you considering? What affects you? Where are you coming from? Where are you going? Where do you live? Where do you roam? Answer me! Human being, answer me in a word! One thing is certain—you have got into trouble today, you have climbed a tree beyond its topmost leaves, you have fallen from a height into a well, you have eaten an unexpected poison, you have found a farmplot full of weeds and planted ground-nuts in it [. . .]. You saw me and I saw you, you were approaching and I was approaching, and yet you did not take to your heels [. . .]. Have you never heard of me? Has no one told you about me? The skulls of greater men than you are in my cooking pot and their backbones are in the corner of my room, while my seat is made from the breast-bones of those who are thoughtless."[1]

Tutuola's less eloquent Satyr says the same:

"Who are you? What are you? Where are you coming from? Where are you going? or don't you know where you are? Answer me! I say answer me now! [. . .] Certainly, you have put yourselves into the mouth of 'death'! You have climbed the tree above its leaves! You see me coming and you too are coming to me instead to run away for your lives!

By the way, have you not been told of my terrible deeds? And that I have killed and eaten so many persons, etc. who were even bold more than you do?" (p. 75).

Both Fagunwa's hero and Tutuola's heroine respond by standing

1. *Ibid.*, pp. 74-75.

their ground and hurling back boasts of their own. In the strenuous wrestling match that ensues the monster is subdued.

It is encouraging to note that Tutuola and Fagunwa differ considerably in their description of this epic struggle and its aftermath. Such differences indicate that Tutuola is not merely translating Fagunwa and that he is sensitive to the demands of his own narrative. They also suggest that even when he follows Fagunwa most faithfully he does so from memory rather than from a printed text, that instead of actually plagiarizing he vividly recreates what he best remembers from Fagunwa's books, knitting the spirit if not the substance of the most suitable material into the loose fibers of his yarn.

Because Fagunwa occasionally makes use of material from Yoruba oral tradition, it is not always easy to tell when Tutuola is borrowing from Fagunwa and when from folktales. For example, both writers use motifs such as the "juju-compass" which helps travelers to find their way,[1] the hall of singing birds which turns out to be a trap,[2] the fierce gatekeeper who must be overcome in combat,[3] and the deer-woman who marries a hunter.[4] Tutuola's handling of these motifs may owe more to Yoruba oral tradition than to Fagunwa. Indeed, it is conceivable that Tutuola seems closest to Fagunwa when Fagunwa is closest to oral tradition. Without folktale texts suitable for comparative study it is impossible to accurately assess Tutuola's debts. But it can be assumed that Fagunwa's books were among those which taught Tutuola how to weave a number of old stories into a flexible narrative pattern that could be stretched into a book. Fagunwa's contribution to Tutuola should perhaps be measured more in terms of overall structure and descriptive technique than in terms of content. Tutuola followed Fagunwa's lead and traveled in the same direction but he did not always walk in Fagunwa's tracks.

Tutuola's first two books, *The Palm-Wine Drinkard* and *My Life in the Bush of Ghosts*, got both good and bad reviews. European and American readers were on the whole very enthusiastic, but a number of Nigerian readers were quite angry that books written in such a manner by a lowly messenger should receive so much publicity and praise abroad. The harshest criticism came from fellow Yoruba

---

1. *Ibid.*, p. 71; *BAH*, p. 48.
2. BEIER, p. 54; *SSDJ*, p. 109.
3. BEIER, p. 52; *MLBG*, pp. 79-80; *BAH*, pp. 48-54.
4. *Odu*, 9 (September 1963), p. 37; *MLBG*, pp. 112-135; "The Elephant Woman", *Chicago Review*, X (Spring 1956), pp. 36-39. Yoruba versions of

who tended to focus on Tutuola's inadequate education, imperfect English, borrowings from Fagunwa and oral tradition, and his damage to the image of Nigeria in Europe and America. Babasola Johnson said that he and his friends who had read *The Palm-Wine Drinkard* had found it a "long tale written in a language we did not understand." Johnson felt that the book "should not have been published at all" for it was

"bad enough to attempt an African narrative in 'good English' [but] worse to attempt it in Mr. Tutuola's strange lingo [. . .]. The book ought to have been written in West African Patois proper, or in Yoruba, but then Mr. Tutuola's literary tactics would have been exposed. Besides the fact that his stories are well-known, and have been published in one form or another, most of his plots were borrowed from Fagunwa's *Ogboju Ode*."[1]

Olawole Olumide, in an article entitled "Amos Tutuola's Reviewers and the Educated Africans," attributed Tutuola's decision to write in English to "daredevilry," an "unflagging belief in himself," and perhaps an awareness that he could not equal Fagunwa writing in Yoruba.[2] I. Adeagbo Akinjogbin, after admitting that he had not read either of Tutuola's books, went on to say that from reviews and descriptions of Tutuola,

"it is clear that the author is not an academic man and therefore I submit that it is not a high literary standard that has attracted so many European and American readers. What then? [. . .] Most Englishmen, and perhaps Frenchmen, are pleased to believe all sorts of fantastic tales about Africa, a continent of which they are profoundly ignorant. The 'extraordinary books' of Mr. Tutuola (which must undoubtedly contain some of the unbelievable things in our folklores) will just suit the temper of his European readers as they seem to confirm their concepts of Africa. No wonder then that they are being read not only in English, but in French as well. And once this harm (I call it harm) is done, it can hardly be undone again."

Akinjogbin concluded that Tutuola's books "are of no literary value [. . .], show no marks of possible future development and [. . .] are incapable of giving accurate information about Africa (or Nigeria for that matter)."[3]

---

this tale, which is known in European oral tradition as a "Swan Maiden" tale (Tale type 465 in the Aarne-Thompson index), can be found in FUJA, pp. 77-82, and WALKER and WALKER, pp. 11-16.

1. JOHNSON, p. 322.
2. *New Nigeria Forum*, I (October 1958), pp. 5-16. I am grateful to Donatus Nwoga for this reference.
3. *West Africa*, June 5, 1954, p. 513.

The Nigerian critics' condemnation of Tutuola's English and suspicion of European motives for praising his books are understandable. J. V. Murra points out that

"to a reader whose excellent English [. . .] is gained at the cost of neglecting his own tongue, mostly in mission schools with their distrust of the pupil's spontaneity and imagination—Shakespeare and the Governor's Annual Report are the proffered models in matters of style—all this recognition for 'translating Yoruba ideas in almost the same sequence as they occur to his mind' must indeed be a puzzle and a shock."[1]

In the early nineteen-fifties such recognition must have been a great embarrassment as well, for educated Nigerians in their growing eagerness for political independence were becoming acutely conscious of their image abroad. They wanted to give an appearance of modernity, maturity, competence and sophistication, but the naive fantasies of the Lagos messenger projected just the opposite image. Gerald Moore suggests that Tutuola aroused the antipathy of some of his countrymen by reminding them of a world from which they wanted to escape.[2] To such readers Tutuola was a disgrace, a setback, a national calamity.

But to readers in Europe and America Tutuola was an exotic delight. Reviewers hailed *The Palm-Wine Drinkard* as "a fantastic primitive,"[3] a book "possessed of an imagination that [. . .] seems to be progressively eradicated as 'civilization' advances."[4] The *New Yorker* went so far as to say: "One catches a glimpse of the very beginning of literature, that moment when writing at last seizes and pins down the myths and legends of an analphabetic culture."[5] In a similar vein, V. S. Pritchett claimed that *My Life in the Bush of Ghosts* "discernibly expresses the unconscious of a race and even moments of the nightmare element of our own unconsciousness [. . .]. Tutuola's voice is like the beginning of man on earth."[6] The image-conscious Nigerians apparently had good reason to worry.

What fascinated many non-African readers of Tutuola was his style. V. S. Pritchett characterized it as "a loose, talking prose,"[7]

---

1. *Nation*, September 25, 1954, p. 261.
2. MOORE, p. 56.
3. Lee ROGOW, *Saturday Review*, October 17, 1953, p. 30.
4. John Henry RALEIGH, *New Republic*, December 14, 1953, p. 21.
5. Anthony WEST, *New Yorker*, December 5, 1953, p. 222.
6. *New Statesman and Nation*, March 6, 1954, p. 291.
7. *Ibid.*

Dylan Thomas as "young English,"[1] another as "naive poetry."[2] One critic even spoke with enthusiasm of the emergence of a "new 'mad' African writing" written by those who "don't learn English; they don't study the rules or grammar; they just tear right into it and let the splinters fly."[3]   To native speakers of English Tutuola's splintered style was an amusing novelty; to educated Nigerians who had spent years honing and polishing their English it was a schoolboy's abomination.

Tutuola's later books were not as enthusiastically received in England and America as his first two.   Reviewers complained that "Tutuola's idiom has lost its charm and spontaneity,"[4] that "his effects are a good deal more calculated than they used to be,"[5] that "there is none of the nightmare fascination of the earlier books,"[6] that "one's attention flags here and there."[7]   Tutuola's writing now seemed repetitive and "deliberately childish" rather than "pleasingly child-like."[8]   Since Faber and Faber no longer took pains to cleanse his manuscripts of their grossest linguistic impurities,[9] he appeared more inarticulate, more splintery, at times almost unintelligible. The *Times Literary Supplement*, in a review of *Feather Woman of the Jungle*, recalled the 'literary sensation' Tutuola's first two books had caused:

"There had been nothing quite like them before, and the strangeness of the African subject matter, the primary colours, the mixture of sophistication, superstition, and primitivism, and above all the incantatory juggling with the English language combined to dazzle and intoxicate.   Novelty-seekers, propagandists for the coloured races, professional rooters for the avant-garde—any avant-garde, anywhere and at any time—were alike delighted, and none more vociferously than the thinning ranks of the Apocalypse."

---

1. London *Observer*, July 6, 1952, p. 7.
2. Selden RODMAN, *New York Times Book Review*, September 20, 1953, p. 29.
3. Tom HOPKINSON, rev. of *An African Treasury*, Langston HUGHES, ed. (London, 1961), London *Observer*, September 17, 1961, p. 28.
4. Simon RAVEN, *Spectator*, May 4, 1962, p. 597.
5. Neal ACHERSON, *New Statesman*, May 11, 1962, p. 683.
6. V. S. NAIPAUL, *ibid.*, April 5, 1958, p. 444.
7. Gene BARO, *New York Herald Tribune Book Review*, January 25, 1959, p. 6.
8. RAVEN, p. 597.
9. *PWD*, p. 24, contains a "page from the author's MS., showing the publisher's 'corrections'."   In a letter to the author dated May 1, 1968, Sarah Lloyd of Faber and Faber says: "Rather less correction was needed for Tutuola's later books as the author has become more practiced in writing." After *MLBG* Tutuola's books contain many more errors in spelling, punctuation and grammar.   For discussion of Tutuola's errors, cf. COLLINS, MS., pp. 156-185.

But now, with the publication of his fifth book, which "very much is the mixture as before [. . .], increasingly one's reaction is irritation, a desire to say 'So what?' in quite the rudest way, and to protest against what is dangerously near a cult of the *faux-naïf*."[1] Clearly, Tutuola's novelty had worn off, and the pendulum of critical opinion had begun to reverse its direction.

Nowadays one of the commonplaces in African literary criticism is that Tutuola has been "either praised or blamed for the wrong reasons."[2] Critics usually make a statement of this sort before throwing their own bouquets and brickbats at him, presumably for the right reasons. Certainly the European and American critics who credit Tutuola with far more originality, sophistication, or naiveté than he possesses are just as wrongheaded as the African critics who belittle him for writing 'bad English' or for borrowing from Fagunwa and Yoruba folktales. Between these two extremes there exists a large middle ground inhabited by old and new explorers intent on determining Tutuola's rightful place in the African literary landscape. Many maps have been drawn, many claims and counter-claims made, but because Tutuola's full dimensions are still not known and his limitations still the subject of lively debate, no firm boundary lines have been established. Since Tutuola's works will no doubt continue to strike African and non-African readers differently for some time to come, it is not likely that the critical battle will end soon. No one denies that Tutuola is an extraordinary writer. The issue seems to be whether he is extraordinarily good, extraordinarily bad, or extraordinarily lucky.

Of course, it could be argued that he is all three. As a raconteur of bizarre Yoruba tales, he is remarkably good. As an undisciplined stylist whose imperfect grasp of English occasionally blocks effective communication, he is at times extremely bad. And as a naive artist who happened to create something original almost by accident, he is extraordinarily lucky. It is Tutuola's rare combination of talent and ineptitude that continues to endear him to many non-African readers.

It could also be argued that in Africa, particularly in Nigeria, Tutuola has been extraordinarily influential. Gerald Moore doesn't think so. He finds Tutuola's books "far more like a fascinating cul-de-sac than the beginning of anything directly useful to other

1. *TLS*, May 25, 1962, p. 369.
2. RAMSARAN, 1963, p. 17. Cf. also MOORE, p. 39.

writers." [1] Certainly in terms of form and technique Moore is right. No one has tried to imitate Tutuola's writing and no one probably ever will. He is not the sort of writer who attracts followers or founds a school. His achievements are unique because his background, imagination and linguistic equipment are unique. In this sense he is a literary dead end.

But it should be remembered that he was the first Nigerian writer to publish a full-length work of fiction in London and that he was a very prolific writer in a decade when Nigerian writers were rare. His second book was published eight months before Cyprian Ekwensi's first novel, *People of the City*.[2] And he had four books to his credit before Chinua Achebe had one.[3] Moreover, Tutuola's first works received immediate international recognition and acclaim; he was the first world-famous black African author.[4] If a Lagos messenger could become a renowned writer, why couldn't a university-educated member of the Nigerian elite? "If he can do it, why can't I?" One wonders how many would-be writers in Nigeria asked themselves this question. Surely Tutuola's astounding success must have been a great spur to someone like Ekwensi, who already considered himself a writer.[5] Such success can easily awaken or reinforce another's urge to write.

Equally important is the fact that Tutuola succeeded by breaking all the rules. He did not write 'good English'. He did not try to create realistic situations and realistic characters. He did not bother with a plot. But blending the only narrative forms he knew—folktales, Fagunwa's *Ogboju Ode Ninu Igbo Irunmale*, the *Arabian Nights*, and Bunyan's *The Pilgrim's Progress*—he created in *The Palm-Wine Drinkard* a thoroughly African literary work that had to be accepted on its own terms. Some have called it a literary bombshell, but few have realized how beneficial an explosion it was for Nigerian letters. Not only did it make much noise and attract much attention,

---

1. MOORE, p. 57.

2. *MLBG* was published on February 5, 1954. EKWENSI's *People of the City* was published on October 11, 1954.

3. *BAH*, TUTUOLA's fourth book, was published on May 28, 1958, and ACHEBE's *Things Fall Apart* on June 9, 1958.

4. Peter Abrahams, a Cape coloured writer from South Africa, was also well-known at this time; by 1955 his early novels had been translated into eleven languages. Leopold Sedar Senghor of Senegal was known chiefly in France and French Africa.

5. EKWENSI spoke of himself as a writer at least as early as August, 1950. Cf. *West African Review*, August, 1950, p. 925.

but it also swept away inhibitions and restraints, reduced real and imagined obstacles, and thus dramatically cleared the way for other Nigerian writers. Best of all it was unorthodox. And Tutuola's writing has remained steadfastly unorthodox, despite his own best efforts to improve himself educationally in order to develop into 'a real writer'.[1] Tutuola's books are *sui generis*. As the *Times Literary Supplement* remarked, "there had been nothing quite like [*The Palm-Wine Drinkard* and *My Life in the Bush of Ghosts*] before."[2] If there has been nothing quite like them since, except his other books, this does not necessarily mean that Tutuola has had no influence on African literature. His originality set an excellent precedent for later writers who might otherwise have followed too parasitically the literary fashions of Europe.

Amos Tutuola is most important as an innovator. He was one of the first African writers to contribute something entirely new to Western literature. Although few of his innovations were conscious or calculated and many were borrowed from Fagunwa and Yoruba oral tradition, he deserves to be called the father of experimentation in Nigerian fiction in English.

1. *West Africa*, May 1, 1954, p. 389.
2. *TLS*, May 25, 1962, p. 369.

AMOS TUTUOLA:
A CHECKLIST OF WORKS,
REVIEWS AND CRITICISM

Amos Tutuola:
A Checklist of Works,
Reviews and Criticism

(*Asterisks denote materials which are reprinted in this book.)

BOOKS

*The Palm-Wine Drinkard and His Dead Palm-Wine Tapster in the Deads'
Town*. London: Faber and Faber, 1952; New York: Grove Press,
1953.

Reviews:

> *Times Literary Supplement*, 9 May 1952, p. 309
> *Dylan Thomas, *The Observer*, 6 July 1952, p. 7
> Cyprian Ekwensi, *African Affairs*, 51 (1952), 257-58
> Cyprian Ekwensi, *West African Review*, July 1952, p. 713
> *[Arthur Calder-Marshall], *The Listener*, 13 November 1952,
>   p. 819
> William Morgan, *West African Review*, December 1952, p.
>   1387
> R. S. Taylor, *Library Journal*, 1 September 1953, p. 1426
> *Selden Rodman, *New York Times Book Review*, 20 Septem-
>   ber 1953, p. 5
> *Time*, 21 September 1953, p. 114
> J. H. Jackson, *San Francisco Chronicle*, 23 September 1953,
>   p. 17
> Anne Fremantle, *Commonweal*, 25 September 1953, p. 616
> Paul Pickrel, *Yale Review*, 43 (1953), xxvi
> Lee Rogow, *Saturday Review*, 17 October 1953, p. 30
> *Anthony West, *New Yorker*, 5 December 1953, p. 206
> J. H. Raleigh, *New Republic*, 14 December 1953, p. 21
> Gene Baro, *New York Herald Tribune Book Review*, 20
>   December 1953, p. 6
> Neal Acherson, *New Statesman*, 11 May 1962, p. 683
> R. G. G. Price, *Punch*, 23 May 1962, p. 805
> *Books for Africa*, 33, 2 (1963), 58

My Life in the Bush of Ghosts. London: Faber and Faber; New York: Grove Press, 1954.

  Reviews:

  Isabel Quigley, *Manchester Guardian*, 9 February 1954, p. 4
  Times Literary Supplement, 19 February 1954, p. 117
  *Kingsley Amis, *Spectator*, 26 February 1954, p. 244
  *Eric Robinson, *West Africa*, 27 February 1954, p. 179
  *V. S. Pritchett, *New Statesman and Nation*, 6 March 1954, p. 291
  Books for Africa, 24, 3 (1954), 58-59
  Jean Holzhauer, *Commonweal*, 8 October 1954, p. 23
  H. V. L. S., *African Affairs*, 53 (1954), 348-49
  Lee Rogow, *Saturday Review*, 13 November 1954, p. 57
  Gene Baro, *New York Herald Tribune Book Review*, 28 November 1954, p. 2
  William Morgan, *West African Review*, December 1954, p. 1217
  Mabel Jolaoso, *Odu*, 1 (1955), 42-43
  Cecil T. Lewis, *Phylon*, 16 (1955), 117-18
  R. D. Jameson, *Western Folklore*, 14 (1955), 302
  Oumar Dodou Thiam, *Présence Africaine*, 51 (1964), 174-75
  O. R. Dathorne, *West African Journal of Education*, 9, 1 (1965), 55

Simbi and the Satyr of the Dark Jungle. London: Faber and Faber, 1955.

  Reviews:

  Times Literary Supplement, 21 October 1955, p. 617
  Books for Africa, 26, 1 (1956), 19
  *Cyprian Ekwensi, *West African Review*, January 1956, p. 45
  Marjorie Nicholson, *African Affairs*, 55 (1956), 62-63
  Gerald Moore, *Odu*, 4 (1956?), 44-47
  T. D., *West Africa*, 29 October 1956, p. 1020

The Brave African Huntress. London: Faber and Faber, 1958; New York: Grove Press, 1970.

  Reviews:

  Stevie Smith, *Spectator*, 28 March 1958, p. 405
  Manchester Guardian, 1 April 1958, p. 4
  *V. S. Naipaul, *New Statesman*, 5 April 1958, p. 444
  Michael Crowder, *West African Review*, June 1958, p. 509

R. V., *New York Times Book Review*, 2 November 1958, p. 41

*Ulli Beier [Akanji], *Black Orpheus*, 4 (1958), 51-53

Books for Africa, 29, 1 (1959), 15

Gene Baro, *New York Herald Tribune Book Review*, 25 January 1959, p. 6

John Henrik Clarke, *Présence Africaine*, 26 (1959), 126-27

Feather Woman of the Jungle. London: Faber and Faber, 1962.

Reviews:

Simon Raven, *Spectator*, 4 May 1962, p. 597

Neal Acherson, *New Statesman*, 11 May 1962, p. 683

Times Weekly Review, 17 May 1962, p. 9

R. G. G. Price, *Punch*, 23 May 1962, p. 805

Times Literary Supplement, 25 May 1962, p. 369

*S. D. D., *West African Review*, August 1962, p. 57

*Mbella Sonne Dipoko, *Présence Africaine*, 44 (1962), 230

John Reed, *Central African Examiner*, 6, 4 (September 1964), 27-28

Ajaiyi and His Inherited Poverty. London: Faber and Faber, 1967.

Reviews:

*Desmond MacNamara, *New Statesman*, 8 December 1967, p. 819

*A. Goldman, *The Listener*, 14 December 1967, p. 20

The Observer, 31 December 1967, p. 20

Times Literary Supplement, 18 January 1968, p. 53

George Awoonor-Williams, *West Africa*, 27 April 1968, pp. 490-91

*Gladys Agbebiyi, *Nigeria Magazine*, 96 (1968), 53

Ola Balogun, *Présence Africaine*, 65 (1968), 180-81

R. E. Morsberger, *Books Abroad*, 42 (1968), 492

Bernth Lindfors, *Journal of the New African Literature and the Arts*, 13/14 (1972), 71-72

For a list of translations of Tutuola's books, see Janheinz Jahn and Claus Peter Dressler, *Bibliography of Creative African Writing*, Nendeln, Liechtenstein: Kraus-Thomson, 1971.

SHORT FICTION

Excerpts from Tutuola's books appear in many anthologies of African literature. Listed here are only those tales which were published originally as short stories.

"The Betrayal," *Radio Times* (Lagos), November 1954, pp. 14, 18.

"The Elephant Woman," *Chicago Review* 10 (1956), 36-39. Published earlier but in a different form in *My Life in the Bush of Ghosts*, pp. 112-35.

"Don't Pay Bad for Bad," *Radio Times* (Lagos), 18 February 1956, p. 7. Reprinted in *Présence Africaine* 30 (1960), 78-81, and in *Reflections: Nigerian Prose and Verse*, ed. Frances Ademola, pp. 33-36. Lagos: African Universities Press, 1962. The story also appears in *Ajaiyi and His Inherited Poverty*, pp. 76-84.

"Ajayi and the Witchdoctor," *Atlantic*, 203 (April 1959), 78-80. A more fully developed version appears in *Black Orpheus*, 19 (1966), 10-14. and in *Ajaiyi and His Inherited Poverty*, pp. 219-35.

"Ajantala, the Noxious Guest," in *An African Treasury*, ed. Langston Hughes, pp. 121-27. New York: Crown, 1960; London: Victor Gollancz, 1961. The character Ajantala reappears in *The Brave African Huntress*, pp. 121-32.

"The Duckling Brothers and Their Disobedient Sister," *Présence Africaine*, 36 (1961), 73-78. A different form of the story appears in *Feather Woman of the Jungle*, pp. 12-35.

"Akanke and the Jealous Pawn Broker," *Afriscope* (Lagos), 4, 1 (1974), 57, 59, 61-62.

"The Pupils of the Eyes: A Folk-lore from Western Nigeria," *Confrontation: A Journal of Third World Literature* (Athens, Ohio), 1, 3 (1974), 78-90.

CRITICISM

Tutuola is mentioned in nearly every book and survey article written on African literature in English. This selected bibliography lists only those published critical and biographical writings in which he and his works are discussed in some detail.

Biographical Studies

Ackerly, Nancy. "WLB Biography: Amos Tutuola," *Wilson Library Bulletin*, 38 (September 1963), 81.

*Anon. "Portrait: A Life in the Bush of Ghosts," *West Africa*, 1 May 1954, pp. 389-90.

Herdeck, Donald E. *African Authors: A Companion to Black African Writing, Volume I: 1300-1973.* Washington, D.C.: Black Orpheus Press, 1973.

Jahn, Janheinz, Ulla Schild and Almut Nordmann. *Who's Who in African Literature: Biographies, Works, Commentaries.* Tübingen: Horst Erdmann, 1972.

Tutuola, Amos. "My Life and Activities," in *The Palm-Wine Drinkard and His Dead Palm-Wine Tapster in the Deads' Town,* pp. 126-30. New York: Grove Press, 1953.

Zell, Hans and Helene Silver, eds. *A Reader's Guide to African Literature.* New York: Africana Publishing Corp., 1971.

Interviews

Nkosi, Lewis. "Conversation with Amos Tutuola," *Africa Report,* 9 (July 1964), 11. Reprinted in *The Classic* (Johannesburg), 1, 4 (1965), 57-60.

[Omotoso, Kole]. "Interview with Amos Tutuola," *Afriscope* (Lagos), 4, 1 (1974), 62, 64.

Literary Criticism

Achonu, Oguike. "Amos Tutuola and English," *Horizon* (Ibadan), 3, 1 (1964?), 19-23.

*Afolayan, A. "Language and Sources of Amos Tutuola," in *Perspectives on African Literature,* ed. Christoper Heywood, pp. 49-63. London: Heinemann; New York: Africana Publishing Corp., 1971.

*Akinjogbin, I. Adeagbo. "The Books of Amos Tutuola," *West Africa,* 5 June 1954, p. 513.

*Anozie, Sunday O. "Amos Tutuola: Littérature et folklore ou le problème de la synthèse," *Cahiers d'études africaines,* 10 (1970), 335-51. Published in this book is an English translation by Judith H. McDowell; a briefer version in English can be found in *Conch,* 2, 2 (1970), 80-88. The same essay appears in Anozie's *Sociologie du roman africaine: Réalisme, structure et détermination dans le roman moderne ouest-africain,* pp. 65-88. Paris: Aubier-Montaigne, 1970.

*Armstrong, Robert P. "The Narrative and Intensive Continuity: *The Palm-Wine Drinkard,*" *Research in African Literatures,* 1 (1970), 9-34. A slightly different version of the same essay appears in Armstrong's *The Affecting Presence: An Essay in Humanistic Anthropology,* pp. 137-73. Urbana: University of Illinois Press, 1971.

Atimono, Emiko. "40 Days in the Jungle," *Sunday Express* (Lagos), 28 February 1960, p. 12.

Awoonor, Kofi. *The Breast of the Earth: A Survey of the History, Culture and Literature of Africa South of the Sahara.* Garden City, N.Y.: Anchor Press/Doubleday, 1975.

Banjo, Ayo. "Aspects of Tutuola's Use of English," in *Essays on African Literature*, ed. W. L. Ballard. Spectrum Monograph Series in the Arts and Sciences, Vol. 3, pp. 155-73. Atlanta: School of Arts and Sciences, Georgia State University, 1973.

Bischofberger, Otto. *Tradition und Wandel aus der Sicht der Romanschriftsteller Kameruns und Nigerias.* Einsiedeln, Switzerland: Etzel Druck, n. d.

Bohannan, Paul. "Translation: A Problem in Anthropology," *The Listener*, 13 May 1954, pp. 815-16. Discusses Tutuola as a translator of culture.

Cartey, Wilfred. *Whispers from a Continent: The Literature of Contemporary Black Africa.* New York: Random House, 1969.

Chakava, Henry M. "Amos Tutuola: The Unselfconscious Eccentric," *Busara*, 3, 3 (1971), 50-57.

*Collins, Harold R. "Founding a New National Literature: The Ghost Novels of Amos Tutuola," *Critique*, 4, 1 (1960-61), 17-28.

——. "The Novel in Nigeria," in *Writers the Other Side of the Horizon: A Guide to Developing Literatures of the World*, ed. Priscilla Tyler, pp. 51-58. Champaign: National Council of Teachers of English, 1964.

——. *Amos Tutuola.* New York: Twayne Publishers, 1969. Reviewed by Donatus I. Nwoga in *Research in African Literatures*, 2, 1 (1971), 94-98.

——. "A Theory of Creative Mistakes and the Mistaking Style of Amos Tutuola," *World Literature Written in English*, 13 (1974), 155-71.

Dathorne, O. R. "Amos Tutuola: The Nightmare of the Tribe," in *Introduction to Nigerian Literature*, ed. Bruce King, pp. 64-76. Lagos: University of Lagos; London: Evans, 1971; New York: Africana Publishing Corp., 1972. A revised version of this essay is reprinted in Dathorne's *The Black Mind: A History of African Literature.* Minneapolis: University of Minnesota Press, 1974.

*Edwards, Paul. "The Farm and the Wilderness in Tutuola's *The Palm-Wine Drinkard*," *Journal of Commonwealth Literature*,

9, 1 (1974), 57-65.

Enekwe, Ossie Onuoro. "Amos Tutuola: An African Surrealist," *Shantih* (Brooklyn, N.Y.) 3, 2 (1974-75), 45.

Enobo Kosso, Martin. "La Rencontre," *Abbia*, 25 (1971), 28-68. On *The Palm-Wine Drinkard*.

Ferris, William R., Jr. "Folklore and the African Novelist: Achebe and Tutuola," *Journal of American Folklore*, 86 (1973), 25-36.

Jahn, Janheinz. *Muntu: An Outline of the New African Culture*. New York: Grove Press, 1961.

_____."An der Tür zum schwarzen Afrika. Amos Tutuola, Nigerias bekanntester Erzähler, verdient sich seinen Lebensunterhalt als Portier," *Der Tagesspiegel,* 12 April 1962.

Jeppesen, Bent Haugaard. *Den Afrikanske Roman*. Copenhagen: Munksgaard, 1971.

*Johnson, Babasola. "The Books of Amos Tutuola," *West Africa*, 10 April 1954, p. 322.

*Jones, Eldred. "Amos Tutuola—*The Palm-Wine Drinkard:* Fourteen Years On," *Bulletin of the Association for African Literature in English*, 4 (1966), 24-30.

King, Bruce. "Two Nigerian Writers: Tutuola and Soyinka," *Southern Review* (Baton Rouge), 6 (1970), 843-52. Review-article discussing *Ajaiyi and His Inherited Poverty*.

Klíma, Vladimír. "Tutuola's Inspiration," *Archiv Orientální*, 35 (1967), 556-62.

_____. *Modern Nigerian Novels.* Prague: Academia, 1969.

*Larrabee, Eric. "Palm-Wine Drinkard Searches for a Tapster," *Reporter*, 12 May 1953, pp. 37-39.

_____. "Amos Tutuola: A Problem in Translation," *Chicago Review*, 10 (Spring 1956), 40-44.

*Larson, Charles R. "Time, Space and Description: The Tutuolan World," *The Emergence of African Fiction*, pp. 93-112. Bloomington: Indiana University Press, 1972. See also pp. 3-11.

Laurence, Margaret. *Long Drums and Cannons: Nigerian Dramatists and Novelists 1952-1966*. London: Macmillan, 1968.

*Leslie, Omolara. "The Palm-Wine Drinkard: A Reassessment of Amos Tutuola." *Journal of Commonwealth Literature*, No. 9 (1970), 48-56. Also published in *Présence Africaine*, 71 (1969), 99-108, and in *Ibadan*, 28 (1970), 22-26.

Lindfors, Bernth. *"The Palm-Wine Drinkard* and Oral Tradition," *Critique*, 11 (1968-69), 42-50.

_____. "Amos Tutuola and His Critics," *Abbia*, 22 (1969),

109-18.

———. "Amos Tutuola and D. O. Fagunwa," *Journal of Commonwealth Literature*, No. 9 (1970), 57-65.

*———. "Amos Tutuola: Debts and Assets," *Cahiers d'études africaines*, 10 (1970), 306-34.

———. "Amos Tutuola's Television-handed Ghostess," *Ariel*, 2, 1 (1971), 68-77. Reprinted in *Readings in Commonwealth Literature*, ed. William Walsh, pp. 142-51. Oxford: Clarendon Press, 1973.

———. "Oral Tradition and the Individual Literary Talent," *Studies in the Novel*, 4 (1972), 200-17.

———. *Folklore in Nigerian Literature*. New York: Africana Publishing Corp., 1973. Reprints *"The Palm-Wine Drinkard* and Oral Tradition," "Amos Tutuola's Television-handed Ghostess" and "Oral Tradition and the Individual Literary Talent."

*Lo Liyong, Taban. "Tutuola, Son of Zinjanthropus," *Busara*, 1, 1 (1968), 3-8. Another version of the same essay can be found in Liyong's *The Last Word: Cultural Synthesism*, pp. 157-70. Nairobi: East African Publishing House, 1969.

*Mackay, Mercedes. "The Books of Amos Tutuola," *West Africa*, 8 May 1954, p. 414.

McDowell, Robert E. "Three Nigerian Storytellers: Okara, Tutuola, and Ekwensi," *Ball State University Forum*, 10, 3 (1969), 67-75.

Mezu, S. Okechukwu, "The Tropical Dawn (II): Amos Tutuola," *Nigerian Students' Voice* (Baltimore), 3 (October 1965), 6-11.

*Moore, Gerald. "Amos Tutuola: A Nigerian Visionary," *Black Orpheus*, 1 (1957), 27-35. Reprinted in *Introduction to African Literature*, ed. Ulli Beier, pp. 179-87. Evanston: Northwestern University Press, 1967. An expanded version of this essay appears in Moore's *Seven African Writers*. London: Oxford University Press, 1962.

———. *The Chosen Tongue: English Writings in the Tropical World*. London: Longmans, 1969.

Murra, John V. "The Unconscious of a Race," *Nation*, 25 September 1954, pp. 261-62. Review-article on *My Life in the Bush of Ghosts*.

*Neumarkt, Paul. "Amos Tutuola: Emerging African Literature," *American Imago*, 28 (1971), 129-45.

Obiechina, E. N. "Transition from Oral to Literary Tradition," *Présence Africaine*, 63 (1967), 140-61.

*——. "Amos Tutuola and the Oral Tradition," *Présence Africaine*, 65 (1968), 85-106.

Obumselu, Ben. "The Background of Modern African Literature," *Ibadan*, 22 (1966), 57.

Olumide, Olawole. "Amos Tutuola's Reviewers and the Educated Africans," *New Nigeria Forum* (London), 1 (October 1958), 5-16.

Olusola, Segun. "The Palm-Wine Drinkard," *Nigeria Magazine*, 77 (1963), 143-49. Review of Kola Ogunmola's opera based on Tutuola's story.

[Omotoso, Kole]. "African Writers and Original Manuscripts," *Afriscope* (Lagos) 4, 1 (1974), 55, 57. On Tutuola's manuscripts and inadequate royalties.

Osunbunmi, Akinbami. "Folklore in African Literature—A Prostitution of the Roots?" *Horizon* (Ibadan), 3, 3 (1965), 25-29.

Parrinder, Geoffrey. "Foreword" to Tutuola's *My Life in the Bush of Ghosts*, pp. 9-15. London: Faber and Faber, 1954.

Priebe, Richard. "Tutuola, Fagunwa, and Shakespeare," *Journal of Commonwealth Literature*, 8, 1 (1973), 110-11.

*——. "Tutuola, the Riddler," paper presented at the Annual Meeting of the African Studies Association held in Chicago in October 1974.

Ramsaran, J. A. "African Twilight: Folktale and Myth in Nigerian Literature," *Ibadan*, 15 (1963), 17-19.

*Robinson, Eric. "The Books of Amos Tutuola," *West Africa*, 17 April 1954, p. 344.

Rønning, Helge. "Amos Tutuola—en nigeriansk eventyrdikter," in *Stemmer fra den tredje verden*, ed. Yngvar Ustvedt, pp. 51-60. Oslo: Gyldendal Norsk Forlag, 1970.

Roscoe, Adrian A. *Mother is Gold: A Study in West African Literature*. London: Cambridge University Press, 1971.

Schmidt, Nancy J. "Nigerian Fiction and the African Oral Tradition," *Journal of the New African Literature and the Arts*, 5/6 (1968), 10-19. Reprinted in *New African Literature and the Arts, Volume 2*, ed. Joseph Okpaku, pp. 25-38. New York: Thomas Y. Crowell, 1970.

——. "Tutuola Joins the Mainstream of Nigerian Novelists," *Africa Today*, 15 (June-July 1968), 22-24. Review-article on *Ajaiyi and His Inherited Poverty*.

*Sodipo, Ade. "The Books of Amos Tutuola," *West Africa*, 5 June 1954, p. 513.

Soyinka, Wole: "Amos Tutuola on Stage," *Ibadan*, 16 (1963),

23-24. Review of Kola Ogunmola's opera based on *The Palm-Wine Drinkard*.

——. "From a Common Back Cloth: Reassessment of the African Literary Image," *American Scholar*, 32 (1963), 387-96.

Takacs, Sherryl. "Oral Tradition in the Works of Amos Tutuola," *Books Abroad*, 44 (1970), 392-98.

Tibble, Anne. *African/English Literature: A Short Survey and Anthology of Prose and Poetry up to 1965*. London: Peter Owen; New York: October House, both 1965.

Tucker, Martin. "Three West African Novelists," *Africa Today*, 12 (November 1965), 10-14. Reprinted in Tucker's *Africa in Modern Literature: A Survey of Contemporary Writing in English*. New York: Frederick Ungar, 1967.

Vavilov, V. N. *Proza Nigerii*. Moscow: Nauka, 1973.

Wade, Michael. "The Writing of Amos Tutuola," *The New East* (Jerusalem), 17 (1967), 75-91. In Hebrew with brief summary in English.

Wästberg, Per. *Afrikas moderna litteratur*. Stockholm: Wahlström & Widstrand och Nordiska Afrikainstitutet, 1969.